John Woolman's Journal

by John Woolman

With an Introduction by Vida D. Scudder

Originally published in 1922.

this very absence of emphasis, so quaintly sober, so sensitive in its unfaltering reticence, becomes the choicest grace of Woolman's style. As is the style, so is the man. Woolman "studied to be quiet," and his steady self-discipline was rewarded by a scrupulous yet instinctive control over the finest shades of verity in speech and life. In the youthful trouble of deep religious feeling, when he "went to meetings," as he expressively tell us, "in an awful frame of mind," he spoke a few words one day, under "a strong exercise of spirit." "But not keeping close to the divine opening, I said more than was required of me, and being soon sensible of my error, I was afflicted in mind some weeks, without any light or comfort, even to such a degree that I could not take satisfaction in anything." The mistake was not often repeated; for as he writes in memorable words: "As I was thus humbled and disciplined under the Cross, my understanding became more strengthened to distinguish the pure spirit that inwardly moves upon the heart, and taught me to wait in silence, sometimes for many weeks together, till I felt that rise which prepares the creature to stand like a trumpet through which the Lord speaks to His flock." A fine passage towards the end of the Journal shows that the danger of speaking without this "pure spirit" was ever present to him. "Many love to hear eloquent orations, and if there is not a careful attention to the Gift, men who have once laboured in the pure Gospel ministry, growing weary of suffering and ashamed of appearing weak, may kindle a fire, compass themselves about with sparks, and walk in the light, not of Christ who is under suffering, but of that fire which they going from the Gift have kindled; and that in hearers which has gone from the meek suffering state into the worldly wisdom, may be warmed with this fire and speak highly of these labours. In this journey, a labour hath attended my mind that the ministers amongst us may be

INTRODUCTION

From the days of Charles Lamb to those of Dr. Eliot of Harvard, the unique charm and worth of the Journal of J[ohn] Woolman have been signalled by a thinker of distinction here and there, and the book, if not widely known, has quietly found its way to many hearts and been reprinted [in] sundry editions. The more formal works, however, in which this gentle and audacious eighteenth-century Quaker-preacher spoke out his whole careful mind have been for the most part neglected. These works are sometimes prosy, always indifferent to style in their unflinching quest for "pure wisdom," often concerned w[ith] the dead issue of negro slavery. Yet even in this last cas[e] they have much value as historic documents; no full knowledge of Woolman's spirit is possible without them and not to know that spirit in its entirety is a distinct los[s].

The present edition, while making no claim to critical completeness, presents the main accessible body of Woolman's writings. Here is a well of purest water, "du[g] deep," to use the Quaker phrase. The mere limpidity of [the] water will be joy enough for some: others gazing into i[t] may feel that they see down to the proverbial Truth—th[e] very origin of things, the foundations of the moral univ[erse].

A studious moderation of utterance is the first quality t[o] make itself felt in Woolman's works. To casual or jade[d] readers who crave the word-embroidery, the heightene[d] note, of the romanticist in style, the result may seem colourless. Here is a lack of adjectives, an entire absen[ce of] emphasis, a systematic habit of under-statement that, i[n the] climax of a paragraph or the crisis of an emotion, seem[s at] times almost ludicrous. Yet to the reader of severer tas[te] preserved in the meek, feeling life of truth." No man could so keenly analyse the snare of fluency and popularity, who had not spent a life on guard. The reserve of his writings is a natural consequence. One searches these pages in vain, often controversial though they be, for a single point in which the note is forced or emotion escapes control.

Yet the emotional intensity concealed beneath this equable habit of soul, is evident from the first line to the last. In the fine phrase of the Friends after his death, Woolman "underwent many deep baptisms;" how deep, the Journal reveals. He was a man of impassioned tenderness. Even as a child he saw "that as the mind is moved by an inward principle to love God as an invisible, incomprehensible Being, so by the same principle it is moved to love Him in all his manifestations in the visible world. That as by his breath the flame of life has kindled in all sensible creatures, to say that we love God as unseen and at the same time exercise cruelty toward the least creature moving by his life, or by life derived from Him, is a contradiction in itself." Woolman did not only say these things, he felt them. He is among the great lovers of the world. His tenderness for animals was always keen, from the days in which, as he has told us, he suffered childish remorse from having killed a robin, to his last voyage, when in the midst of personal suffering, he noted pityingly the dull and pining appearance of the "dunghill fowls" on board. "I believe," he writes, "where the love of God is verily perfected, a care will be felt that we do not lessen that sweetness of life in the animal creation which the great Creator intends for them under our government."

He who so sympathised with the robin and the cock was filled with a yearning compassion for the sorrows of humanity. Of him as of Shelley it might well be said, "He was as a nerve o'er which do creep the else unfelt oppressions of the earth." We read of his appetite failing through the agitation of his mind over human pain and his relations to it. In his last illness he broke forth in words that might have been uttered by S. Catherine of Siena: "O Lord my God! The amazing horrors of darkness were gathered around me and covered me all over, and I saw no way to go forth. I felt the misery of my fellow-beings separated from the divine harmony, and it was heavier than I could bear; I was crushed down under it." All great lovers are great sufferers: Woolman was no exception to the rule.

If he knew deep sorrow he knew deep joy also, as all must do who like him "live under the Cross and simply follow the operations of Truth." More is unuttered than uttered in the Journal, yet through its silences we may read an inner experience akin to that of Bunyan or Pascal. Like these great protagonists of the Spirit, he knew a peace given "not as the world giveth." For peace can be where ease is not. Decorous son of an unillumined century, John Woolman is of the company of the Mystics. He is of those led by the Shepherd of Souls beside the still waters. He has suggested his own secret: "Some glances of real beauty may be seen in their faces who dwell in true meekness. There is a harmony in the sound of that voice to which Divine love gives utterance, and some appearance of right order in their temper and conduct whose passions are regulated. Yet all these do not fully show forth that inward life to those who have not felt it; but this white stone and new name are known rightly only to such as have them." "Pure" is the central word of the Journal, and the beauty of pure contemplative quietude is the final impression conveyed by this record so full of anguish over the sorrows of humanity and of unflinching witness against wickedness, borne at the expense of the crucifixion of the natural man.

A chief value of Woolman's works consists in his serene application of his mystical intuitions to the affairs of this world. He who "dwelt deep in an inward stillness" studied his age with a penetrating sagacity that allowed no evasions. The man so carefully on his guard against extravagance was a reformer who pushed his demands, as some would think, almost beyond the border of sanity. No temper was ever more opposed to fanaticism: yet many readers may question whether he escaped the doom of the fanatic. And the most pertinent reason for a re-issue of his works at this juncture is, that in our own day so many hearts are troubled like his own. A generation seeking guidance on the path of social duty will find here a precursor of Ruskin and Tolstoi, a man whose thought, despite the quaintness of his diction, has a quite extraordinary modernness, and whose searchings of conscience are none of them familiar.

The main contemporary issue that agitated Woolman was of course the slave-trade, and he was long regarded all but exclusively as a herald of the anti-slavery movement. But the Fabian Society did well to suggest, in reprinting one of his tracts, the broader scope of his thinking. It will be evident from this edition that his horror of chattel slavery was one incident only in that general attitude toward civilisation which drew from him the bitter cry: "Under a sense of deep revolt and an overflowing stream of unrighteousness, my life has often been a life of mourning." The central evil which he opposed was, in brief, the exploitation of labour: the ideal which he sought was a society in which no man should need to profit by the degradation of his fellow-men. For economic analysis of the modern type one naturally looks in vain; moral analysis of social relations has, however, rarely been carried farther. These little essays "On Labour," "On the Right Use of the

Lord's Outward Gifts," "On Loving our Neighbour," these "Considerations on the True Harmony of Mankind," this "Word of Remembrance and Caution to the Rich," reveal through their quaint formalities of phrase a searching spirit not to be outdone to-day.

Woolman felt "a concern in the spring of pure love, that all who have plenty of outward substance may example others in the right use of things, may carefully look into the condition of poor people, and beware of exacting of them in regard to their wages." He was solicitous, as many have been since his day, over the perplexities of those who seek to combine a due care for their own families with consideration for the wage-earner, "in a fruitful land where the wages bear so small a proportion to the necessaries of life." "There are few if any," he says truly, "could behold their fellow-creatures lie long in distress and forbear to help them when they could do it without any inconvenience; but customs, requiring much labour to support them, do often lie heavy upon the poor, while they who live in these customs are so entangled in a multitude of unnecessary concerns that they think but little of the hardships the poor people go through." To lessen these "concerns," thus to emancipate the labourer from a part of the crushing burden of production, became his central thought. "In beholding that unnecessary toil which many go through in supporting outward greatness, and procuring delicacies; in beholding how the true calmness of life is changed into hurry, and that many, by eagerly pursuing outward treasure, are in danger of withering as to the inward state of the mind; in meditating on the works of this spirit, and the desolations it makes among the professors of Christianity, I may thankfully acknowledge that I often feel pure love beget longings in my mind for the exaltation of the peaceable Kingdom of Christ, and an engagement to labour according to the Gift bestowed upon me for promoting an humble, plain, temperate way of living."

The Simple Life is then Woolman's plea, and the necessity for social sacrifice the burden of his teaching. This plea he presents with no vagueness or Wagnerian sentimentality, but with an alarming precision of outline.

No man ever described better the insensible growth of worldly convention into that custom which "lies upon us with a weight heavy as frost and deep almost as life." Noting the gradual lapse of the Friends from their earlier standards of unworldliness, he says: "These things, though done in calmness without any show of disorder, do yet deprave the mind in like manner and with as great certainty as prevailing cold congeals water." And again, "Though the change from day to night is by a motion so gradual as scarcely to be perceived, yet when night is come we behold it very different from the day; and thus as people become wise in their own eyes and prudent in their own sight, customs rise up from the spirit of this world and spread, by little and little, till a departure from the simplicity that is in Christ becomes as distinguishable as light from darkness to such who are crucified to the world." So the generations as they pass slip further and further from "pure wisdom," for "the customs of their parents, and their neighbours, working upon their minds, and they from thence conceiving ideas of things and modes of conduct, the entrance into their hearts becomes in a great measure shut up against the gentle movings of Uncreated Purity." Woolman is too wise to feel resentment against those so hardened; rather he says, "Compassion hath filled my heart toward my fellow-creatures involved in customs, grown up in the wisdom of this world, which is foolishness with God."

To his own spirit, we may well apply the description in the little essay on "Merchandising," of the growing sensitiveness among the faithful friends of Christ, who "inwardly breathe that His Kingdom may come on earth" and "learn to be very attentive to the means He may appoint for promoting pure righteousness." His ideal is "that state in which Christ is the Light of our life," so that "our labours stand in the true harmony of society." "In this state," he writes, "a care is felt for a reformation in general, that our own posterity, with the rest of mankind in succeeding ages, may not be entangled by oppressive customs, transmitted to them through our hands." When we consider the deepening desire in our own day to lessen for the next generation that intolerable burden of social compunction which rests upon ourselves, may we perhaps dare to hope that this blessed "state," in which John Woolman himself constantly abode, is becoming common?

The definite issues suggested in these pages are often surprisingly modern. Now the fine old Quaker is perturbed over the question of tainted money: "Have the gifts and possessions received by me from others been conveyed in a way free from all unrighteousness so far as I have seen?" Now he notes the evils of over-work: "I have observed that too much labour not only makes the understanding dull, but so intrudes upon the harmony of the body that, after ceasing from our toil, we have another to pass through before we can enjoy the sweetness of rest," and proceeds to plead with energy for mercy and moderation in the standard of toil exacted from the poor. "The condition of many who dwell in cities," had "affected him with brotherly sympathy." Again we find him touching on the problem of dangerous trades, or analysing with the puzzle of the pioneer the ancient fallacy that the production of luxuries relieves economic distress—a fallacy to which he gives in quaint phrase a sound refutal. In the fifth chapter of the "Word of Remembrance," the interested reader will find a remarkable and very beautiful prophecy of the central principle of the settlement movement. And so we might go on.

In the twelfth century Woolman's solution would probably have been found in withdrawal from the evil world to the purity of desert or convent. Not so in the eighteenth. He remained among his brethren, bearing on his heart the burden of the common guilt: he was one of the first people to perceive that the moral sense must control not only our obvious but also our hidden relations with our fellows. And his experience may be said to mark the exact point where the individualism of the Puritan age broke down, unable to stand the strain of the growing sense of social solidarity. The intense but often naïvely self-centred conception of the religious life common to a Bunyan and an Edwardes had proved inadequate, and a new demand for an extension of Christianity to the remotest reaches of practical life, till human society be transformed in its depth and its breadth by a supernatural power, was consciously born.

Yet if Woolman's problem be social, his solution is individualistic. It is found in a resolute endeavour to clear his own life of any dependence on evil. Among the many experiments on the same lines, none more thorough-going is recorded; he pushed consistency to a farther point than Tolstoi or Thoreau. It is the story of this experiment that he tells us in the Journal, with a rare sincerity. See him as a lad, starting out peaceably at his trade of tailor, easily reaching commercial success—for Woolman possessed practical ability,—but "perceiving merchandise to be attended with much cumber," and deciding accordingly not to develop his business. Watch from this time the interaction of two co-operating forces, a craving for personal purity, and a horror of profiting by human pain,—and note that while the first impulse never waned, the second became more and more constraining. The record of his various "concerns" is delightfully human and appealing. He hated to be morally fussy, and the necessity of violating good breeding at the call of conscience caused him acute distress, for he had an ingrained instinct of good manners. Yet though "the exercise was heavy," he bravely took his elders to task on occasion: refused to accept free hospitality from slave-holders, forcing money on them for his entertainment; and, what is still harder, laboured with his friends. "Thou who travels in the work of the ministry, and art made very welcome by thy friends, it is good for thee to dwell deep that thou mayest feel and understand the spirits of people.... I have seen that in the midst of kindness and smooth conduct, to speak close and home to them who entertain us on points that relate to their outward interest, is hard labour, and sometimes when I have felt Truth lead toward it I have found myself disqualified by a superficial friendship.... To see the failings of our friends and think hard of them without opening that which we ought to open, and still carry a face of friendship, this tends to undermine the foundation of true unity." A man, sensitive, humble, and well-bred as Woolman evidently was, who can write thus, is pretty sure to know "deep exercises that are mortifying to the creaturely will." Some of his concerns, as those relating to the payment of taxes and the entertainment of soldiers, were common to the Friends; others are apparently inventions of his own. As time went on they increased and multiplied, all practically springing from the common root, the desire to avoid the oppression of the poor. Greed and the wish for ease came to seem a root of all evil. Travelling among the Indians, he felt the intimate relation of their misfortunes to the hunger of the English race for luxury and land. The use of dyes harmful to the worker forced him to wear undyed garments, even though to his meek distress a passing fashion of white hats made him run the danger of being confounded with the children of this world. A concern came upon him to go on foot in his preaching journeys: at first apparently that he might, like his Master, appear in the form of a servant; later, that he might have no complicity in the miseries suffered by the little post-boys employed in the chaises. Nothing is clearer to the reader of the Journal than the rapid increase of this holy or foolish sensitiveness. Seeking not to trade with oppressors, he refuses to gratify his palate with sugars prepared by the slave labour: under inward pressure to visit the West Indies, he has anxious scruples about taking passage on a ship owned by the West India Company, but decides that he may do so if he pays a sum sufficiently larger than that demanded to compensate the labour involved on another basis than that of slavery. At last—and here the crisis of his experience draws near—he feels himself inwardly bound to go to England; and decides that it is his duty to travel in the steerage, because forsooth the adornments of the cabin have cost vain and degrading labour. The horrors of a steerage passage in those days are well known to us from other sources; and among our visions of the martyrs of Truth we may well preserve the picture of John Woolman, his patient Quaker face upturned at midnight through the hatch, panting for a breath of air. Through the studied quiet of the narrative, the shrinking of the flesh can plainly be felt. The whole story at this point palpitates with a solemn pain and an exceeding peace. As usual, the sufferings of others form the larger part of his pain: he is wracked with sympathy for the sailors, and moved to a grieved indignant study of their temptations and afflictions which is good reading still to-day. Arrived in England, his experience deepens. As usual, he writes without emphasis: but his distress and tenderness are in every line. In a passage that reads as if penned by Engels or Rowntree, he makes careful pitying note of the scale of wages and cost of living, and cries out sharply, "Oh, may the wealthy consider the poor! May those who have plenty lay these things to heart!" We perceive that he is realising with increasing perplexity the extraordinary intricacy with which "the spirit of oppression" is entwined with the most innocent and necessary pursuits. "Silence as to every motion proceeding from the love of money and an humble waiting upon God to know his will concerning us appear necessary: 'He alone is able' so to direct us in our outward employments that pure universal love may shine forth in our proceedings." In "bowedness of spirit" he proceeds northward, and it is evident that the body is growing weaker as he makes his silent laborious way on foot, bearing from town to town the message of his Lord. He is offered to drink when thirsty, in silver vessels, and declines, "telling his case with weeping." Disgusted, "being but weakly," with "the scent arising from that filth which more or less infects the air of all closely settled towns," he feels distress both in body and mind with that which is impure, and a longing "that people might come in to cleanness of spirit, cleanness of person, and cleanness about their houses and garments:" noting at the same time, with his accustomed sagacity, that "some who are great carry delicacy to a great height themselves, and yet real cleanliness is not generally promoted." So continues his travail of soul, recorded in these pathetic and illumined pages, and before long the fatal disorder, small-pox, seizes upon him. He dies among strangers after lying patiently through his illness in the spirit of prayer, still saying characteristically to the young apothecary Friend with whom he had "found a freedom to confer," "that if anything should be proposed as to medicine that did not come through defiled channels or oppressive hands, he should be willing to consider and take it so far as he found freedom." Almost his last words, when already he could hardly be understood, are charged with his steady social compunction.

Dear John Woolman! Pure and high spirit, incapable of evasion, noteworthy no less for restraint and gentleness than for the resolute determination to translate the undimmed vision of the Perfect Right into terms of our daily existence! Whither would his "concerns" have carried him, had not the Angel of Small-Pox ended his wistful and unrelenting quest? He died in 1772, having lived his life before the industrial revolution, in days which we are wont to envy as simpler and less beset by social problems than our own. Certainly they were days in which the network of human relations was far less intricate than now. Yet the process in which he was engaged reached out to limits beyond our power to scan, and his experience is in one point of view an heroic reductio ad absurdum. No more instructive attempt was ever made to attain personal purity while neither withdrawing from the world nor transforming it. To-day the number is on the increase of persons who suffer under the sense of social guilt. All who know such suffering and are inclined to think the conversion of individuals adequate as an ultimate remedy, will do well to ponder these pages. For the conclusion is forced on us that Woolman was in an impasse: and while we love and reverence the heavenly sturdiness of soul possessed by this eighteenth-century saint, we must recognise with amusement touched by tenderness the hopelessness of his efforts to attain personal purity, the ridiculous extremes of isolation into which such a conscientious effort, if logically carried out, would lead us. The definite inference from Woolman's life and thought will be for most modern people the conviction of the hopelessness of the attempt to achieve, by individual means and private effort, a satisfying social righteousness in an unchanged world.

After all, Woolman's trouble and sorrow and tumult of spirit, so suggestive, so helpful to modern souls, were transitory. At the heart of his "endless agitation" subsisted a "central peace." His was the grace to know that "deep humility is a strong bulwark," and to "look less at the effects of the labour than at the pure motion and reality of the concern." The gentleness with which he delivered his fiery message was more than a manner due to Quaker training, or even than a result of resolute self-discipline: it was the index of an inward stillness in which his soul dwelt undisturbed. Let us hope that the days may come when the "concern" about profiting by the painful or degrading labour of others will have an interest as exclusively historic as the "concern" about holding slaves has already attained. Tremulously it may be, yet soberly and joyously, many clear-minded and practical people are beginning to hope for such a day. When it comes, the immediate message of Woolman will be less cogent, but he will still continue to be read by those who care for the revelations of a beautiful soul. These pages offer more than light on the path of social duty; they offer fellowship with a spirit that "dwelt deep," and attained an abiding loveliness because responsive through all turmoil of spirit and all outward suffering, to the "gentle movings of Uncreated Purity." "That purity of life," wrote he, "which proceeds from faithfulness in following the Spirit of Truth, this habitation has often been opened before me as a place of retirement for the children of the light, where we may stand separated from that which disordereth and confuseth the affairs of society." Such a "place of retirement for the Children of the Light," this book affords. -VIDA D. SCUDDER.

BIBLIOGRAPHY

Some Considerations on the Keeping of Negroes, recommended to the Professors of Christianity of every Denomination, Part I., 1754; Part II., 1762; many later issues of both parts; Considerations on Pure Wisdom and Human Policy, on Labour, Schools, and the Right Use of the Lord's Outward Gifts, 1768, and numerous later reprints; Considerations on the True Harmony of Mankind, and how it is to be Maintained, 1770, and later reprints; an Epistle to the Quarterly and Monthly Meetings of Friends, 1772; Remarks on Sundry Subjects, 1773, and later reprints; Serious Considerations on Various Subjects of Importance (containing the four above works, and some expressions of John Woolman in his last illness), 1773; A First Book for Children, 1774 (?); A Journal of the Life, Gospel, Labours, and Christian Experiences of John Woolman, 1774, and many later editions; with Introduction by John Greenleaf Whittier, 1871; with Introduction by A. Smellie, and Appreciation by J. G. Whittier (Books of the Heart), 1898; new century edition, with bibliography, etc., 1900; with foreword by Rev. R. J. Campbell, 1903; A Word of Remembrance and Caution to the Rich, 1793; later editions, published by Fabian Society, 1898, 1908.

Letters: Edited by J. Kendall (Letters on Religious Subjects, vol. ii.), 1820; by J. and I. Comly (Friends' Miscellany, vol. i.), 1834; in Journal, and in Friends' Review, vols. v.-xxviii.

Works: 1774; 5th edition, 1818.

Life: Saint John Woolman (Eclectic Review), 1861; David Duncan, paper read at Manchester Friends' Institute, 1871;

Dora Greenwell, 1871; W. Garrett Horder, A Quaker Saint (The Young Man), 1874; reprinted in Quaker Worthies, 1896; T. Green, 1885, with Introduction by H. C. G. Moule, 1897; Sketch of the Life of John Woolman (Booklet Series, No. 6), 1896; in Present Day Papers, vol. iii., 1900; a poem by Bernard Barton, "A Tribute to the Memory of John Woolman," appeared in vol. iii. of The Friend, and references to Woolman are found in Lamb, and in H. Crabb Robinson's Diary.

CONTENTS

Advertisement to the Reader

The Testimony of Friends in Yorkshire

A Testimony of the Monthly-Meeting of Friends

A Journal of the Life and Travels of John Woolman

The Last Epistle and Other Writings

Considerations on the True Harmony of Mankind

An Epistle to the Quarterly and Monthly-Meetings of Friends

Remarks on Sundry Subjects

Some Expressions of John Woolman in his Last Illness

ADVERTISEMENT TO THE READER

The manuscript JOURNAL of our late Friend John Woolman, was ended in England; where he also finished all his Labours. It appears, by a Letter which he sent, in his last Illness, to a Friend in London, that he did not intend the whole should be printed, and that he desired the said Friend to revise what he had written in this Nation, and leave out such Parts as he should think proper. It was, notwithstanding, sent entire, without any Alteration, to America; where it was soon after printed, together with several Tracts which had been published in his Life-time. But, as some Passages in the Journal contain Observations which appear to have been intended as private Memorandums only, and others relate to Circumstances which happened in his native Country, not expedient to be preserved on Record in this Nation, it is apprehended that the following Abridgement of it will be acceptable to Friends, and may be of general Service; and, as many weighty Arguments and pertinent Advices, relative to Slavery and the Oppression of the Negroes in the Plantations, are contained in the Journal, it was therefore apprehended that two small Tracts on that Subject might be omitted in this Abridgement.

THE TESTIMONY OF FRIENDS IN YORKSHIRE

At their Quarterly-meeting held at York, the 24th and 25th of the third Month 1773, concerning

JOHN WOOLMAN

Of Mount-Holly, in the Province of New-Jersey, in America; who departed this Life at the House of our Friend, Thomas Priestman, in the Suburbs of this City, the 7th of the tenth month 1772, and was interred in the Burying-ground of Friends, the 9th of the same, aged about fifty-two Years.

This our valuable Friend, having been under a religious Engagement for some Time to visit Friends in this Nation, and more especially us in the northern Parts, undertook the same in full Concurrence and near Sympathy with his Friends and Brethren at home, as appeared by Certificates from the monthly and quarterly Meetings to which he belonged, and from the Spring-meeting of Ministers and Elders, held at Philadelphia for Pennsylvania and New-Jersey.

He arrived in the City of London the beginning of the last Yearly-meeting, and, after attending that Meeting, travelled northward, visiting the Quarterly-meetings of Hertfordshire, Buckinghamshire, Northamptonshire, Oxfordshire, and Worcestershire, and divers particular Meetings in his Way.

He visited many Meetings on the West Side of this County; also some in Lancashire and Westmorland; from whence he came to our Quarterly-meeting in the last ninth Month; and though much out of Health, yet was enabled to attend all the Sittings of that Meeting except the last.

His Disorder, then, which proved the Small-pox, increased speedily upon him, and was very afflicting; under which he was supported in much Meekness, Patience, and Christian Fortitude. To those who attended him in his Illness his Mind appeared to be centered in divine Love; under the precious Influence whereof, we believe, he finished his Course, and entered into the Mansions of everlasting Rest.

In the early Part of his Illness he requested a Friend to write, and he broke forth thus:

"O Lord, my God! the amazing Horrors of Darkness were gathered around me and covered me all over, and I saw no Way to go forth: I felt the Misery of my Fellow-creatures separated from the divine Harmony, and it was heavier than I could bear, and I was crushed down under it: I lifted up my Hand, and stretched out my Arm, but there was none to help me: I looked round about, and was amazed: In the Depths of Misery, O Lord! I remembered that thou art omnipotent; that I had called thee Father; and I felt that I loved thee, and I was made quiet in thy Will, and I waited for Deliverance from thee; thou hadst Pity upon me when no Man could help me: I saw that Meekness under suffering was shewed to us in the most affecting Example of thy Son, and thou wast teaching me to follow him, and I said, Thy Will, O Father, be done."

Many more of his weighty Expressions might have been inserted here, but it was deemed unnecessary, they being already published in Print.

He was a Man endued with a large natural Capacity; and, being obedient to the Manifestations of divine Grace, having in Patience and Humility endured many deep Baptisms, he became thereby sanctified and fitted for the Lord's Work, and was truly serviceable in his Church: Dwelling in awful Fear and Watchfulness, he was careful, in his public Appearances, to feel the putting forth of the divine Hand, so that the Spring of the Gospel-ministry often flowed through him with great Sweetness and Purity, as a refreshing Stream to the weary Travellers toward the City of God: Skilful in dividing the Word, he was furnished by Him, in whom are hid all the Treasures of Wisdom and Knowledge, to communicate freely to the several States of the People where his Lot was cast. His Conduct at other Times was seasoned with the like watchful Circumspection and Attention to the Guidance of divine Wisdom, which rendered his whole Conversation uniformly edifying.

He was fully perswaded that as the Life of Christ comes to reign in the Earth, all Abuse and unnecessary Oppression, both of the human and brute Creation, will come to an End; but, under the Sense of a deep Revolt and overflowing Stream of Unrighteousness, his Life has been often a Life of mourning.

He was deeply concerned on account of that inhuman and iniquitous Practice of making Slaves of the People of Africa, or holding them in that State; and, on that Account, we understand he hath not only written some Books, but travelled much on the Continent of America, in order to make the Negro-masters (especially those in Profession with us) sensible of the evil of such a Practice; and though, in his Journey to England, he was far removed from the outward Sight of their Sufferings, yet his deep Exercise of Mind remained, as appears by a short Treatise he wrote in this Journey, and his frequent Concern to open the miserable State of this deeply-injured People. His Testimony in the last Meeting he attended was on this Subject; wherein he remarked, that as we, as a Society, when under outward Sufferings, had often found it our Concern to lay them before those in Authority, and thereby, in the Lord's Time, had obtained Relief, so he recommended this oppressed Part of the Creation to our Notice, that we may, as way may open, represent their Sufferings, in an Individual, if not a Society Capacity, to those in Authority.

Deeply sensible that the Desire to gratify People's Inclinations in Luxury and Superfluities is the principal Ground of Oppression, and the Occasion of many unnecessary Wants, he believed it to be his Duty to be a Pattern of great Self-denial with Respect to the Things of this Life, and earnestly to labour with Friends in the Meekness of Wisdom, to impress on their Minds the great Importance of our Testimony in these Things, recommending to the Guidance of the blessed Truth in this and all other Concerns, and cautioning such as are experienced therein against contenting themselves with acting up to the Standard of others, but to be careful to make the Standard of Truth, manifested to them, the Measure of their Obedience; for, said he, "that Purity of Life which proceeds from Faithfulness in following the Spirit of Truth, that State where our Minds are devoted to serve God, and all our Wants are bounded by his Wisdom,—this Habitation has often been opened before me, as a Place of retirement for the Children of the Light, where they may stand separated from that which disordereth and confuseth the Affairs of Society, and where we may have a Testimony of our Innocence in the Hearts of those who behold us."

We conclude with fervent Desires that we, as a People, may thus, by our Example, promote the Lord's Work in the Earth; and, our Hearts being prepared, may unite in Prayer to the great Lord of the Harvest, that as, in his infinite Wisdom, he hath greatly stripped the Church, by removing of late divers faithful Ministers and Elders, he may be pleased to send forth many more faithful Labourers into his Harvest.

Signed in, by Order, and on Behalf of, said Meeting:

Thomas Bennett,

John Storr,

Joseph Eglin,

Thomas Perkinson,

Joseph Wright,

Samuel Briscoe,

John Turner,

Joshua Robinson,

Thomas Priestman, and

divers other Friends.

A TESTIMONY OF THE MONTHLY-MEETING OF FRIENDS

Held in Burlington, the first Day of the eighth Month, in the Year of our Lord 1774, concerning our esteemed Friend,

JOHN WOOLMAN, DECEASED

He was born in Northampton, in the County of Burlington, and Province of West-New-Jersey, in the eighth Month, 1720, of religious Parents, who instructed him very early in the Principles of the Christian Religion, as professed by the People called Quakers, which he esteemed a Blessing to him, even in his young Years, tending to preserve him from the Infection of wicked Children; but, through the Workings of the Enemy, and Levity incident to Youth, he frequently deviated from those parental Precepts, by which he laid a renewed Foundation for Repentance, that was finally succeeded by a godly Sorrow not to be repented of, and so became acquainted with that sanctifying Power which qualifies for true Gospel Ministry, into which he was called about the twenty-second year of his Age; and, by a faithful Use of the Talents committed to him, he experienced an Increase, until he arrived at the State of a Father, capable of dividing the Word aright to the different States he ministered unto; dispensing Milk to Babes, and Meat to those of riper Years. Thus he found the Efficacy of that Power to arise, which, in his own Expressions, "prepares the Creature to stand like a Trumpet through which the Lord speaks to his People."—He was a loving Husband, a tender Father, and very humane to every Part of the Creation under his Care.

His Concern for the Poor and those in Affliction was evident by his Visits to them; whom he frequently relieved by his Assistance and Charity. He was for many Years deeply exercised on Account of the poor enslaved Africans, whose Cause, as he sometimes mentioned, lay almost continually upon him, and to obtain Liberty to those Captives, he laboured both in public and private; and was favoured to see his Endeavours crowned with considerable Success. He was particularly desirous that Friends should not be instrumental to lay Burthens on this oppressed People, but remember the Days of suffering from which they had been providentially delivered; that, if Times of Trouble should return, no Injustice dealt to those in Slavery might rise in Judgment against us, but, being clear, we might on such Occasions address the Almighty with a degree of Confidence, for his Interposition and Relief; being particularly careful, as to himself, not to countenance Slavery even by the Use of those Conveniences of Life which were furnished by their Labour.

He was desirous to have his own, and the Minds of others, redeemed from the Pleasures and immoderate Profits of this World, and to fix them on those Joys which fade not away; his principal Care being after a Life of Purity, endeavouring to avoid not only the grosser Pollutions, but those also which, appearing in a more refined Dress, are not sufficiently guarded against by some well-disposed People. In the latter Part of his Life he was remarkable for the Plainness and Simplicity of his Dress, and, as much as possible, avoided the Use of Plate, costly Furniture, and feasting; thereby endeavouring to become an Example of Temperance and Self-denial, which he believed himself called unto, and was favoured with Peace therein, although it carried the Appearance of great Austerity in the View of some. He was very moderate in his Charges in the Way of

Business, and in his Desires after Gain; and, though a Man of Industry, avoided, and strove much to lead others out of extreme Labour and Anxiousness after perishable Things; being desirous that the Strength of our Bodies might not be spent in procuring Things unprofitable, and that we might use Moderation and Kindness to the brute Animals under our Care, to prize the Use of them as a great Favour, and by no Means abuse them; that the Gifts of Providence should be thankfully received and applied to the Uses they were designed for.

He several Times opened a School at Mount-Holly, for the Instruction of poor Friends Children and others, being concerned for their Help and Improvement therein: His Love and Care for the rising Youth among us were truly great, recommending to Parents and those who have the Charge of them, to chuse conscientious and pious Tutors, saying, "It is a lovely Sight to behold innocent Children," and that "to labour for their Help against that which would mar the Beauty of their Minds, is a Debt we owe them."

His Ministry was sound, very deep and penetrating, sometimes pointing out the dangerous Situation which Indulgence and Custom lead into; frequently exhorting others, especially the Youth, not to be discouraged at the Difficulties which occur, but press after Purity. He often expressed an earnest Engagement that pure Wisdom should be attended to, which would lead into Lowliness of Mind and Resignation to the divine Will, in which State small Possessions here would be sufficient.

In transacting the Affairs of Discipline, his Judgment was sound and clear, and he was very useful in treating with those who had done amiss; he visited such in a private Way in that Plainness which Truth dictates, shewing great

Tenderness and Christian Forbearance. He was a constant Attender of our Yearly-meeting, in which he was a good Example, and particularly useful; assisting in the Business thereof with great Weight and Attention. He several Times visited most of the Meetings of Friends in this and the neighbouring Provinces, with the Concurrence of the Monthly-meeting to which he belonged, and, we have Reason to believe, had good Service therein, generally or always expressing, at his Return, how it had fared with him, and the Evidence of Peace in his Mind for thus performing his Duty. He was often concerned with other Friends in the important Service of visiting Families, which he was enabled to go through to Satisfaction.

In the Minutes of the Meeting of Ministers and Elders for this Quarter, at the Foot of a List of the Members of that Meeting, made about five Years before his Death, we find in his Hand-writing the following Observations and Reflections. "As looking over the Minutes, made by Persons who have put off this Body, hath sometimes revived in me a Thought how Ages pass away; so this List may probably revive a like Thought in some, when I and the rest of the Persons above-named are centered in another State of Being.—The Lord, who was the Guide of my Youth, hath in tender Mercies helped me hitherto; he hath healed me of Wounds, he hath helped me out of grievous Entanglements; he remains to be the Strength of my Life; to whom I desire to devote myself in Time and in Eternity."— Signed, John Woolman.

In the twelfth Month, 1771, he acquainted this Meeting that he found his Mind drawn towards a religious Visit to Friends in some Parts of England, particularly in Yorkshire. In the first Month, 1772, he obtained our Certificate, which was approved and endorsed by our Quarterly-meeting, and by the Half-year's-meeting of Ministers and Elders at Philadelphia. He embarked on his Voyage in the fifth, and arrived in London in the sixth, Month following, at the Time of their annual Meeting in that City. During his short Visit to Friends in that Kingdom, we are informed that his Services were acceptable and edifying. In his last Illness he uttered many lively and comfortable Expressions, being "perfectly resigned, having no Will either to live or die," as appears by the Testimony of Friends at York in Great-Britain, in the Suburbs whereof, at the House of our Friend, Thomas Priestman, he died of the Small-pox, on the seventh Day of the tenth Month, 1772, and was buried in Friends Burying-ground in that City, on the ninth of the same, after a large and solid Meeting held on the Occasion at their great Meeting-house, aged near fifty-two Years; a Minister upwards of thirty Years, during which Time he belonged to Mount-Holly Particular-meeting, which he diligently attended when at Home and in Health of Body, and his Labours of Love, and pious Care for the Prosperity of Friends in the blessed Truth, we hope may not be forgotten, but that his good Works may be remembered to Edification.

Signed in, and by Order of, the said Meeting, by

Samuel Allinson, Clerk.

Read and approved at our Quarterly-meeting, held at Burlington the 29th of the eighth Month, 1774.

Signed, by Order of said Meeting,

Daniel Smith, Clerk.

A JOURNAL OF THE LIFE, GOSPEL-LABOURS, AND CHRISTIAN EXPERIENCES, OF THAT FAITHFUL MINISTER OF JESUS CHRIST,

JOHN WOOLMAN;

Late of Mount-Holly, in the Province of New-Jersey.

Isaiah xxxii. 17.

"The Work of Righteousness shall be Peace; and the Effect of Righteousness, Quietness and Assurance for ever."

LONDON:

Printed and sold by James Phillips, in

George-Yard, Lombard-Street.

M.DCC.LXXV.

A JOURNAL OF THE LIFE AND TRAVELS OF JOHN WOOLMAN,

In the Service of the Gospel

CHAPTER I

His Birth and Parentage, with some Account of the Operations of divine Grace on his Mind in his Youth—His first Appearance in the Ministry—And his Considerations, while young, on the keeping of Slaves

I have often felt a Motion of Love to leave some Hints in Writing of my Experience of the Goodness of God; and now, in the thirty-sixth Year of my Age, I begin this Work.

I was born in Northampton, in Burlington County, West-Jersey, in the Year 1720; and before I was seven Years old I began to be acquainted with the Operations of divine Love. Through the Care of my Parents, I was taught to read nearly as soon as I was capable of it; and, as I went from School one seventh Day, I remember, while my Companions went to play by the Way, I went forward out of Sight, and, sitting down, I read the 22d Chapter of the Revelations: "He shewed me a pure River of Water of Life, clear as Chrystal, proceeding out of the Throne of God and of the Lamb, etc." and, in reading it, my Mind was drawn to seek after that pure Habitation, which, I then believed, God had prepared for his Servants. The Place where I sat, and the Sweetness that attended my Mind, remain fresh in my Memory.

This, and the like gracious Visitations, had that Effect upon me, that when Boys used ill Language it troubled me; and, through the continued Mercies of God, I was preserved from it.

The pious Instructions of my Parents were often fresh in my Mind when I happened to be among wicked Children, and were of Use to me. My Parents, having a large Family of Children, used frequently, on first Days after Meeting, to put us to read in the holy Scriptures, or some religious Books, one after another, the rest sitting by without much Conversation; which, I have since often thought, was a good Practice. From what I had read and heard, I believed there had been, in past Ages, People who walked in Uprightness before God, in a Degree exceeding any that I knew, or heard of, now living: And the Apprehension of there being less Steadiness and Firmness, amongst People in this Age than in past Ages, often troubled me while I was a Child.

A Thing remarkable in my Childhood was, that once, going to a Neighbour's House, I saw, on the Way, a Robin sitting on her Nest, and as I came near she went off, but, having young ones, flew about, and with many Cries expressed her Concern for them; I stood and threw Stones at her, till, one striking her, she fell down dead: At first I was pleased with the Exploit, but after a few Minutes was seized with Horror, as having, in a sportive Way, killed an innocent Creature while she was careful for her Young: I beheld her lying dead, and thought these young ones, for which she was so careful, must now perish for want of their Dam to nourish them; and, after some painful Considerations on the Subject, I climbed up the Tree, took all the young Birds, and killed them; supposing that better than to leave them to pine away and die miserably: And believed, in this Case, that Scripture-proverb was fulfilled, "The tender Mercies of the Wicked are cruel." I then went on my Errand, but, for some Hours, could think of little else but the Cruelties I had committed, and was much troubled. Thus he, whose tender Mercies are over all his Works, hath placed a Principle in the human Mind, which incites to exercise Goodness towards every living Creature; and this being singly attended to, People become tender hearted and sympathising; but being frequently and totally rejected, the Mind becomes shut up in a contrary Disposition.

About the twelfth Year of my Age, my Father being abroad, my Mother reproved me for some Misconduct, to which I made an undutiful Reply; and, the next first Day, as I was with my Father returning from Meeting, he told me he understood I had behaved amiss to my Mother, and advised me to be more careful in future. I knew myself blameable, and in Shame and Confusion remained silent. Being thus awakened to a Sense of my Wickedness, I felt Remorse in my Mind, and, getting home, I retired and prayed to the Lord to forgive me; and do not remember that I ever, after that, spoke unhandsomely to either of my Parents, however foolish in some other Things.

Having attained the Age of sixteen Years, I began to love wanton Company; and though I was preserved from prophane Language, or scandalous Conduct, still I perceived a Plant in me which produced much wild Grapes; yet my merciful Father forsook me not utterly, but, at Times, through his Grace, I was brought seriously to consider my Ways; and the Sight of my Backslidings affected me with Sorrow; but, for want of rightly attending to the Reproofs of Instruction, Vanity was added to Vanity, and Repentance to Repentance: Upon the whole, my Mind was more and more alienated from the Truth, and I hastened toward Destruction. While I meditate on the Gulph towards which I travelled, and reflect on my youthful Disobedience, for these Things I weep, mine Eyes run down with Water.

Advancing in Age, the Number of my Acquaintances increased, and thereby my Way grew more difficult; though I had found Comfort in reading the holy Scriptures, and thinking on heavenly Things, I was now estranged therefrom: I knew I was going from the Flock of Christ, and had no Resolution to return; hence serious Reflections were uneasy to me, and youthful Vanities and Diversions my greatest Pleasure. Running in this Road I found many like myself; and we associated in that which is the reverse of true Friendship.

But in this swift Race it pleased God to visit me with Sickness, so that I doubted of recovering; and then did Darkness, Horror, and Amazement, with full Force, seize me, even when my Pain and Distress of Body was very great. I thought it would have been better for me never to have had a Being, than to see the Day which I now saw. I was filled with Confusion; and in great Affliction, both of Mind and Body, I lay and bewailed myself. I had not Confidence to lift up my Cries to God, whom I had thus offended; but, in a deep Sense of my great Folly, I was humbled before him; and, at length, that Word which is as a Fire and a Hammer, broke and dissolved my rebellious Heart, and then my Cries were put up in Contrition; and in the multitude of his Mercies I found inward Relief, and felt a close Engagement, that, if he was pleased to restore my Health, I might walk humbly before him.

After my Recovery, this Exercise remained with me a considerable Time; but, by Degrees, giving Way to youthful Vanities, they gained Strength, and, getting with wanton young People, I lost Ground. The Lord had been very gracious, and spoke Peace to me in the Time of my Distress; and I now most ungratefully turned again to Folly; on which Account, at Times, I felt sharp Reproof. I was not so hardy as to commit Things scandalous; but to exceed in Vanity, and promote Mirth, was my chief Study. Still I retained a Love for pious People, and their Company brought an Awe upon me. My dear Parents, several Times, admonished me in the Fear of the Lord, and their Admonition entered into my Heart, and had a good Effect for a Season; but, not getting deep enough to pray rightly, the Tempter, when he came, found Entrance. I remember once, having spent a Part of the Day in Wantonness, as I went to Bed at Night, there lay in a Window, near my Bed, a Bible, which I opened, and first cast my Eye on this Text, "We lie down in our Shame, and our Confusion covers us:" This I knew to be my Case; and, meeting with so unexpected a Reproof, I was somewhat affected with it, and went to Bed under Remorse of Conscience; which I soon cast off again.

Thus Time passed on: My Heart was replenished with Mirth and Wantonness, and pleasing Scenes of Vanity were presented to my Imagination, till I attained the Age of eighteen Years; near which Time I felt the Judgments of God, in my Soul, like a consuming Fire; and, looking over my past Life, the Prospect was moving.—I was often sad, and longed to be delivered from those Vanities; then again, my Heart was strongly inclined to them, and there was in me a sore Conflict: At Times I turned to Folly, and then again, Sorrow and Confusion took hold of me. In a while, I resolved totally to leave off some of my Vanities; but there was a secret Reserve, in my Heart, of the more refined Part of them, and I was not low enough to find true Peace. Thus, for some Months, I had great Troubles; there remaining in me an unsubjected Will, which rendered my Labours fruitless, till at length, through the merciful Continuance of heavenly Visitations, I was made to bow down in Spirit before the Lord. I remember one Evening I had spent some Time in reading a pious Author; and walking out alone, I humbly prayed to the Lord for his Help, that I might be delivered from all those Vanities which so ensnared me. Thus, being brought low, he helped me; and, as I learned to bear the Cross, I felt Refreshment to come from his Presence; but, not keeping in that Strength which gave Victory, I lost Ground again; the Sense of which greatly affected me; and I sought Desarts and lonely Places, and there, with Tears, did confess my Sins to God, and humbly craved Help of him. And I may say with Reverence, he was near to me in my Troubles, and in those Times of Humiliation opened my Ear to Discipline. I was now led to look seriously at the Means by which I was drawn from the pure Truth, and learned this, that, if I would live in the Life which the faithful Servants of God lived in, I must not go into Company as heretofore in my own Will; but all the Cravings of Sense must be governed by a divine Principle. In Times of Sorrow and Abasement these Instructions were sealed upon me, and I felt the Power of Christ prevail over selfish Desires, so that I was preserved in a good degree of Steadiness; and, being young, and believing at that Time that a single Life was best for me, I was strengthened to keep from such Company as had often been a Snare to me.

I kept steadily to Meetings; spent First-day Afternoons chiefly in reading the Scriptures and other good Books; and was early convinced in Mind, that true Religion consisted in an inward Life, wherein the Heart doth love and reverence God the Creator, and learns to exercise true Justice and Goodness, not only toward all Men, but also toward the brute Creatures.—That as the Mind was moved, by an inward Principle, to love God as an invisible incomprehensible Being, by the same Principle it was moved to love him in all his Manifestations in the visible World.—That, as by his Breath the Flame of Life was kindled in all animal sensible Creatures, to say we love God, and, at the same Time exercise Cruelty toward the least Creature, is a Contradiction in itself.

I found no Narrowness respecting Sects and Opinions; but believed, that sincere upright-hearted People, in every Society, who truly love God, were accepted of him.

As I lived under the Cross, and simply followed the Openings of Truth, my Mind, from Day to Day, was more enlightened; my former Acquaintance were left to judge of me as they would, for I found it safest for me to live in private, and keep these Things sealed up in my own Breast. While I silently ponder on that Change wrought in me, I find no Language equal to it, nor any Means to convey to another a clear Idea of it. I looked on the Works of God in this visible Creation, and an Awfulness covered me; my Heart was tender and often contrite, and universal Love to my Fellow-creatures increased in me: This will be understood by such as have trodden the same Path. Some Glances of real Beauty may be seen in their Faces, who dwell in true Meekness. There is a Harmony in the Sound of that Voice to which divine Love gives Utterance, and some Appearance of right Order in their Temper and Conduct, whose Passions are regulated; yet all these do not fully shew forth that inward Life to such as have not felt it: But this white Stone and new Name is known rightly to such only as have it.

Though I had been thus strengthened to bear the Cross, I still found myself in great Danger, having many Weaknesses attending me, and strong Temptations to wrestle with; in the feeling whereof I frequently withdrew into private Places, and often with Tears besought the Lord to help me, whose gracious Ear was open to my Cry.

All this Time I lived with my Parents, and wrought on the Plantation; and, having had Schooling pretty well for a Planter, I used to improve it in Winter Evenings, and other leisure Times; and, being now in the twenty-first Year of my Age, a Man, in much Business at shop-keeping and baking, asked me, if I would hire with him to tend Shop and keep Books. I acquainted my Father with the Proposal; and, after some Deliberation, it was agreed for me to go.

At Home I had lived retired; and now, having a Prospect of being much in the Way of Company, I felt frequent and fervent Cries in my Heart to God, the Father of Mercies, that he would preserve me from all Corruption; that in this more publick Employment, I might serve him, my gracious Redeemer, in that Humility and Self-denial, with which I had been, in a small Degree, exercised in a more private Life. The Man, who employed me, furnished a Shop in Mount-Holly, about five Miles from my Father's House, and six from his own; and there I lived alone, and tended his Shop. Shortly after my Settlement here I was visited by several young People, my former Acquaintance, who knew not but Vanities would be as agreeable to me now as ever; and, at these Times, I cried to the Lord in secret, for Wisdom and Strength; for I felt myself encompassed with Difficulties, and had fresh Occasion to bewail the Follies of Time past, in contracting a Familiarity with libertine People; and, as I had now left my Father's House outwardly, I found my heavenly Father to be merciful to me beyond what I can express.

By Day I was much amongst People, and had many Trials to go through; but, in the Evenings, I was mostly alone, and may with Thankfulness acknowledge, that, in those Times, the Spirit of Supplication was often poured upon me; under which I was frequently exercised, and felt my Strength renewed.

In a few Months after I came here, my Master bought several Scotchmen, Servants, from on-board a Vessel, and brought them to Mount-Holly to sell; one of which was taken sick, and died.

In the latter Part of his Sickness, he, being delirious, used to curse and swear most sorrowfully; and, the next Night after his Burial, I was left to sleep alone in the same Chamber where he died; I perceived in me a Timorousness; I knew, however, I had not injured the Man, but assisted in taking Care of him according to my Capacity; and was not free to ask any one, on that Occasion, to sleep with me: Nature was feeble; but every Trial was a fresh Incitement to give myself up wholly to the Service of God, for I found no Helper like him in Times of Trouble.

After a While, my former Acquaintance gave over expecting me as one of their Company; and I began to be known to some whose Conversation was helpful to me: And now, as I had experienced the Love of God, through Jesus Christ, to redeem me from many Pollutions, and to be a Succour to me through a Sea of Conflicts, with which no Person was fully acquainted; and as my Heart was often enlarged in this heavenly Principle, I felt a tender Compassion for the Youth, who remained entangled in

Snares, like those which had entangled me from one Time to another: This Love and Tenderness increased; and my Mind was more strongly engaged for the Good of my Fellow-creatures. I went to Meetings in an awful Frame of Mind, and endeavoured to be inwardly acquainted with the Language of the true Shepherd; and, one Day, being under a strong Exercise of Spirit, I stood up, and said some Words in a Meeting; but, not keeping close to the divine Opening, I said more than was required of me; and being soon sensible of my Error, I was afflicted in Mind some Weeks, without any Light or Comfort, even to that Degree that I could not take Satisfaction in any Thing: I remembered God, and was troubled, and, in the Depth of my Distress, he had Pity upon me, and sent the Comforter: I then felt Forgiveness for my Offence, and my Mind became calm and quiet, being truly thankful to my gracious Redeemer for his Mercies; and, after this, feeling the Spring of divine Love opened, and a Concern to speak, I said a few Words in a Meeting, in which I found Peace; this, I believe, was about six Weeks from the first Time: And, as I was thus humbled and disciplined under the Cross, my Understanding became more strengthened to distinguish the pure Spirit which inwardly moves upon the Heart, and taught me to wait in Silence sometimes many Weeks together, until I felt that rise which prepares the Creature.

From an inward purifying, and stedfast abiding under it, springs a lively operative Desire for the Good of others: All the Faithful are not called to the public Ministry; but whoever are, are called to minister of that which they have tasted and handled spiritually. The outward Modes of Worship are various; but, wherever any are true Ministers of Jesus Christ, it is from the Operation of his Spirit upon their Hearts, first purifying them, and thus giving them a just Sense of the Conditions of others.

This Truth was clearly fixed in my Mind; and I was taught to watch the pure Opening, and to take Heed, lest, while I was standing to speak, my own Will should get uppermost, and cause me to utter Words from worldly Wisdom, and depart from the Channel of the true Gospel-Ministry.

In the Management of my outward Affairs, I may say, with Thankfulness, I found Truth to be my Support; and I was respected in my Master's Family, who came to live in Mount-Holly within two Years after my going there.

About the twenty-third Year of my Age, I had many fresh and heavenly Openings, in respect to the Care and Providence of the Almighty over his Creatures in general, and over Man as the most noble amongst those which are visible. And being clearly convinced in my Judgment, that to place my whole Trust in God was best for me, I felt renewed Engagements, that in all Things I might act on an inward Principle of Virtue, and pursue worldly Business no farther, than as Truth opened my Way therein.

About the Time called Christmas, I observed many People from the Country, and Dwellers in Town, who, resorting to Public-Houses, spent their Time in drinking and vain Sports, tending to corrupt one another; on which Account I was much troubled. At one House, in particular, there was much Disorder; and I believed it was a Duty incumbent on me to go and speak to the Master of that House. I considered I was young, and that several elderly Friends in town had Opportunity to see these Things; but though I would gladly have been excused, yet I could not feel my Mind clear.

The Exercise was heavy; and as I was reading what the Almighty said to Ezekiel, respecting his Duty as a Watchman, the Matter was set home more clearly; and then, with Prayers and Tears, I besought the Lord for his Assistance, who, in Loving-kindness, gave me a resigned Heart: Then, at a suitable Opportunity, I went to the Public-house, and, seeing the Man amongst much Company, I went to him, and told him, I wanted to speak with him; so we went aside, and there, in the Fear of the Almighty, I expressed to him what rested on my Mind; which he took kindly, and afterward shewed more Regard to me than before. In a few Years afterwards he died, middle-aged; and I often thought that, had I neglected my Duty in that Case, it would have given me great Trouble; and I was humbly thankful to my gracious Father, who had supported me herein.

My Employer having a Negro Woman, sold her, and desired me to write a Bill of Sale, the Man being waiting who bought her: The Thing was sudden; and, though the Thoughts of writing an Instrument of Slavery for one of my Fellow-creatures felt uneasy, yet I remembered I was hired by the Year, that it was my Master who directed me to do it, and that it was an elderly Man, a Member of our Society, who bought her; so, through Weakness, I gave way, and wrote; but, at the executing it, I was so afflicted in my Mind, that I said, before my Master and the Friend, that I believed Slave-keeping to be a Practice inconsistent with the Christian Religion: This in some Degree abated my Uneasiness; yet, as often as I reflected seriously upon it, I thought I should have been clearer, if I had desired to have been excused from it, as a Thing against my Conscience; for such it was. And, some Time after this, a young Man, of our Society, spoke to me to write a Conveyance of a Slave to him, he having lately taken a Negro into his House: I told him I was not easy to write it; for, though many of our Meeting and in other Places kept Slaves, I still believed the Practice was not right, and desired to be excused from the writing. I spoke to him in Good-will; and he told me that keeping Slaves was not altogether agreeable to his Mind; but that the Slave being a Gift to his Wife, he had accepted of her.

CHAPTER II

His first Journey, on a religious Visit, into East-Jersey, in Company with Abraham Farrington—His Thoughts on merchandizing, and his learning a Trade—His second Journey, with Isaac Andrews, into Pennsylvania, Maryland, Virginia, and North Carolina—His third Journey, with Peter Andrews, through Part of West and East-Jersey—Some Account of his Sister Elizabeth, and her Death—His fourth Journey, with Peter Andrews, through New-York and Long-Island, to New-England—And his fifth Journey, with John Sykes, to the eastern Shore of Maryland, and the lower Counties on Delaware

My esteemed Friend, Abraham Farrington, being about to make a Visit to Friends on the eastern Side of this Province, and having no Companion, he proposed to me to go with him; and, after a Conference with some elderly Friends, I agreed to go: We set out the fifth Day of the ninth Month, in the Year 1743; had an Evening-meeting at a Tavern in Brunswick, a Town in which none of our Society dwelt; the Room was full, and the People quiet. Thence to Amboy, and had an Evening-meeting in the Court-house; to which many People came, amongst whom were several Members of the Assembly, they being in Town on public Affairs of the Province: In both these Meetings my ancient Companion was enlarged to preach, in the Love of the Gospel. Thence we went to Woodbridge, Raway, and Plainfield; and had six or seven Meetings in Places where Meetings of Friends are not usually held, being made up chiefly of Presbyterians; and my beloved Companion was frequently strengthened to publish the

Word of Life amongst them: As for me, I was often silent; and, when I spake, it was with much Care, that I might speak only what Truth opened: And I learned some profitable Lessons.—We were out about two Weeks.

Near this Time, being on some outward Business in which several Families were concerned, and which was attended with Difficulties, some Things relating thereto not being clearly stated, nor rightly understood by all, there arose some Heat in the Minds of the Parties, and one valuable Friend got off his Watch; I had a great Regard for him, and felt a strong Inclination, after Matters were settled, to speak to him concerning his Conduct in that case: But I being a Youth, and he far advanced in Age and Experience, my Way appeared difficult; but, after some Days Deliberation, and inward seeking to the Lord for Assistance, I was made subject; so that I expressed what lay upon me in a Way which became my Youth and his Years: And, though it was a hard Task to me, it was well taken, and, I believe, useful to us both.

Having now been several Years with my Employer, and he doing less at Merchandize than heretofore, I was thoughtful of some other Way of Business; perceiving Merchandize to be attended with much Cumber, in the Way of trading in these Parts.

My mind, through the Power of Truth, was in a good degree weaned from the Desire of outward Greatness, and I was learning to be content with real Conveniences, that were not costly; so that a Way of Life, free from much Entanglement, appeared best for me, though the Income might be small. I had several Offers of Business that appeared profitable, but did not see my Way clear to accept of them; as believing the Business proposed would be attended with more outward Care than was required of me to engage in.

I saw that a humble Man, with the blessing of the Lord, might live on a little; and that where the Heart was set on Greatness, Success in Business did not satisfy the craving; but that commonly, with an Increase of Wealth, the Desire of Wealth increased. There was a Care on my Mind so to pass my Time, that nothing might hinder me from the most steady Attention to the Voice of the true Shepherd.

My Employer, though now a Retailer of Goods, was by Trade a Taylor, and kept a Servant-man at that Business; and I began to think about learning the Trade, expecting that, if I should settle, I might, by this Trade and a little retailing of Goods, get a Living in a plain Way, without the Load of great Business: I mentioned it to my Employer, and we soon agreed on Terms; and then, when I had Leisure from the Affairs of Merchandize, I worked with his Man. I believed the Hand of Providence pointed out this Business for me; and was taught to be content with it, though I felt, at Times, a Disposition that would have sought for something greater: But, through the Revelation of Jesus Christ, I had seen the Happiness of Humility, and there was an earnest Desire in me to enter deep into it; and, at Times, this Desire arose to a Degree of fervent Supplication, wherein my Soul was so environed with heavenly Light and Consolation, that Things were made easy to me which had been otherwise.

After some Time, my Employer's Wife died; she was a virtuous Woman, and generally beloved of her Neighbours; and, soon after this, he left shop-keeping, and we parted. I then wrought at my Trade, as a Taylor; carefully attended Meetings for Worship and Discipline; and found an

Enlargement of Gospel-love in my Mind, and therein a Concern to visit Friends in some of the Back-settlements of Pennsylvania and Virginia; and, being thoughtful about a Companion, I expressed it to my beloved Friend, Isaac Andrews, who then told me that he had Drawings to the same Places; also to go through Maryland, Virginia, and Carolina. After considerable Time past, and several Conferences with him, I felt easy to accompany him throughout, if Way opened for it. I opened the Case in our Monthly-meeting; and, Friends expressing their Unity therewith, we obtained Certificates to travel as Companions; his from Haddonfield, and mine from Burlington.

We left our Province on the twelfth Day of the third Month, in the Year 1746, and had several Meetings in the upper Part of Chester County, and near Lancaster; in some of which, the Love of Christ prevailed, uniting us together in his Service. Then we crossed the River Susquehannah, and had several Meetings in a new Settlement, called the Red-Lands; the oldest of which, as I was informed, did not exceed ten Years. It is the poorer Sort of People that commonly begin to improve remote Desarts: With a small Stock they have Houses to build, Lands to clear and fence, Corn to raise, Clothes to provide, and Children to educate; that Friends, who visit such, may well sympathise with them in their Hardships in the Wilderness; and though the best Entertainment such can give may seem coarse to some who are used to Cities, or old settled Places, it becomes the Disciples of Christ to be content with it. Our Hearts were sometimes enlarged in the Love of our heavenly Father amongst these People; and the sweet Influence of his Spirit supported us through some Difficulties: To him be the Praise!

We passed on to Monoquacy, Fairfax, Hopewell, and Shanando, and had Meetings; some of which were comfortable and edifying. From Shanando we set off in the Afternoon for the old Settlements of Friends in Virginia; and, the first Night, we, with our Pilot, lodged in the Woods, our Horses feeding near us; but he being poorly provided with a Horse, and we young and having good Horses, were free the next Day to part with him; and did so. In two Days after, we reached to our Friend John Cheagle's, in Virginia; so we took the Meetings in our Way through Virginia; were, in some Degree, baptized into a feeling Sense of the Conditions of the People; and our Exercise in general was more painful in these old Settlements, than it had been amongst the back Inhabitants: But, through the Goodness of our heavenly Father, the Well of living Waters was, at Times, opened to our Encouragement and the Refreshment of the sincere-hearted. We went on to Perquimons, in North-Carolina, had several Meetings, which were large, and found some Openness in those Parts, and a hopeful Appearance amongst the young People. So we turned again to Virginia, and attended most of the Meetings which we had not been at before, labouring amongst Friends in the Love of Jesus Christ, as Ability was given; and thence went to the Mountains, up James-River, to a new Settlement, and had several Meetings amongst the People, some of whom had lately joined in Membership with our Society.

In our journeying to and fro, we found some honest-hearted Friends, who appeared to be concerned for the Cause of Truth among a backsliding People.

From Virginia, we crossed over the River Patowmac, at Hoe's Ferry, and made a general Visit to the Meetings of Friends on the Western Shore of Maryland; and were at their Quarterly-meeting. We had some hard Labour amongst them, endeavouring to discharge our Duty honestly as Way opened, in the Love of Truth: And thence taking sundry Meetings in our Way, we passed homeward; where, through the Favour of divine Providence we reached the sixteenth Day of the sixth Month, in the Year 1746; and I may say that, through the Assistance of the Holy Spirit, my Companion and I travelled in Harmony, and parted in the Nearness of true brotherly Love.

Two Things were remarkable to me in this Journey; first, in Regard to my Entertainment, when I ate, drank, and lodged at free-cost, with People who lived in Ease on the hard Labour of their Slaves, I felt uneasy; and, as my Mind was inward to the Lord, I found, from Place to Place, this Uneasiness return upon me, at Times, through the whole Visit. Where the Masters bore a good Share of the Burthen, and lived frugally, so that their Servants were well provided for, and their Labour moderate, I felt more easy; but where they lived in a costly Way, and laid heavy Burthens on their Slaves, my Exercise was often great, and I frequently had Conversation with them, in private, concerning it. Secondly; this Trade of importing Slaves from their native Country being much encouraged amongst them, and the white People and their Children so generally living without much Labour, was frequently the Subject of my serious Thoughts: And I saw in these southern Provinces so many Vices and Corruptions, increased by this Trade and this Way of Life, that it appeared to me as a Gloom over the Land; and though now many willingly run into it, yet, in future, the Consequence will be grievous to Posterity: I express it as it hath appeared to me, not at once nor twice, but as a Matter fixed on my Mind.

Soon after my Return Home, I felt an increasing Concern for Friends on our Sea-coast; and, on the eighth Day of the eighth Month, in the Year 1746, with the Unity of Friends, and in Company with my beloved Friend and Neighbour, Peter Andrews, Brother to my Companion before-mentioned, we set forward, and visited Meetings generally about Salem, Cape May, Great and Little Egg-Harbour; and had Meetings at Barnagat, Mannahocking, and Mane-Squan, and so to the Yearly-meeting at Shrewsbury. Through the Goodness of the Lord Way was opened, and the Strength of divine Love was sometimes felt in our Assemblies, to the Comfort and Help of those who were rightly concerned before him. We were out twenty-two Days, and rode, by Computation, three hundred and forty Miles. At Shrewsbury Yearly-meeting, we met with our dear Friends Michael Lightfoot and Abraham Farrington, who had good Service there.

The Winter following my eldest Sister, Elizabeth Woolman, jun. died of the Small-pox, aged thirty-one Years. She was, from her Youth, of a thoughtful Disposition; and very compassionate to her Acquaintance in their Sickness or Distress, being ready to help as far as she could. She was dutiful to her Parents; one Instance whereof follows:—It happened that she, and two of her Sisters, being then near the Estate of young Women, had an Inclination, one First-day after Meeting, to go on a Visit to some other young Women at some Distance off; whose Company, I believe, would have done them no Good. They expressed their Desire to our Parents; who were dissatisfied with the Proposal, and stopped them. The same Day, as my Sisters and I were together, and they talking about their Disappointment, Elizabeth expressed her Contentment under it; signifying, she believed it might be for their Good.

A few Years after she attained to mature-Age, through the gracious Visitations of God's Love, she was strengthened to live a self-denying exemplary Life, giving herself much to Reading and Meditation.

The following Letter may shew, in some Degree, her Disposition.

Haddonfield, 1st Day, 11th Month, 1743.

Beloved Brother, John Woolman,—In that Love which desires the Welfare of all Men, I write unto thee: I received thine, dated second Day of the tenth Month last, with which I was comforted. My Spirit is bowed with Thankfulness that I should be remembered, who am unworthy; but the Lord is full of Mercy, and his Goodness is extended to the meanest of his Creation; therefore, in his infinite Love, he hath pitied, and spared, and shewed Mercy, that I have not been cut off nor quite lost; but, at Times, I am refreshed and comforted as with the Glimpse of his Presence, which is more to the immortal Part, than all which this World can afford: So, with Desires for thy Preservation with my own, I remain

Thy affectionate Sister,

Eliz. Woolman, jun.

In the fore Part of her Illness she was in great Sadness and Dejection of Mind, of which she told one of her intimate Friends, and said, When I was a young Girl I was wanton and airy, but I thought I had thoroughly repented of it; and added, I have of late had great Satisfaction in Meetings. Though she was thus disconsolate, still she retained a

Hope, which was as an Anchor to her: And sometime after, the same Friend came again to see her, to whom she mentioned her former Expressions, and said, It is otherwise now, for the Lord hath rewarded me seven fold; and I am unable to express the Greatness of his Love manifested to me. Her Disorder appearing dangerous, and our Mother being sorrowful, she took Notice of it, and said, Dear Mother, weep not for me; I go to my God: And, many Times, with an audible Voice, uttered Praise to her Redeemer.

A Friend, coming some Miles to see her the Morning before she died, asked her, how she did? She answered, I have had a hard Night, but shall not have another such, for I shall die, and it will be well with my Soul; and accordingly died the next Evening.

The following Ejaculations were found amongst her Writings; written, I believe, at four Times:

I. Oh! that my Head were as Waters, and mine Eyes as a Fountain of Tears, that I might weep Day and Night, until acquainted with my God.

II. O Lord, that I may enjoy thy Presence! or else my Time is lost, and my Life a Snare to my Soul.

III. O Lord, that I may receive Bread from thy Table, and that thy Grace may abound in me!

IV. O Lord, that I may be acquainted with thy Presence, that I may be seasoned with thy Salt, that thy Grace may abound in me!

Of late I found Drawings in my Mind to visit Friends in New-England, and, having an Opportunity of joining in Company with my beloved Friend, Peter Andrews, we, having obtained Certificates from our Monthly-meeting, set forward on the sixteenth Day of the third Month, in the Year 1747, and reached the Yearly-meeting at Long-Island; at which were our Friends Samuel Nottingham, from England, John Griffith, Jane Hoskins, and Elizbeth Hudson, from Pennsylvania, and Jacob Andrews, from Chesterfield. Several of whom were favoured in their publick Exercise; and, through the Goodness of the Lord, we had some edifying Meetings. After this, my Companion and I visited Friends on Long-Island; and, through the Mercies of God we were helped in the Work.

Besides going to the settled Meetings of Friends, we were at a general Meeting at Setawket, chiefly made up of other Societies; and had a Meeting at Oyster-Bay in a Dwelling-house, at which were many People: At the first of which there was not much said by way of Testimony; but it was I believe, a good Meeting: At the latter, through the springing up of living Waters, it was a Day to be thankfully remembered. Having visited the Island, we went over to the Main, taking Meetings in our Way, to Oblong, Nine Partners, and New-Milford.—In these back Settlements we met with several People, who, through the immediate Workings of the Spirit of Christ in their Minds, were drawn from the Vanities of the World, to an inward Acquaintance with him: They were educated in the Way of the Presbyterians. A considerable Number of the Youth, Members of that Society, used to spend their Time often together in merriment; but some of the principal young Men of that Company being visited by the powerful Workings of the Spirit of Christ, and thereby led humbly to take up his Cross, could no longer join in those Vanities;

and, as these stood stedfast to that inward Convincement, they were made a Blessing to some of their former Companions; so that, through the Power of Truth, several were brought into a close Exercise concerning the eternal Well-being of their Souls. These young People continued for a Time to frequent their publick Worship; and, besides that, had Meetings of their own; which Meetings were a while allowed by their Preacher, who, sometimes, met with them: But, in Time, their Judgment, in Matters of Religion, disagreeing with some of the Articles of the Presbyterians, their Meetings were disapproved by that Society; and such of them as stood firm to their Duty, as it was inwardly manifested, had many Difficulties to go through. And their Meetings were in a while dropped; some of them returning to the Presbyterians; and others of them, after a Time, joined our religious Society. I had Conversation with some of the latter, to my Help and Edification; and believe several of them are acquainted with the Nature of that Worship, which is performed in Spirit and in Truth.

From hence, accompanied by Amos Powel, a Friend from Long-Island, we rode through Connecticut, chiefly inhabited by Presbyterians, who were generally civil to us; and, after three Days riding, we came amongst Friends in the Colony of Rhode-Island. We visited Friends in and about Newport, and Dartmouth, and generally in those Parts; and then to Boston; and proceeded eastward as far as Dover; and then returned to Newport; and, not far from thence, we met our Friend, Thomas Gawthrop, from England, who was then on a Visit to these Provinces. From Newport we sailed to Nantucket; were there near a Week; and from thence came over to Dartmouth: And having finished our Visit in these Parts, we crossed the Sound from New-London to Long-Island; and, taking some Meetings on the Island, proceeded homeward; where we reached the thirteenth Day of the seventh Month, in the Year 1747, having rode about fifteen hundred Miles, and sailed about one hundred and fifty.

In this Journey, I may say, in general, we were sometimes in much Weakness, and laboured under Discouragements; and at other Times, through the renewed Manifestations of divine Love, we had seasons of Refreshment, wherein the Power of Truth prevailed.

We were taught, by renewed Experience, to labour for an inward Stillness; at no Time to seek for Words, but to live in the Spirit of Truth, and utter that to the People which Truth opened in us. My beloved Companion and I belonged to one Meeting, came forth in the Ministry near the same Time, and were inwardly united in the Work; he was about thirteen Years older than I, bore the heaviest Burthen, and was an Instrument of the greatest Use.

Finding a Concern to visit Friends in the lower Counties on Delaware, and on the eastern Shore of Maryland, and having an Opportunity to join with my well-beloved ancient Friend, John Sykes, we obtained Certificates, and set off the seventh Day of the eighth Month, in the Year 1748; were at the Meetings of Friends in the lower Counties, attended the Yearly-meeting at Little-Creek, and made a Visit to the chief of the Meetings on the eastern Shore; and so Home by Way of Nottingham: Were abroad about six Weeks, and rode, by Computation, about five hundred and fifty Miles.

Our Exercise, at Times, was heavy; but, through the Goodness of the Lord, we were often refreshed; and I may say, by Experience, He is a strong Hold in the Day of Trouble. Though our Society, in these Parts, appeared to me to be in a declining Condition; yet, I believe, the Lord hath a People amongst them, who labour to serve him uprightly, but have many Difficulties to encounter.

CHAPTER III

His Marriage—The Death of his Father—His Journies into the upper Part of New-Jersey, and afterwards into Pennsylvania—Considerations on keeping Slaves, and his Visits to the Families of Friends at several Times and Places—An Epistle from the General Meeting—His Journey to Long-Island—Considerations on Trading, and on the Use of spirituous Liquors and costly Apparel—And his Letter to a Friend

About this Time, believing it good for me to settle, and thinking seriously about a Companion, my Heart was turned to the Lord with Desires that he would give me Wisdom to proceed therein agreeable to his Will; and he was pleased to give me a well-inclined Damsel, Sarah Ellis; to whom I was married the eighteenth Day of the eighth Month, in the Year 1749.

In the fall of the Year 1750 died my Father, Samuel Woolman, with a Fever, aged about sixty Years.

In his Life-time he manifested much Care for us his Children, that in our Youth we might learn to fear the Lord; often endeavouring to imprint in our Minds the true Principles of Virtue, and particularly to cherish in us a Spirit of Tenderness, not only towards poor People, but also towards all Creatures of which we had the Command.

After my Return from Carolina, in the Year 1746, I made some Observations on keeping Slaves, which some Time before his Decease I shewed him; and he perused the

Manuscript, proposed a few Alterations, and appeared well satisfied that I found a Concern on that Account: And in his last Sickness, as I was watching with him one Night, he being so far spent that there was no Expectation of his Recovery, but having the perfect Use of his Understanding, he asked me concerning the Manuscript, whether I expected soon to proceed to take the Advice of Friends in publishing it? And, after some Conversation thereon, said, I have all along been deeply affected with the Oppression of the poor Negroes; and now, at last, my Concern for them is as great as ever.

By his Direction I had wrote his Will in a Time of Health, and that Night he desired me to read it to him, which I did; and he said it was agreeable to his Mind. He then made mention of his End, which he believed was near; and signified, that, though he was sensible of many Imperfections in the Course of his Life, yet his Experience of the Power of Truth, and of the Love and Goodness of God from Time to Time, even till now, was such, that he had no Doubt but that, in leaving this Life, he should enter into one more happy.

The next Day his Sister Elizabeth came to see him, and told him of the Decease of their Sister Ann, who died a few Days before: He then said, I reckon Sister Ann was free to leave this World: Elizabeth said, she was. He then said, I also am free to leave it; and, being in great Weakness of Body, said, I hope I shall shortly go to Rest. He continued in a weighty Frame of Mind, and was sensible till near the last.

On the second Day of the ninth Month, in the Year 1751, feeling Drawings in my Mind to visit Friends at the Great-Meadows, in the upper Part of West-Jersey, with the Unity of our Monthly-meeting, I went there; and had some searching laborious Exercise amongst Friends in those Parts, and found inward Peace therein.

In the ninth Month of the Year 1753, in Company with my well-esteemed Friend John Sykes, and with the Unity of Friends, we travelled about two Weeks, visiting Friends in Bucks-County. We laboured in the Love of the Gospel, according to the Measure received; and, through the Mercies of him, who is Strength to the Poor who trust in him, we found Satisfaction in our Visit: And, in the next Winter, Way opening to visit Friends Families within the Compass of our Monthly-meeting, partly by the Labours of two Friends from Pennsylvania, I joined in some Part of the Work; having had a Desire some Time that it might go forward amongst us.

About this Time, a Person at some Distance lying sick, his Brother came to me to write his Will: I knew he had Slaves; and, asking his Brother, was told he intended to leave them as Slaves to his Children. As Writing is a profitable Employ, and as offending sober People was disagreeable to my Inclination, I was straitened in my Mind; but, as I looked to the Lord, he inclined my Heart to his Testimony: And I told the Man, that I believed the Practice of continuing Slavery to this People was not right; and had a Scruple in my Mind against doing Writings of that Kind; that, though many in our Society kept them as Slaves, still I was not easy to be concerned in it; and desired to be excused from going to write the Will. I spake to him in the Fear of the Lord; and he made no Reply to what I said, but went away: He, also, had some Concerns in the Practice; and I thought he was displeased with me. In this Case I had a fresh Confirmation, that acting contrary to present outward Interest, from a Motive of divine Love, and in Regard to Truth and Righteousness, opens the Way to a Treasure better than Silver, and to a Friendship exceeding the Friendship of Men.

The Manuscript before-mentioned having lain by me several Years, the Publication of it rested weightily upon me; and this Year I offered it to the Revisal of Friends, who, having examined and made some small Alterations in it, directed a Number of Copies thereof to be published, and dispersed amongst Friends.

In the Year 1754, I found my Mind drawn to join in a Visit to Friends Families belonging to Chesterfield Monthly-meeting; and having the Approbation of our own, I went to their Monthly-meeting in order to confer with Friends, and see if Way opened for it: I had Conference with some of their Members, the Proposal having been opened before in their Meeting, and one Friend agreed to join with me as a Companion for a Beginning; but, when Meeting was ended, I felt great Distress of Mind, and doubted what Way to take, or whether to go Home and wait for greater Clearness: I kept my Distress secret; and, going with a Friend to his House, my Desires were to the great Shepherd for his heavenly Instruction; and in the Morning I felt easy to proceed on the Visit, being very low in my Mind: And as mine Eye was turned to the Lord, waiting in Families in deep Reverence before him, he was pleased graciously to afford Help; so that we had many comfortable Opportunities, and it appeared as a fresh Visitation to some young People. I spent several Weeks this Winter in the Service, Part of which Time was employed near Home. And again, in the following Winter, I was several Weeks in the same Service; some Part of the Time at Shrewsbury, in Company with my beloved Friend, John Sykes; and have Cause humbly to acknowledge, that, through the Goodness of the Lord, our Hearts were, at Times, enlarged in his Love; and Strength was given to go through the Trials which, in the Course of our Visit, attended us.

From a Disagreement between the Powers of England and France, it was now a Time of Trouble on this Continent; and an Epistle to Friends went forth from our General Spring-meeting, which I thought good to give a Place in this Journal.

An EPISTLE from our General Spring-meeting of Ministers and Elders for Pennsylvania and New-Jersey, held at Philadelphia, from the 29th of the third Month, to the first of the fourth Month, inclusive, 1755.

To Friends on the Continent of America.

Dear Friends,—In an humble Sense of divine Goodness, and the gracious Continuation of God's Love to his People, we tenderly salute you; and are at this Time therein engaged in Mind, that all of us who profess the Truth, as held forth and published by our worthy Predecessors in this latter Age of the World, may keep near to that Life which is the Light of Men, and be strengthened to hold fast the Profession of our Faith without wavering, that our Trust may not be in Man but in the Lord alone, who ruleth in the Army of Heaven, and in the Kingdoms of Men, before whom the Earth is as the Dust of the Balance, and her Inhabitants as Grasshoppers. Isa. xl. 22.

We (being convinced that the gracious Design of the Almighty in sending his Son into the World, was to repair the Breach made by Disobedience, to finish Sin and Transgression, that his Kingdom might come, and his Will be done on Earth as it is in Heaven) have found it to be our

Duty to cease from those national Contests productive of Misery and Bloodshed, and submit our Cause to him, the Most High, whose tender Love to his Children exceeds the most warm Affections of natural Parents, and who hath promised to his Seed throughout the Earth, as to one Individual, "I will never leave thee, nor forsake thee." Heb. xiii. 5. And as we, through the gracious Dealings of the Lord our God, have had Experience of that Work which is carried on, "not by earthly Might, nor by Power, but by my Spirit, saith the Lord of Hosts:" Zech. iv. 6. By which Operation, that spiritual Kingdom is set up, which is to subdue and break in pieces all Kingdoms that oppose it, and shall stand for ever; in a deep Sense thereof, and of the Safety, Stability, and Peace, there is in it, we are desirous that all who profess the Truth, may be inwardly acquainted with it, and thereby be qualified to conduct ourselves in all Parts of our Life as becomes our peaceable Profession: And we trust, as there is a faithful Continuance to depend wholly upon the Almighty Arm, from one Generation to another, the peaceable Kingdom will gradually be extended "from Sea to Sea, and from the River to the Ends of the Earth." Zech. ix. 10. to the Completion of those Prophecies already begun, that "Nation shall not lift up a Sword against Nation, nor learn War any more." Isa. ii. 4. Micah iv. 3.

And, dearly beloved Friends, seeing we have these Promises, and believe that God is beginning to fulfil them, let us constantly endeavour to have our Minds sufficiently disintangled from the surfeiting Cares of this Life, and redeemed from the Love of the World, that no earthly Possessions nor Enjoyments may bias our Judgments, or turn us from that Resignation, and entire Trust in God, to which his Blessing is most surely annexed; then may we say, "Our Redeemer is mighty, he will plead our Cause for us." Jer. 1. 34. And if, for the farther promoting his most gracious Purposes in the Earth, he should give us to taste of that bitter Cup which his faithful Ones have often partaken of; O! that we may be rightly prepared to receive it.

And now, dear Friends, with Respect to the Commotions and Stirrings of the Powers of the Earth at this Time near us, we are desirous that none of us may be moved thereat; "but repose ourselves in the Munition of that Rock that all these Shakings shall not move, even in the Knowledge and Feeling of the eternal Power of God, keeping us subjectly given up to his heavenly Will, and feel it daily to mortify that which remains in any of us which is of this World; for the worldly Part, in any, is the changeable Part, and that is up and down, full and empty, joyful and sorrowful, as Things go well or ill in this World; for as the Truth is but one, and many are made Partakers of its Spirit, so the World is but one, and many are made Partakers of the Spirit of it; and so many as do partake of it, so many will be straitened and perplexed with it: But they who are single to the Truth, waiting daily to feel the Life and Virtue of it in their Hearts, these shall rejoice in the midst of Adversity," and have to experience, with the Prophet, that "Although the Fig-tree shall not blossom, neither shall Fruit be in the Vines; the Labour of the Olive shall fail, and the Fields shall yield no Meat; the Flock shall be cut off from the Fold, and there shall be no Herd in the Stalls; yet will they rejoice in the Lord, and joy in the God of their Salvation." Hab. iii. 17, 18.

If, contrary to this, we profess the Truth, and, not living under the Power and Influence of it, are producing Fruits disagreeable to the Purity thereof, and trust to the Strength of Man to support ourselves, therein our Confidence will be vain. For he, who removed the Hedge from his Vineyard, and gave it to be trodden under Foot, by reason of the wild Grapes it produced, (Isa. v. 5.) remains unchangeable; And if, for the Chastisement of Wickedness, and the farther promoting his own Glory, he doth arise, even to shake terribly the Earth, who then may oppose him, and prosper!

We remain, in the Love of the Gospel, your Friends and Brethren.

Signed by fourteen Friends.

Scrupling to do Writings, relative to keeping Slaves, having been a Means of sundry small Trials to me, in which I have so evidently felt my own Will set aside, I think it good to mention a few of them.—Tradesmen and Retailers of Goods, who depend on their Business for a Living, are naturally inclined to keep the Good-will of their Customers; nor is it a pleasant Thing for young Men to be under any Necessity to question the Judgment or Honesty of elderly Men, and more especially of such as have a fair Reputation. Deep-rooted Customs, though wrong, are not easily altered; but it is the Duty of every one to be firm in that which they certainly know is right for them. A charitable benevolent Man, well acquainted with a Negro, may, I believe, under some Circumstances, keep him in his Family as a Servant, from no other Motives than the Negro's Good; but Man, as Man, knows not what shall be after him, nor hath Assurance that his Children will attain to that Perfection in Wisdom and Goodness necessary rightly to exercise such Power: It is clear to me, that I ought not to be the Scribe where Wills are drawn, in which some Children are made absolute Masters over others during Life.

About this Time, an ancient Man, of good Esteem in the Neighbourhood, came to my House to get his Will written; he had young Negroes; and I asked him privately, how he purposed to dispose of them? He told me: I then said, I cannot write thy Will without breaking my own Peace; and respectfully gave him my Reasons for it: He signified that he had a Choice that I should have written it; but as I could not, consistent with my Conscience, he did not desire it: And so he got it written by some other Person. And, a few Years after, there being great Alterations in his Family, he came again to get me to write his Will: His Negroes were yet young; and his Son, to whom he intended to give them, was, since he first spoke to me, from a Libertine, become a sober young Man; and he supposed, that I would have been free, on that Account, to write it. We had much friendly Talk on the Subject, and then deferred it: A few Days after, he came again, and directed their Freedom; and then I wrote his Will.

Near the Time the last-mentioned Friend first spoke to me, a Neighbour received a bad Bruise in his Body, and sent for me to bleed him; which being done, he desired me to write his Will: I took Notes; and, amongst other Things, he told me to which of his Children he gave his young Negro: I considered the Pain and Distress he was in, and knew not how it would end; so I wrote his Will, save only that Part concerning his Slave, and carrying it to his Bed side, read it to him; and then told him, in a friendly Way, that I could not write any Instruments by which my Fellow-creatures were made Slaves, without bringing Trouble on my own Mind: I let him know that I charged nothing for what I had done; and desired to be excused from doing the other Part in the Way he proposed: We then had a serious Conference on the Subject; at length he agreeing to set her free, I finished his Will.

Having found Drawings in my Mind to visit Friends on Long-Island, after obtaining a Certificate from our Monthly-meeting, I set off on the twelfth Day of the fifth Month, in the Year 1756. When I reached the Island, I lodged the first Night at the House of my dear Friend, Richard Hallet; the next Day, being the first of the Week, I was at the Meeting in New-town; in which we experienced the renewed Manifestations of the Love of Jesus Christ, to the Comfort of the honest-hearted. I went that Night to Flushing; and the next Day, in Company with my beloved Friend, Matthew Franklin, we crossed the Ferry at White-stone; were at three Meetings on the Main, and then returned to the Island; where I spent the Remainder of the Week in visiting Meetings. The Lord, I believe, hath a People in those Parts, who are honestly inclined to serve him; but many, I fear, are too much clogged with the Things of this Life, and do not come forward bearing the Cross in such Faithfulness as he calls for.

My Mind was deeply engaged in this Visit, both in publick and private; and, at several Places, observing that they had Slaves, I found myself under a Necessity in a friendly Way, to labour with them on that Subject; expressing, as Way opened, the Inconsistency of that Practice with the Purity of the Christian Religion, and the ill Effects of it manifested amongst us.

The Latter-end of the Week, their Yearly-meeting began; at which were our Friends John Scarborough, Jane Hoskins, and Susanna Brown, from Pennsylvania: The publick Meetings were large, and measurably favoured with divine Goodness.

The Exercise of my Mind, at this Meeting, was chiefly on Account of those who were considered as the foremost

Rank in the Society; and, in a Meeting of Ministers and Elders, Way opened, that I expressed in some Measure what lay upon me; and, at a Time when Friends were met for transacting the Affairs of the Church, having set a while silent, I felt a Weight on my Mind, and stood up; and, through the gracious Regard of our heavenly Father, Strength was given fully to clear myself of a Burthen, which, for some Days, had been increasing upon me.

Through the humbling Dispensations of divine Providence, Men are sometimes fitted for his Service. The Messages of the Prophet Jeremiah, were so disagreeable to the People, and so reverse to the Spirit they lived in, that he became the Object of their Reproach; and, in the Weakness of Nature, thought of desisting from his prophetic Office; but, saith he, "His Word was in my Heart as a burning Fire shut up in my Bones; and I was weary with forbearing, and could not stay." I saw at this Time, that if I was honest in declaring that which Truth opened in me, I could not please all Men; and laboured to be content in the Way of my Duty, however disagreeable to my own Inclination. After this I went homeward, taking Woodbridge, and Plainfield in my Way; in both which Meetings, the pure Influence of divine Love was manifested; in an humbling Sense whereof I went Home, having been out about twenty-four Days, and rode about three hundred and sixteen Miles.

While I was out on this Journey, my Heart was much affected with a Sense of the State of the Churches in our southern Provinces; and, believing the Lord was calling me to some farther Labour amongst them, I was bowed in Reverence before him, with fervent Desires that I might find Strength to resign myself up to his heavenly Will.

Until this Year, 1756, I continued to retail Goods, besides following my Trade as a Taylor; about which Time, I grew uneasy on Account of my Business growing too cumbersome: I had begun with selling Trimmings for Garments, and from thence proceeded to sell Cloths and Linens; and, at length, having got a considerable Shop of Goods, my Trade increased every Year, and the Road to large Business appeared open; but I felt a Stop in my Mind.

Through the Mercies of the Almighty, I had, in a good degree, learned to be content with a plain Way of Living: I had but a small Family; and, on serious Consideration, I believed Truth did not require me to engage in much cumbering Affairs: It had been my general Practice to buy and sell Things really useful: Things that served chiefly to please the vain Mind in People, I was not easy to trade in; seldom did it; and, whenever I did, I found it weaken me as a Christian.

The Increase of Business became my Burthen; for, though my natural Inclination was toward Merchandize, yet I believed Truth required me to live more free from outward Cumbers: and there was now a Strife in my Mind between the two; and in this Exercise my Prayers were put up to the Lord, who graciously heard me, and gave me a Heart resigned to his holy Will: Then I lessened my outward Business; and, as I had Opportunity, told my Customers of my Intention, that they might consider what Shop to turn to: And, in a while, wholly laid down Merchandize, following my Trade, as a Taylor, myself only, having no Apprentice. I also had a Nursery of Appletrees; in which I employed some of my Time in hoeing, grafting, trimming, and inoculating. In Merchandize it is the Custom, where I lived, to sell chiefly on Credit, and poor People often get in Debt; and when Payment is expected, not having wherewith to pay, their Creditors often sue for it at Law. Having often observed Occurrences of this Kind, I found it good for me to advise poor People to take such Goods as were most useful and not costly.

In the Time of Trading, I had an Opportunity of seeing, that the too liberal Use of spirituous Liquors, and the Custom of wearing too costly Apparel, led some People into great Inconveniences; and these two Things appear to be often connected; for, by not attending to that Use of Things which is consistent with universal Righteousness, there is an Increase of Labour which extends beyond what our heavenly Father intends for us: And by great Labour, and often by much Sweating, there is, even among such as are not Drunkards, a craving of some Liquors to revive the Spirits; that, partly by the luxurious Drinking of some, and partly by the Drinking of others (led to it through immoderate Labour), very great Quantities of Rum are every Year expended in our Colonies; the greater Part of which we should have no Need of, did we steadily attend to pure Wisdom.

Where Men take Pleasure in feeling their Minds elevated with Strong-drink, and so indulge their Appetite as to disorder their Understandings, neglect their Duty as Members in a Family or Civil Society, and cast off all Regard to Religion, their Case is much to be pitied; and where such, whose Lives are for the most Part regular, and whose Examples have a strong Influence on the Minds of others, adhere to some Customs which powerfully draw to the Use of more Strong-liquor than pure Wisdom allows; this also, as it hinders the spreading of the Spirit of Meekness, and strengthens the Hands of the more excessive Drinkers, is a Case to be lamented.

As every Degree of Luxury hath some Connection with Evil, those who profess to be Disciples of Christ, and are looked upon as Leaders of the People, should have that Mind in them which was also in Christ, and so stand separate from every wrong Way, as a Means of Help to the Weaker. As I have sometimes been much spent in the Heat, and taken Spirits to revive me, I have found, by Experience, that in such Circumstances the Mind is not so calm, nor so fitly disposed for divine Meditation, as when all such Extremes are avoided; and I have felt an increasing Care to attend to that holy Spirit which sets Bounds to our Desires, and leads those, who faithfully follow it, to apply all the Gifts of divine Providence to the Purposes for which they were intended. Did such, as have the Care of great Estates, attend with Singleness of Heart to this heavenly Instructor, which so opens and enlarges the Mind, that Men love their Neighbours as themselves, they would have Wisdom given them to manage, without finding Occasion to employ some People in the Luxuries of Life, or to make it necessary for others to labour too hard; but, for want of steadily regarding this Principle of divine Love, a selfish Spirit takes Place in the Minds of People, which is attended with Darkness and manifold Confusion in the World.

Though trading in Things useful is an honest Employ; yet, through the great Number of Superfluities which are bought and sold, and through the Corruption of the Times, they, who apply to merchandize for a Living, have great Need to be well experienced in that Precept which the Prophet Jeremiah laid down for his Scribe: "Seekest thou great Things for thyself? seek them not."

In the Winter, this Year, I was engaged with Friends in visiting Families; and, through the Goodness of the Lord, we had oftentimes Experience of his Heart-tendering Presence amongst us.

A Copy of a Letter written to a Friend.

In this thy late Affliction I have found a deep Fellow-feeling with thee; and had a secret Hope throughout, that it might please the Father of Mercies to raise thee up, and sanctify thy Troubles to thee; that thou, being more fully acquainted with that Way which the World esteems foolish, mayst feel the Clothing of divine Fortitude, and be strengthened to resist that Spirit which leads from the Simplicity of the everlasting Truth.

We may see ourselves crippled and halting, and, from a strong Bias to Things pleasant and easy, find an Impossibility to advance forward; but Things impossible with Men are possible with God; and, our Wills being made subject to his, all Temptations are surmountable.

This Work of subjecting the Will is compared to the Mineral in the Furnace; "He refines them as Silver is refined.—He shall sit as a Refiner and Purifier of Silver." By these Comparisons we are instructed in the Necessity of the Operation of the Hand of God upon us, to prepare our Hearts truly to adore him, and manifest that Adoration, by inwardly turning away from that Spirit, in all its Workings, which is not of him. To forward this Work, the all-wise God is sometimes pleased, through outward Distress, to bring us near the Gates of Death; that, Life being painful and afflicting, and the Prospect of Eternity open before us, all earthly Bonds may be loosened, and the Mind prepared for that deep and sacred Instruction, which otherwise would not be received. If Parents love their Children and delight in their Happiness, then he, who is perfect Goodness, in sending abroad mortal Contagions, doth assuredly direct their Use: Are the Righteous removed by it? Their Change is happy: Are the Wicked taken away in their Wickedness? The Almighty is clear: Do we pass through with Anguish and great Bitterness, and yet recover, he intends that we should be purged from Dross, and our Ears opened to Discipline.

And now that, on thy Part, after thy sore Affliction and Doubts of Recovery, thou art again restored, forget not him who hath helped thee; but in humble Gratitude hold fast his Instructions, thereby to shun those By-paths which lead from the firm Foundation. I am sensible of that Variety of Company, to which one in thy Business must be exposed: I have painfully felt the Force of Conversation proceeding from Men deeply rooted in an earthly Mind, and can sympathize with others in such Conflicts, in that much Weakness still attends me.

I find that to be a Fool as to worldly Wisdom, and commit my Cause to God, not fearing to offend Men, who take Offence at the Simplicity of Truth, is the only Way to remain unmoved at the Sentiments of others.

The Fear of Man brings a Snare; by halting in our Duty, and giving back in the Time of Trial, our Hands grow weaker, our Spirits get mingled with the People, our Ears grow dull as to hearing the Language of the true Shepherd; that when we look at the Way of the Righteous, it seems as though it was not for us to follow them.

There is a Love clothes my Mind, while I write, which is superior to all Expressions; and I find my Heart open to encourage a holy Emulation, to advance forward in

Christian Firmness. Deep Humility is a strong Bulwark; and, as we enter into it, we find Safety: The Foolishness of God is wiser than Man, and the Weakness of God is stronger than Man. Being unclothed of our own Wisdom, and knowing the Abasement of the Creature, therein we find that Power to arise, which gives Health and Vigour to us.

CHAPTER IV

His Journey to Pennsylvania, Maryland, Virginia, and North-Carolina: Considerations on the State of Friends there; and the Exercise he was under in travelling among those so generally concerned in keeping Slaves: With some Observations in Conversation, at several Times, on this Subject—His Epistle to Friends at New-Garden and Cane-Creek—His Thoughts on the Neglect of a religious Care in the Education of the Negroes

Feeling an Exercise in Relation to a Visit to the southern Provinces, I acquainted our Monthly-meeting therewith, and obtained their Certificate: Expecting to go alone, one of my Brothers, who lived in Philadelphia, having some Business in North-Carolina, proposed going with me Part of the Way; but, as he had a View of some outward Affairs, to accept of him as a Companion seemed some Difficulty with me, whereupon I had Conversation with him at sundry Times; and, at length, feeling easy in my Mind, I had Conversation with several elderly Friends of Philadelphia on the Subject; and he obtaining a Certificate suitable to the Occasion, we set off in the fifth Month of the Year 1757; and, coming to Nottingham Week-day Meeting, lodged at John Churchman's; and here I met with our Friend Benjamin Buffington, from New-England, who was returning from a Visit to the southern Provinces. Thence we crossed the River Susquehannah, and lodged at William Cox's in Maryland; and, soon after I entered this Province, a deep and painful Exercise came upon me, which I often had some Feeling of since my Mind was drawn towards these Parts, and with which I had acquainted my Brother before we agreed to join as Companions.

As the People in this and the southern Provinces live much on the Labour of Slaves, many of whom are used hardly, my Concern was, that I might attend with Singleness of Heart to the Voice of the true Shepherd, and be so supported as to remain unmoved at the Faces of Men.

The Prospect of so weighty a Work brought me very low; and such were the Conflicts of my Soul, that I had a near Sympathy with the Prophet, in the Time of his Weakness, when he said, "If thou deal thus with me, kill me, I pray thee, if I have found Favour in thy Sight," Numb. xi. 15. But I soon saw that this proceeded from the Want of a full Resignation to the divine Will. Many were the Afflictions which attended me; and in great Abasement, with many Tears, my Cries were to the Almighty, for his gracious and Fatherly Assistance; and then, after a Time of deep Trial, I was favoured to understand the State mentioned by the Psalmist, more clearly than ever I had before; to wit: "My Soul is even as a weaned Child." Psalm cxxxi. 2. Being thus helped to sink down into Resignation, I felt a Deliverance from that Tempest in which I had been sorely exercised, and in Calmness of Mind went forward, trusting that the Lord Jesus Christ, as I faithfully attended to him, would be a Counsellor to me in all Difficulties.

The seventh Day of the fifth Month, in the Year 1757, I lodged at a Friend's House; and the next Day, being the first of the Week, was at Potapsco Meeting; then crossed Patuxent River, and lodged at a Public-house. On the ninth breakfasted at a Friend's House; who, afterward, putting us a little on our Way, I had Conversation with him, in the Fear of the Lord, concerning his Slaves; in which my Heart was tender, and I used much Plainness of Speech with him, which he appeared to take kindly. We pursued our Journey without appointing Meetings, being pressed in Mind to be at the Yearly-meeting in Virginia; and, in my travelling on the Road, I often felt a Cry rise from the Center of my Mind, thus: O Lord, I am a Stranger on the Earth, hide not thy Face from me.

On the eleventh Day of the fifth Month, we crossed the Rivers Patowmack and Rapahannock, and lodged at Port-Royal; and on the Way we happening in Company with a Colonel of the Militia, who appeared to be a thoughtful Man, I took Occasion to remark on the Difference in general betwixt a People used to labour moderately for their Living, training up their Children in Frugality and Business, and those who live on the Labour of Slaves; the former, in my View, being the most happy Life: With which he concurred, and mentioned the Trouble arising from the untoward, slothful, Disposition of the Negroes; adding, that one of our Labourers would do as much in a Day as two of their Slaves. I replied, that free Men, whose Minds were properly on their Business, found a Satisfaction in improving, cultivating, and providing for their Families; but Negroes, labouring to support others who claim them as their Property, and expecting nothing but Slavery during Life, had not the like Inducement to be industrious.

After some farther Conversation, I said, that Men having Power too often misapplied it; that though we made Slaves of the Negroes, and the Turks made Slaves of the Christians, I believed that Liberty was the natural Right of all Men equally: Which he did not deny; but said, the Lives of the Negroes were so wretched in their own Country, that many of them lived better here than there: I only said, there are great odds, in regard to us, on what Principle we act; and so the Conversation on that Subject ended: And I may here add, that another Person, some Time afterward, mentioned the Wretchedness of the Negroes, occasioned by their intestine Wars, as an Argument in Favour of our fetching them away for Slaves: To which I then replied, if Compassion on the Africans, in Regard to their domestic Troubles, were the real Motive of our purchasing them, that Spirit of Tenderness, being attended to, would incite us to use them kindly; that, as Strangers brought out of Affliction, their Lives might be happy among us; and as they are human Creatures, whose Souls are as precious as ours, and who may receive the same Help and Comfort from the holy Scriptures as we do, we could not omit suitable Endeavours to instruct them therein: But while we manifest, by our Conduct, that our Views in purchasing them are to advance ourselves; and while our buying Captives taken in War animates those Parties to push on that War, and increase Desolation amongst them, to say they live unhappy in Africa, is far from being an Argument in our Favour: And I farther said, the present Circumstances of these Provinces to me appear difficult; that the Slaves look like a burthensome Stone to such who burthen themselves with them; and that if the white People retain a Resolution to prefer their outward Prospects of Gain to all other Considerations, and do not act conscientiously toward them as fellow Creatures, I believe that Burthen will grow heavier and heavier, till Times change in a Way disagreeable to us: At which the Person appeared very serious, and owned, that, in considering their Condition, and the Manner of their Treatment in these Provinces, he had sometimes thought it might be just in the Almighty so to order it.

Having thus travelled through Maryland, we came amongst Friends at Cedar-Creek in Virginia, on the 12th Day of the fifth Month; and the next Day rode, in Company with several Friends, a Day's Journey to Camp-Creek. As I was riding along in the Morning, my Mind was deeply affected in a Sense I had of the Want of divine Aid to support me in the various Difficulties which attended me; and, in an uncommon Distress of Mind, I cried in secret to the Most High, O Lord, be merciful, I beseech thee, to thy poor afflicted Creature. After some Time, I felt inward Relief; and, soon after, a Friend in Company began to talk in Support of the Slave-Trade, and said, the Negroes were understood to be the Offspring of Cain, their Blackness being the Mark God set upon him after he murdered Abel his Brother; that it was the Design of Providence they should be Slaves, as a Condition proper to the Race of so wicked a Man as Cain was: Then another spake in Support of what had been said. To all which, I replied in Substance as follows: That Noah and his Family were all who survived the Flood, according to Scripture; and, as Noah was of Seth's Race, the Family of Cain was wholly destroyed. One of them said, that after the Flood Ham went to the Land of Nod, and took a Wife; that Nod was a Land far distant, inhabited by Cain's Race, and that the Flood did not reach it; and as Ham was sentenced to be a Servant of Servants to his Brethren, these two Families, being thus joined, were undoubtedly fit only for Slaves. I replied, the Flood was a Judgment upon the World for its Abominations; and it was granted, that Cain's Stock was the most wicked, and therefore unreasonable to suppose they were spared: As to Ham's going to the Land of Nod for a Wife, no Time being fixed, Nod might be inhabited by some of Noah's Family, before Ham married a second Time; moreover the Text saith, "That all Flesh died that moved upon the Earth." Gen. vii. 21. I farther reminded them, how the Prophets repeatedly declare, "That the Son shall not suffer for the Iniquity of the Father; but every one be answerable for his own Sins." I was troubled to perceive the Darkness of their Imaginations; and in some Pressure of Spirit said, the Love of Ease and Gain is the Motive in general for keeping Slaves, and Men are wont to take hold of weak Arguments to support a Cause which is unreasonable; and added, I have no Interest on either Side, save only the Interest which I desire to have in the Truth: And as I believe Liberty is their Right, and see they are not only deprived of it, but treated in other Respects with Inhumanity in many Places, I believe he, who is a Refuge for the Oppressed, will, in his own Time, plead their Cause; and happy will it be for such as walk in Uprightness before him: And thus our Conversation ended.

On the fourteenth Day of the fifth Month I was at Camp-Creek Monthly-meeting, and then rode to the Mountains up James-River, and had a Meeting at a Friend's House; in both which I felt Sorrow of Heart, and my Tears were poured out before the Lord, who was pleased to afford a Degree of Strength, by which Way was opened to clear my Mind amongst Friends in those Places. From thence I went to Fort-Creek, and so to Cedar-Creek again; at which Place I had a Meeting; here I found a tender Seed: And as I was preserved in the Ministry to keep low with the Truth, the same Truth in their Hearts answered it, that it was a Time of mutual Refreshment from the Presence of the Lord. I lodged at James Standley's, Father of William Standley, one of the young Men who suffered Imprisonment at Winchester, last Summer, on Account of their Testimony against Fighting; and I had some satisfactory Conversation with him concerning it. Hence I went to the Swamp Meeting, and to Wayanoke Meeting; and then crossed James-River, and lodged near Burleigh. From the Time of my entering Maryland I had been much under Sorrow, which so increased upon me, that my Mind was almost overwhelmed; and I may say with the Psalmist, "In my Distress I called upon the Lord, and cried to my God;" who, in infinite Goodness, looked upon my Affliction, and in my private Retirement sent the Comforter for my Relief: For which I humbly bless his holy Name.

The Sense I had of the State of the Churches brought a Weight of Distress upon me: The Gold to me appeared dim, and the fine Gold changed; and though this is the Case too generally, yet the Sense of it in these Parts hath, in a particular Manner, borne heavy upon me. It appeared to me, that, through the prevailing of the Spirit of this World, the Minds of many were brought to an inward Desolation; and, instead of the Spirit of Meekness, Gentleness, and heavenly Wisdom, which are the necessary Companions of the true Sheep of Christ, a Spirit of Fierceness, and the Love of Dominion, too generally prevailed. From small Beginnings in Errors, great Buildings, by degrees, are raised; and from one Age to another are more and more strengthened by the general Concurrence of the People; and, as Men obtain Reputation by their Profession of the Truth, their Virtues are mentioned as Arguments in Favour of general Error, and those of less Note, to justify themselves, say, such and such good Men did the like. By what other Steps could the People of Judah arise to that Height in Wickedness, as to give just Ground for the Prophet Isaiah to declare, in the Name of the Lord, "that none calleth for Justice, nor any pleadeth for Truth." Isaiah lix. 4. Or for the Almighty to call upon the great City of Jerusalem, just before the Babylonish Captivity: "If ye can find a Man, if there be any who executeth Judgment, that seeketh the Truth, and I will pardon it." Jer. v. 1. The Prospect of a Road lying open to the same Degeneracy, in some Parts of this newly-settled Land of America, in Respect to our Conduct toward the Negroes, deeply bowed my Mind in this Journey; and, though, to briefly relate how these People are treated is no agreeable Work; yet, after often reading over the Notes I made as I travelled, I find my Mind engaged to preserve them. Many of the white People in those Provinces take little or no Care of Negro Marriages; and, when Negroes marry after their own Way, some make so little Account of those Marriages, that, with Views of outward Interest, they often part Men from their Wives by selling them far asunder; which is common when Estates are sold by Executors at Vendue. Many, whose Labour is heavy, being followed, at their Business in the Field, by a Man with a Whip, hired for that Purpose, have, in common, little else allowed but one Peck of Indian Corn and some Salt for one Week, with a few Potatoes; the Potatoes they commonly raise by their Labour on the first Day of the Week.

The Correction, ensuing on their Disobedience to Overseers, or Slothfulness in Business, is often very severe, and sometimes desperate.

The Men and Women have many Times scarce Clothes enough to hide their Nakedness, and Boys and Girls, ten and twelve Years old, are often quite naked amongst their Master's Children: Some of our Society, and some of the Society called New-Lights, use some Endeavours to instruct those they have in reading; but, in common, this is not only neglected, but disapproved. These are the People by whose Labour the other Inhabitants are in a great Measure supported, and many of them in the Luxuries of Life: These are the People who have made no Agreement to serve us, and who have not forfeited their Liberty that we know of: These are Souls for whom Christ died, and, for our Conduct toward them, we must answer before him who is no Respecter of Persons.

They who know the only true God, and Jesus Christ whom he hath sent, and are thus acquainted with the merciful, benevolent Gospel Spirit, will therein perceive that the Indignation of God is kindled against Oppression and Cruelty; and, in beholding the great Distress of so numerous a People, will find Cause for Mourning.

From my Lodging I went to Burleigh Meeting, where I felt my Mind drawn into a quiet resigned State; and, after long Silence, I felt an Engagement to stand up; and, through the powerful Operation of divine Love, we were favoured with an edifying Meeting. The next Meeting we had was at Black-Water; and so to the Yearly-meeting at the western Branch: When Business began, some Queries were considered, by some of their Members, to be now produced; and, if approved, to be answered hereafter by their respective Monthly-meetings. They were the Pennsylvania Queries, which had been examined by a Committee of Virginia Yearly-meeting appointed the last Year, who made some Alterations in them; one of which Alterations was made in Favour of a Custom which troubled me. The Query was, "Are there any concerned in the Importation of Negroes, or buying them after imported?" Which they altered thus: "Are there any concerned in the Importation of Negroes, or buying them to trade in?" As one Query admitted with Unanimity was, "Are any concerned in buying or vending Goods unlawfully imported, or prize Goods?" I found my Mind engaged to say, that as we professed the Truth, and were there assembled to support the Testimony of it, it was necessary for us to dwell deep, and act in that Wisdom which is pure, or otherwise we could not prosper. I then mentioned their

Alteration; and, referring to the last-mentioned Query, added, as purchasing any Merchandize, taken by the Sword, was always allowed to be inconsistent with our Principles; Negroes being Captives of War, or taken by Stealth, those Circumstances make it inconsistent with our Testimony to buy them; and their being our Fellow-creatures, who are sold as Slaves, adds greatly to the Iniquity. Friends appeared attentive to what was said; some expressed a Care and Concern about their Negroes; none made any Objection, by Way of Reply to what I said; but the Query was admitted as they had altered it. As some of their Members have heretofore traded in Negroes, as in other Merchandize, this Query being admitted, will be one Step farther than they have hitherto gone: And I did not see it my Duty to press for an Alteration; but felt easy to leave it all to him, who alone is able to turn the Hearts of the Mighty, and make Way for the spreading of Truth on the Earth, by Means agreeable to his infinite Wisdom. But, in Regard to those they already had, I felt my Mind engaged to labour with them; and said, that, as we believe the Scriptures were given forth by holy Men, as they were moved by the Holy Ghost, and many of us know by Experience that they are often helpful and comfortable, and believe ourselves bound in Duty to teach our Children to read them, I believe, that, if we were divested of all selfish Views, the same good Spirit, that gave them forth, would engage us to teach the Negroes to read, that they might have the Benefit of them: Some, amongst them, at this Time, manifested a Concern in Regard to taking more Care in the Education of their Negroes.

On the twenty-ninth Day of the fifth Month, at the House where I lodged, was a Meeting of Ministers and Elders, at the ninth Hour in the Morning; at which Time I found an Engagement to speak freely and plainly to them concerning their Slaves; mentioning, how they, as the first Rank in the Society, whose Conduct in that Case was much noticed by others, were under the stronger Obligations to look carefully to themselves: Expressing how needful it was for them, in that Situation, to be thoroughly divested of all selfish Views; that living in the pure Truth, and acting conscientiously toward those People in their Education and otherwise, they might be instrumental in helping forward a Work so necessary, and so much neglected amongst them. At the twelfth Hour the Meeting of Worship began, which was a solid Meeting.

On the thirtieth Day, about the tenth Hour, Friends met to finish their Business, and then the meeting for Worship ensued, which to me was a laborious Time; but, through the Goodness of the Lord, Truth, I believe, gained some Ground; and it was a strengthening Opportunity to the Honest-hearted.

About this Time I wrote an Epistle to Friends in the Back-settlements of North-Carolina, as follows:

To Friends at their Monthly-meeting at New-Garden and Cane-Creek, in North-Carolina.

Dear Friends,—It having pleased the Lord to draw me forth on a Visit to some Parts of Virginia and Carolina, you have often been in my Mind; and though my Way is not clear to come in Person to visit you, yet I feel it in my Heart to communicate a few Things, as they arise in the Love of Truth. First, my dear Friends, dwell in Humility, and take Heed that no Views of outward Gain get too deep hold of you, that so your Eyes being single to the Lord, you may be preserved in the Way of Safety. Where People let loose their Minds after the Love of outward Things, and are more engaged in pursuing the Profits, and seeking the Friendships, of this World, than to be inwardly acquainted with the Way of true Peace; such walk in a vain Shadow, while the true Comfort of Life is wanting: Their Examples are often hurtful to others; and their Treasures, thus collected, do many Times prove dangerous Snares to their Children.

But where People are sincerely devoted to follow Christ, and dwell under the Influence of his holy Spirit, their Stability and Firmness, through a divine Blessing, is at Times like Dew on the tender Plants round about them, and the Weightiness of their Spirits secretly works on the Minds of others; and in this Condition, through the spreading Influence of divine Love, they feel a Care over the Flock; and Way is opened for maintaining good Order in the Society: And though we meet with Opposition from another Spirit, yet, as there is a dwelling in Meekness, feeling our Spirits subject, and moving only in the gentle peaceable Wisdom, the inward Reward of Quietness will be greater than all our Difficulties. Where the pure Life is kept to, and Meetings of Discipline are held in the Authority of it, we find by Experience that they are comfortable, and tend to the Health of the Body.

While I write, the Youth come fresh in my Way:—Dear young People, choose God for your Portion; love his Truth, and be not ashamed of it: Choose for your Company such as serve him in Uprightness; and shun, as most dangerous, the Conversation of those whose Lives are of an ill Savour; for, by frequenting such Company, some hopeful young People have come to great Loss, and have been drawn from less Evils to greater, to their utter Ruin. In the Bloom of Youth no Ornament is so lovely as that of Virtue, nor any Enjoyments equal to those which we partake of, in fully resigning ourselves to the divine Will: These Enjoyments add Sweetness to all other Comforts, and give true Satisfaction in Company and Conversation, where People are mutually acquainted with it; and, as your Minds are thus seasoned with the Truth, you will find Strength to abide stedfast to the Testimony of it, and be prepared for Services in the Church.

And now, dear Friends and Brethren, as you are improving a Wilderness, and may be numbered amongst the first Planters in one Part of a Province, I beseech you, in the Love of Jesus Christ, to wisely consider the Force of your Examples, and think how much your Successors may be thereby affected: It is a Help in a Country, yea, and a great Favour and a Blessing, when Customs, first settled, are agreeable to sound Wisdom; so, when they are otherwise, the Effect of them is grievous; and Children feel themselves encompassed with Difficulties prepared for them by their Predecessors.

As moderate Care and Exercise, under the Direction of true Wisdom, are useful both to Mind and Body; so by this Means in general, the real Wants of Life are easily supplied: Our gracious Father having so proportioned one to the other, that keeping in the true Medium we may pass on quietly. Where Slaves are purchased to do our Labour, numerous Difficulties attend it. To rational Creatures Bondage is uneasy, and frequently occasions Sourness and Discontent in them; which affects the Family, and such as claim the Mastery over them: And thus People and their Children are many Times encompassed with Vexations, which arise from their applying to wrong Methods to get a Living.

I have been informed that there is a large Number of Friends in your Parts, who have no Slaves; and in tender and most affectionate Love, I beseech you to keep clear from purchasing any. Look, my dear Friends, to divine Providence; and follow in Simplicity that Exercise of Body, that Plainness and Frugality, which true Wisdom leads to; so will you be preserved from those Dangers which attend such as are aiming at outward Ease and Greatness.

Treasures, though small, attained on a true Principle of Virtue, are sweet in the Possession, and, while we walk in the Light of the Lord, there is true Comfort and Satisfaction. Here, neither the Murmurs of an oppressed People, nor an uneasy Conscience, nor anxious Thoughts about the Events of Things, hinder the Enjoyment of it.

When we look toward the End of Life, and think on the Division of our Substance among our Successors; if we know that it was collected in the Fear of the Lord, in Honesty, in Equity, and in Uprightness of Heart before him, we may consider it as his Gift to us; and with a single Eye to his Blessing, bestow it on those we leave behind us. Such is the Happiness of the plain Ways of true Virtue. "The Work of Righteousness shall be Peace; and the Effect of Righteousness, Quietness and Assurance for ever." Isa. xxxii. 17.

Dwell here, my dear Friends; and then, in remote and solitary Desarts, you may find true Peace and Satisfaction. If the Lord be our God, in Truth and Reality, there is Safety for us; for he is a Stronghold in the Day of Trouble, and knoweth them that trust in him.

Isle of Wight County, in Virginia,

29th of the 5th Month, 1757.

From the Yearly-meeting in Virginia, I went to Carolina; and, on the first Day of the sixth Month, was at Wells Monthly-meeting, where the Spring of the Gospel Ministry was opened, and the Love of Jesus Christ experienced amongst us: To his Name be the Praise!

Here my Brother joined with some Friends from New-Garden, who were going homeward; and I went next to Simond's Creek Monthly-meeting, where I was silent during the Meeting for Worship: When Business came on, my Mind was exercised concerning the poor Slaves; but did not feel my Way clear to speak: In this Condition I was bowed in Spirit before the Lord; and with Tears and inward Supplication besought him so to open my Understanding, that I might know his Will concerning me; and, at length, my mind was settled in Silence: Near the End of their Business, a Member of their Meeting expressed a Concern, that had some Time lain upon him, on Account of Friends so much neglecting their Duty in the Education of their Slaves; and proposed having Meetings sometimes appointed for them on a Week-day, to be only attended by some Friends to be named in their Monthly-meetings: Many present appeared to unite with the Proposal: One said, he had often wondered that they, being our Fellow-creatures, and capable of religious Understanding, had been so exceedingly neglected: Another expressed the like Concern, and appeared zealous, that Friends, in future, might more closely consider it: At length a Minute was made; and the farther Consideration of it referred to their next Monthly-meeting. The Friend who made this Proposal had Negroes: He told me, that he was at New-Garden, about two hundred and fifty Miles from Home, and came back alone; and that in this solitary Journey, this Exercise, in Regard to the Education of their Negroes, was, from Time to Time, renewed in his Mind. A Friend of some Note in Virginia, who had Slaves, told me, that he being far from Home on a lonesome Journey, had many serious Thoughts about them; and that his Mind was so impressed therewith, that he believed that he saw a Time coming, when divine Providence would alter the Circumstances of these People, respecting their Condition as Slaves.

From hence I went to Newbegun Creek, and sat a considerable Time in much Weakness; then I felt Truth open the Way to speak a little in much Plainness and Simplicity, till, at length, through the Increase of divine Love amongst us, we had a seasoning Opportunity. From thence to the Head of Little-River, on a First-day, where was a crowded Meeting; and, I believe, it was, through divine Goodness, made profitable to some. Thence to the Old-Neck; where I was led into a careful searching out the secret Workings of the Mystery of Iniquity, which, under a Cover of Religion, exalts itself against that pure Spirit, which leads in the Way of Meekness and Self-denial. From thence to Pineywoods: This was the last Meeting I was at in Carolina, and was large; and, my Heart being deeply engaged, I was drawn forth into a fervent Labour amongst them.

From hence I went back into Virginia, and had a Meeting near James Cowpland's; it was a Time of inward Suffering; but, through the Goodness of the Lord, I was made content: Then to another Meeting; where, through the Renewings of pure Love, we had a very comfortable Season.

Travelling up and down of late, I have had renewed Evidences, that to be faithful to the Lord, and content with his Will concerning me, is a most necessary and useful Lesson for me to be learning; looking less at the Effects of my Labour, than at the pure Motion and Reality of the Concern, as it arises from heavenly Love. In the Lord Jehovah is everlasting Strength; and as the Mind, by a humble Resignation, is united to him; and we utter Words from an inward Knowledge that they arise from the heavenly Spring, though our Way may be difficult, and require close Attention to keep in it; and though the Manner in which we may be led may tend to our own Abasement; yet, if we continue in Patience and Meekness, heavenly Peace is the Reward of our Labours.

From thence I went to Curles Meeting; which, though small, was reviving to the Honest-hearted. Thence to Black-Creek and Caroline Meetings; from whence, accompanied by William Standley, before-mentioned, we rode to Goose-Creek, being much through the Woods, and about one hundred Miles.—We lodged the first Night at a Publick-house; the second, in the Woods; and, the next Day, we reached a Friend's House, at Goose-Creek. In the Woods we lay under some Disadvantage, having no Fire-works nor Bells for our Horses; but we stopped a little before Night, and let them feed on the wild Grass which was in plenty; in the mean Time cutting with our Knives a Store against Night, and then tying them, and gathering some Bushes under an Oak, we lay down; but, the Musquettoes being plenty, and the Ground damp, I slept but little: Thus, lying in the Wilderness, and looking at the Stars, I was led to contemplate on the Condition of our first Parents, when they were sent forth from the Garden; but the Almighty, though they had been disobedient, continued to be a Father to them, and shewed them what tended to their Felicity, as intelligent Creatures, and was acceptable to him. To provide Things relative to our outward Living, in the Way of true Wisdom, is good; and the Gift of improving in Things useful is a good Gift, and comes from the Father of Lights. Many have had this Gift; and, from Age to Age, there have been Improvements of this Kind made in the World: But some, not keeping to the pure Gift, have, in the creaturely Cunning and Self-Exaltation, sought out many Inventions; which Inventions of Men are distinct from that Uprightness in which Man was created; as the first Motion to them was evil, so the Effects have been and are evil. At this Day, it is as necessary for us constantly to attend on the heavenly Gift, to be qualified to use rightly the good Things in this Life amidst great Improvements, as it was for our first Parents, when they were without any Improvements, without any Friend or Father but God only.

I was at a Meeting at Goose-Creek; and next at a Monthly-meeting at Fairfax; where, through the gracious Dealing of the Almighty with us, his Power prevailed over many Hearts. Thence to Manoquacy and Pipe-Creek, in Maryland; at both which Places I had Cause humbly to adore him, who supported me through many Exercises, and by whose Help I was enabled to reach the true Witness in the Hearts of others: There were some hopeful young People in those Parts. Thence I had Meetings at John Everit's in Monalen, and at Huntingdon; and I was made humbly thankful to the Lord, who opened my Heart amongst the People in these new Settlements, so that it was a Time of Encouragement to the Honest-minded.

At Monalen, a Friend gave me some Account of a religious Society among the Dutch, called Mennonists; and, amongst other Things, related a Passage in Substance as follows:—
One of the Mennonists having Acquaintance with a Man of another Society at a considerable Distance, and being with his Waggon on Business near the House of his said

Acquaintance, and Night coming on, he had Thoughts of putting up with him; but passing by his Fields, and observing the distressed Appearance of his Slaves, he kindled a Fire in the Woods hard by, and lay there that Night: His said Acquaintance hearing where he lodged, and afterward meeting the Mennonist, told him of it; adding, he should have been heartily welcome at his House; and, from their Acquaintance in former Time, wondered at his Conduct in that Case. The Mennonist replied, Ever since I lodged by thy Field, I have wanted an Opportunity to speak with thee: The Matter was; I intended to have come to thy House for Entertainment, but, seeing thy Slaves at their Work, and observing the Manner of their Dress, I had no liking to come to partake with thee: Then admonished him to use them with more Humanity; and added, As I lay by the Fire that Night, I thought that, as I was a Man of Substance, thou wouldst have received me freely; but, if I had been as poor as one of thy Slaves, and had no Power to help myself, I should have received from thy Hand no kinder Usage than they.

Hence I was at three Meetings in my Way; and so I went Home, under a humbling Sense of the gracious Dealings of the Lord with me, in preserving me through many Trials and Afflictions in my Journey. I was out about two Months, and travelled about eleven hundred and fifty Miles.

CHAPTER V

The draughting of the Militia in New-Jersey to serve in the Army; with some Observations on the State of the Members of our Society at that Time—His Visit to Friends in Pennsylvania, accompanied by Benjamin Jones—Proceedings at the Monthly, Quarterly, and Yearly-Meetings, in Philadelphia, respecting those who keep Slaves

On the ninth Day of the eighth Month, in the Year 1757, at Night, Orders came to the military Officers in our County (Burlington), directing them to draught the Militia, and prepare a Number of Men to go off as Soldiers, to the Relief of the English at Fort-William-Henry, in New-York Government: A few Days after which there was a general Review of the Militia at Mount-Holly, and a Number of Men chosen and sent off under some Officers. Shortly after, there came Orders to draught three Times as many, to hold themselves in Readiness to march when fresh Orders came: And, on the 17th Day of the eighth Month, there was a Meeting of the military Officers at Mount-Holly, who agreed on a Draught; and Orders were sent to the Men, so chosen, to meet their respective Captains at set Times and Places; those in our Township to meet at Mount-Holly; amongst whom was a considerable Number of our Society. My Mind being affected herewith, I had fresh Opportunity to see and consider the Advantage of living in the real Substance of Religion, where Practice doth harmonize with Principle. Amongst the Officers are Men of Understanding, who have some Regard to Sincerity where they see it; and in the Execution of their Office, when they have Men to deal with whom they believe to be upright-hearted, to put them to Trouble, on account of Scruples of Conscience, is a painful Task, and likely to be avoided as much as easily may be: But where Men profess to be so meek and heavenly-minded, and to have their Trust so firmly settled in God, that they cannot join in Wars, and yet, by their Spirit and Conduct in common Life, manifest a contrary Disposition, their Difficulties are great at such a Time.

Officers, in great Anxiety, endeavouring to get Troops to answer the Demands of their Superiors, seeing Men, who are insincere, pretend Scruple of Conscience in Hopes of being excused from a dangerous Employment, such are likely to be roughly handled. In this Time of Commotion some of our young Men left the Parts, and tarried abroad till it was over; some came, and proposed to go as Soldiers; others appeared to have a real tender Scruple in their Minds against joining in Wars, and were much humbled under the Apprehension of a Trial so near: I had Conversation with several of them to my Satisfaction. At the set Time when the Captain came to Town, some of those last-mentioned went and told him in Substance as follows:—That they could not bear Arms for Conscience-sake; nor could they hire any to go in their Places, being resigned as to the Event of it: At length the Captain acquainted them all, that they might return Home for the present, and, required them to provide themselves as Soldiers, and to be in Readiness to march when called upon. This was such a Time as I had not seen before; and yet I may say, with Thankfulness to the Lord, that I believed this Trial was intended for our Good; and I was favoured with Resignation to him. The French Army, taking the Fort they were besieging, destroyed it and went away: The Company of Men first draughted, after some Days march, had Orders to return Home; and those on the second Draught were no more called upon on that Occasion.

On the fourth Day of the fourth Month, in the Year 1758, Orders came to some Officers in Mount-Holly, to prepare Quarters, a short Time, for about one hundred Soldiers: And an Officer and two other Men, all Inhabitants of our Town, came to my House; and the Officer told me, that he came to speak with me, to provide Lodging and Entertainment for two Soldiers, there being six Shillings a Week per Man allowed as Pay for it. The Case being new and unexpected, I made no Answer suddenly; but sat a Time silent, my Mind being inward: I was fully convinced, that the Proceedings in Wars are inconsistent with the Purity of the Christian Religion: And to be hired to entertain Men, who were then under Pay as Soldiers, was a Difficulty with me. I expected they had legal Authority for what they did; and, after a short Time, I said to the Officer, If the Men are sent here for Entertainment, I believe I shall not refuse to admit them into my House; but the Nature of the Case is such, that I expect I cannot keep them on Hire: One of the Men intimated, that he thought I might do it consistent with my religious Principles; To which I made no Reply; as believing Silence at that Time best for me. Though they spake of two, there came only one, who tarried at my House about two Weeks, and behaved himself civilly; and when the Officer came to pay me, I told him I could not take Pay for it, having admitted him into my House in a passive Obedience to Authority. I was on Horseback when he spake to me: And, as I turned from him, he said, he was obliged to me: To which I said nothing; but, thinking on the Expression, I grew uneasy; and afterwards, being near where he lived, I went and told him on what Grounds I refused taking Pay for keeping the Soldier.

Near the Beginning of the Year 1758, I went one Evening, in Company with a Friend, to visit a sick Person; and, before our Return, we were told of a Woman living near, who, of late, had several Days been disconsolate, occasioned by a Dream; wherein Death, and the Judgments of the Almighty after Death, were represented to her Mind in a moving Manner: Her Sadness on that Account, being worn off, the Friend, with whom I was in Company, went to see her, and had some religious Conversation with her and her Husband: With this Visit they were somewhat affected; and the Man, with many Tears, expressed his Satisfaction; and, in a short Time after, the poor Man being on the River in a Storm of Wind, he, with one more, was drowned.

In the eighth Month of the Year 1758, having had Drawings in my Mind to be at the Quarterly-meeting in Chester County, and at some Meetings in the County of Philadelphia, I went first to said Quarterly-meeting, which was large, and several weighty Matters came under Consideration and Debate; and the Lord was pleased to qualify some of his Servants with Strength and Firmness to bear the Burthen of the Day: Though I said but little, my Mind was deeply exercised; and, under a Sense of God's Love, in the Anointing and fitting some young Men for his Work, I was comforted, and my Heart was tendered before him. From hence I went to the Youth's Meeting at Darby, where my beloved Friend and Brother, Benjamin Jones, met me, by an Appointment before I left Home, to join in the Visit: And we were at Radnor, Merion, Richland, North-Wales, Plymouth, and Abington Meetings; and had Cause to bow in Reverence before the Lord, our gracious God, by whose Help Way was opened for us from day to day. I was out about two Weeks, and rode about two hundred Miles.

The Monthly-meeting of Philadelphia having been under a Concern on Account of some Friends who this Summer (1758) had bought Negro Slaves, the said Meeting moved it to their Quarterly-meeting, to have the Minute reconsidered in the Yearly-meeting, which was made last on that Subject: And the said Quarterly-meeting appointed a Committee to consider it, and report to their next; which Committee having met once and adjourned, I going to Philadelphia to meet a Committee of the Yearly-meeting, was in Town the Evening on which the Quarterly-meeting's Committee met the second Time; and, finding an Inclination to sit with them, was, with some others, admitted; and Friends had a weighty Conference on the Subject: And, soon after their next Quarterly-meeting, I heard that the Case was coming to our Yearly-meeting; which brought a weighty Exercise upon me, and under a Sense of my own Infirmities, and the great Danger I felt of turning aside from perfect Purity, my Mind was often drawn to retire alone, and put up my Prayers to the Lord, that he would be graciously pleased to strengthen me; that, setting aside all Views of Self-interest, and the Friendship of this World, I might stand fully resigned to his holy Will.

In this Yearly-meeting, several weighty Matters were considered; and, toward the last, that in Relation to dealing with Persons who purchase Slaves. During the several Sittings of the said Meeting, my Mind was frequently covered with inward Prayer, and I could say with David, that Tears were my Meat Day and Night. The Case of Slave-keeping lay heavy upon me; nor did I find any Engagement to speak directly to any other Matter before the Meeting. Now, when this Case was opened, several faithful Friends spake weightily thereto, with which I was comforted; and, feeling a Concern to cast in my Mite, I said in Substance as follows:

"In the Difficulties attending us in this Life, nothing is more precious than the Mind of Truth inwardly manifested; and it is my earnest Desire that, in this weighty Matter we may be so truly humbled as to be favoured with a clear Understanding of the Mind of Truth, and follow it; this would be of more Advantage to the Society, than any Medium not in the Clearness of divine Wisdom. The Case is difficult to some who have them; but if such set aside all Self-interest, and come to be weaned from the Desire of getting Estates, or even from holding them together, when Truth requires the Contrary, I believe Way will open that they will know how to steer through those Difficulties."

Many Friends appeared to be deeply bowed under the Weight of the Work; and manifested much Firmness in their Love to the Cause of Truth and universal Righteousness on the Earth: And, though none did openly justify the Practice of Slave-keeping in general, yet some appeared concerned, lest the Meeting should go into such Measures as might give Uneasiness to many Brethren; alledging, that if Friends patiently continued under the Exercise, the Lord, in Time to come might open a Way for the Deliverance of these People: And, I finding an Engagement to speak, said, "My Mind is often led to consider the Purity of the divine Being, and the Justice of his Judgments; and herein my Soul is covered with Awfulness: I cannot omit to hint of some Cases, where People have not been treated with the Purity of Justice, and the Event hath been lamentable: Many Slaves on this Continent are oppressed, and their Cries have reached the Ears of the Most High. Such are the Purity and Certainty of his Judgments, that he cannot be partial in our Favour. In infinite Love and Goodness, he hath opened our Understandings, from one Time to another, concerning our Duty towards this People; and it is not a Time for Delay.

Should we now be sensible of what he requires of us, and, through a Respect to the private Interest of some Persons, or through a Regard to some Friendships which do not stand on an immutable Foundation, neglect to do our Duty in Firmness and Constancy, still waiting for some extraordinary Means to bring about their Deliverance, it may be by terrible Things in Righteousness God may answer us in this Matter."

Many faithful Brethren laboured with great Firmness; and the Love of Truth, in a good Degree, prevailed. Several Friends, who had Negroes, expressed their Desire that a Rule might be made, to deal with such Friends as Offenders who bought Slaves in future: To this it was answered, that the Root of this Evil would never be effectually struck at, until a thorough Search was made into the Circumstances of such Friends as kept Negroes, with respect to the Righteousness of their Motives in keeping them, that impartial Justice might be administered throughout. Several Friends expressed their Desire, that a Visit might be made to such Friends as kept Slaves; and many Friends said, that they believed Liberty was the Negroes Right: To which, at length, no Opposition was made publickly. A Minute was made more full on that Subject than any heretofore; and the Names of several Friends entered, who were free to join in a Visit to such as kept Slaves.

CHAPTER VI

His visiting the Quarterly-meetings in Chester County; and afterwards joining with Daniel Stanton and John Scarborough in a Visit to such as kept Slaves there—Some Observations on the Conduct such should maintain as are concerned to speak in Meetings for Discipline—Several more Visits to such as kept Slaves; and to Friends near Salem—Some Account of the Yearly-meeting in the Year 1759; and of the increasing Concern, in divers Provinces, to labour against buying and keeping Slaves—The Yearly-meeting Epistle

On the eleventh Day of the eleventh Month, in the Year 1758, I set out for Concord; the Quarterly-meeting, heretofore held there, was now, by reason of a great Increase of Members, divided into two by the Agreement of Friends, at our last Yearly-meeting. Here I met with our beloved Friends, Samuel Spavold and Mary Kirby, from England, and with Joseph White, from Bucks County, who had taken Leave of his Family in order to go on a religious Visit to Friends in England; and, through divine Goodness, we were favoured with a strengthening Opportunity together.

After this Meeting I joined with my Friends, Daniel Stanton and John Scarborough, in visiting Friends who had Slaves; and at Night we had a Family-meeting at William Trimble's, many young People being there; and it was a precious reviving Opportunity. Next Morning we had a comfortable Sitting with a sick Neighbour; and thence to the Burial of the Corpse of a Friend at Uwchland Meeting, at which were many People, and it was a Time of divine Favour; after which, we visited some who had Slaves; and, at Night, had a Family-meeting at a Friend's House, where the Channel of Gospel-love was opened, and my Mind was comforted after a hard Day's Labour. The next Day we were at Goshen Monthly-meeting; and thence, on the eighteenth Day of the eleventh Month, in the Year 1758, attended the Quarterly-meeting at London-Grove, it being the first held at that Place. Here we met again with all the before-mentioned Friends, and had some edifying Meetings: And, near the Conclusion of the Meeting for Business, Friends were incited to Constancy in supporting the Testimony of Truth, and reminded of the Necessity which the Disciples of Christ are under to attend principally to his Business, as he is pleased to open it to us: And to be particularly careful to have our Minds redeemed from the Love of Wealth; to have our outward Affairs in as little Room as may be; that no temporal Concerns may entangle our Affections, or hinder us from diligently following the Dictates of Truth, in labouring to promote the pure Spirit of Meekness and Heavenly-mindedness amongst the Children of Men in these Days of Calamity and Distress, wherein God is visiting our Land with his just Judgments.

Each of these Quarterly-meetings was large, and sat near eight Hours. Here I had Occasion to consider, that it was a weighty Thing to speak much in large Meetings for Business: First, except our Minds are rightly prepared, and we clearly understand the Case we speak to, instead of forwarding, we hinder, Business, and make more Labour for those on whom the Burthen of the Work is laid.

If selfish Views, or a partial Spirit, have any Room in our Minds, we are unfit for the Lord's Work; if we have a clear

Prospect of the Business, and proper Weight on our Minds to speak, it behoves us to avoid useless Apologies and Repetitions: Where People are gathered from far, and adjourning a Meeting of Business is attended with great Difficulty, it behoves all to be cautious how they detain a Meeting; especially when they have sat six or seven Hours, and have a great Distance to ride Home. After this Meeting I rode Home.

In the Beginning of the twelfth Month of the Year 1758 I joined in Company with my Friends, John Sykes and Daniel Stanton, in visiting such as had Slaves: Some, whose Hearts were rightly exercised about them, appeared to be glad of our Visit; but in some Places our Way was more difficult; and I often saw the Necessity of keeping down to that Root from whence our Concern proceeded; and have Cause, in reverent Thankfulness, humbly to bow down before the Lord, who was near to me, and preserved my Mind in Calmness under some sharp Conflicts, and begat a Spirit of Sympathy and Tenderness in me toward some who were grievously entangled by the Spirit of this World.

In the first Month of the Year 1759, having found my Mind drawn to visit some of the more active Members, in our Society at Philadelphia, who had Slaves, I met my Friend John Churchman there, by an Agreement: And we continued about a Week in the City. We visited some that were sick, and some Widows and their Families; and the other Part of our Time was mostly employed in visiting such as had Slaves.—It was a Time of deep Exercise, looking often to the Lord for his Assistance; who, in unspeakable Kindness, favoured us with the Influence of that Spirit, which crucifies to the Greatness and Splendour of this World, and enabled us to go through some heavy Labours, in which we found Peace.

On the twenty-fourth Day of the third Month of this Year, I was at our general Spring-meeting at Philadelphia: After which, I again joined with John Churchman on a Visit to some more who had Slaves in Philadelphia; and, with Thankfulness to our heavenly Father, I may say, that divine Love and a true sympathising Tenderness of Heart prevailed at Times in this Service.

Having, at Times, perceived a Shyness in some Friends, of considerable Note, towards me, I found an Engagement in Gospel Love to pay a Visit to one of them; and, as I dwelt under the Exercise, I felt a Resignedness in my Mind to go; So I went, and told him, in private, I had a Desire to have an Opportunity with him alone; to which he readily agreed: And then, in the Fear of the Lord, Things relating to that Shyness were searched to the Bottom; and we had a large Conference, which, I believe, was of Use to both of us, and am thankful that Way was opened for it.

On the fourteenth Day of the sixth Month, in the same Year, having felt Drawings in my Mind to visit Friends about Salem, and having the Approbation of our Monthly-meeting therein, I attended their Quarterly-meeting, and was out seven Days, and at seven Meetings; in some of which I was chiefly silent, and in others, through the baptizing Power of Truth, my Heart was enlarged in heavenly Love, and found a near Fellowship with the Brethren and Sisters, in the manifold Trials attending their Christian Progress through this World.

In the seventh Month, I found an increasing Concern on my Mind to visit some active Members in our Society who had

Slaves; and, having no Opportunity of the Company of such as were named on the Minutes of the Yearly-meeting, I went alone to their Houses, and, in the Fear of the Lord, acquainted them with the Exercise I was under: And thus, sometimes, by a few Words, I found myself discharged from a heavy Burthen.

After this, our Friend John Churchman, coming into our Province with a View to be at some Meetings, and to join again in the Visit to those who had Slaves, I bore him Company in the said Visit to some active Members, and found inward Satisfaction.

At our Yearly-meeting, in the Year 1759, we had some weighty Seasons; where the Power of Truth was largely extended, to the strengthening of the Honest-minded. As Friends read over the Epistles, to be sent to the Yearly-meetings along this Continent, I observed in most of them, both this Year and last, it was recommended to Friends to labour against buying and keeping Slaves; and in some of them closely treated upon. This Practice had long been a heavy Exercise to me, and I have often waded through mortifying Labours on that Account; and, at Times, in some Meetings been almost alone therein. Now, observing the increasing Concern in our religious Society, and seeing how the Lord was raising up and qualifying Servants for his Work, not only in this Respect, but for promoting the Cause of Truth in general, I was humbly bowed in Thankfulness before him.

This Meeting continued near a Week; and, for several Days, in the fore Part of it, my Mind was drawn into a deep inward Stillness; and being, at Times, covered with the Spirit of Supplication, my Heart was secretly poured out before the Lord: And, near the Conclusion of the Meeting for Business, Way opened, that, in the pure Flowings of divine Love, I expressed what lay upon me; which, as it then arose in my Mind, was "first to shew how Deep answers to Deep in the Hearts of the Sincere and Upright; though, in their different Growths, they may not all have attained to the same Clearness in some Points relating to our Testimony: And I was led to mention the Integrity and Constancy of many Martyrs, who gave their Lives for the Testimony of Jesus; and yet, in some Points, held Doctrines distinguishable from some which we hold: And that, in all Ages, where People were faithful to the Light and Understanding which the Most High afforded them, they found Acceptance with him; and that now, though there are different Ways of Thinking amongst us in some Particulars, yet, if we mutually kept to that Spirit and Power which crucifies to the World, which teaches us to be content with Things really needful, and to avoid all Superfluities, giving up our Hearts to fear and serve the Lord, true Unity may still be preserved amongst us: And that if such, as were, at Times, under Sufferings on Account of some Scruples of Conscience, kept low and humble, and in their Conduct in Life manifested a Spirit of true Charity, it would be more likely to reach the Witness in others, and be of more Service in the Church, than if their Sufferings were attended with a contrary Spirit and Conduct." In which Exercise I was drawn into a sympathizing Tenderness with the Sheep of Christ, however distinguished one from another in this World; and the like Disposition appeared to spread over others in the Meeting. Great is the Goodness of the Lord toward his poor Creatures!

An Epistle went forth from this Yearly-meeting, which I think good to give a Place in this Journal; being as follows:

From the Yearly-meeting held at Philadelphia, for Pennsylvania and New-Jersey, from the twenty-second Day of the ninth Month, to the twenty-eighth Day of the same, inclusive, 1759.

To the Quarterly and Monthly-meetings of Friends belonging to the said Yearly-meeting.

"Dearly beloved Friends and Brethren,—In an awful Sense of the Wisdom and Goodness of the Lord our God, whose tender Mercies have long been continued to us in this Land, we affectionately salute you, with sincere and fervent Desires, that we may reverently regard the Dispensations of his Providence, and improve under them.

The Empires and Kingdoms of the Earth are subject to his almighty Power: He is the God of the Spirits of all Flesh, and deals with his People agreeable to that Wisdom, the Depth whereof is to us unsearchable: We, in these Provinces, may say, he hath, as a gracious and tender Parent, dealt bountifully with us, even from the Days of our Fathers: It was he who strengthened them to labour through the Difficulties attending the Improvement of a Wilderness, and made Way for them in the Hearts of the Natives; so that by them they were comforted in Times of Want and Distress: It was by the gracious Influences of his holy Spirit, that they were disposed to work Righteousness, and walk uprightly one towards another, and towards the Natives, and in Life and Conversation to manifest the Excellency of the Principles and Doctrines of the Christian Religion; and thereby they retain their Esteem and Friendship: Whilst they were labouring for the Necessaries of Life, many of them were fervently engaged to promote Piety and Virtue in the Earth, and educate their Children in the Fear of the Lord.

If we carefully consider the peaceable Measures pursued in the first Settlement of the Land, and that Freedom from the Desolations of Wars which for a long Time we enjoyed, we shall find ourselves under strong Obligations to the Almighty, who, when the Earth is so generally polluted with Wickedness, gave us a Being in a Part so signally favoured with Tranquility and Plenty, and in which the Glad-tidings of the Gospel of Christ are so freely published, that we may justly say with the Psalmist, "What shall we render unto the Lord for all his Benefits?"

Our own real Good, and the Good of our Posterity, in some Measure, depend on the Part we act; and it nearly concerns us to try our Foundations impartially. Such are the different Rewards of the Just and Unjust in a future State, that, to attend diligently to the Dictates of the Spirit of Christ, to devote ourselves to his Service, and engage fervently in his Cause, during our short Stay in this World, is a Choice well becoming a free intelligent Creature; we shall thus clearly see and consider that the Dealings of God with Mankind in a national Capacity, as recorded in Holy Writ, do sufficiently evidence the Truth of that Saying, "It is Righteousness which exalteth a Nation;" and though he doth not at all Times suddenly execute his Judgments on a sinful People in this Life, yet we see, by many Instances, that where "Men follow lying Vanities, they forsake their own Mercies;" and as a proud selfish Spirit prevails and spreads among a People, so partial Judgment, Oppression, Discord, Envy, and Confusions, increase, and Provinces and Kingdoms are made to drink the Cup of Adversity as a Reward of their own Doings. Thus the inspired Prophet, reasoning with the degenerated Jews, saith, "Thine own Wickedness shall correct thee, and thy Backslidings shall reprove thee: Know, therefore, that it is an evil Thing and bitter, that thou hast forsaken the Lord thy God, and that my Fear is not in thee, saith the Lord God of Hosts." Jer. ii. 19.

The God of our Fathers, who hath bestowed on us many Benefits, furnished a Table for us in the Wilderness, and made the Desarts and solitary Places to rejoice; he doth now mercifully call upon us to serve him more faithfully.— We may truly say, with the Prophet, "It is his Voice which crieth to the City, and Men of Wisdom see his Name: They regard the Rod, and him who hath appointed it."—People, who look chiefly at Things outward, too little consider the original Cause of the present Troubles; but such as fear the Lord, and think often upon his Name, see and feel that a wrong Spirit is spreading among the Inhabitants of our Country; that the Hearts of many are waxed fat, and their Ears dull of hearing; that the Most High, in his Visitations to us, instead of calling, lifteth up his Voice and crieth; he crieth to our Country, and his Voice waxeth louder and louder. In former Wars between the English and other Nations, since the Settlement of our Provinces, the Calamities attending them have fallen chiefly on other Places, but now of late they have reached to our Borders; many of our fellow Subjects have suffered on and near our Frontiers, some have been slain in Battle, some killed in their Houses, and some in their Fields, some wounded and left in great Misery, and others separated from their Wives and little Children, who have been carried Captives among the Indians: We have seen Men and Women, who have been Witnesses of these Scenes of Sorrow, and been reduced to Want, have come to our Houses asking Relief.—It is not long since it was the Case of many young Men, in one of these Provinces, to be draughted, in order to be taken as Soldiers; some were at that Time in great Distress, and had Occasion to consider that their Lives had been too little conformable to the Purity and Spirituality of that Religion which we profess, and found themselves too little acquainted with that inward Humility, in which true Fortitude to endure Hardness for the Truth's Sake is experienced.—Many Parents were concerned for their Children, and in that Time of Trial were led to consider, that their Care, to get outward Treasure for them, had been greater than their Care for their Settlement in that Religion which crucifieth to the World, and enableth to bear a clear Testimony to the peaceable Government of the Messiah. These Troubles are removed, and for a Time we are released from them.

Let us not forget that "The Most High hath his Way in the Deep, in Clouds and in thick Darkness"—that it is his Voice which crieth to the City and to the Country; and oh! that these loud and awakening Cries may have a proper Effect upon us, that heavier Chastisement may not become necessary! For though Things, as to the Outward, may, for a short Time, afford a pleasing Prospect; yet, while a selfish Spirit, that is not subject to the Cross of Christ, continueth to spread and prevail, there can be no long Continuance in outward Peace and Tranquility. If we desire an Inheritance incorruptible, and to be at Rest in that State of Peace and Happiness, which ever continues; if we desire, in this Life, to dwell under the Favour and Protection of that almighty Being, whose Habitation is in Holiness, whose Ways are all equal, and whose Anger is now kindled because of our Backslidings; let us then awfully regard these Beginnings of his fore Judgments, and, with Abasement and Humiliation turn to him, whom we have offended.

Contending with one equal in Strength is an uneasy Exercise; but if the Lord is become our Enemy, if we persist to contend with him who is omnipotent, our Overthrow will be unavoidable.

Do we feel an affectionate Regard to Posterity; and are we employed to promote their Happiness? Do our Minds, in Things outward, look beyond our own Dissolution; and are we contriving for the Prosperity of our Children after us? Let us then, like wise Builders, lay the Foundation deep; and, by our constant uniform Regard to an inward Piety and Virtue, let them see that we really value it: Let us labour, in the Fear of the Lord, that their innocent Minds, while young and tender, may be preserved from Corruptions; that, as they advance in Age, they may rightly understand their true Interest, may consider the Uncertainty of temporal Things, and, above all, have their Hope and Confidence firmly settled in the Blessing of that Almighty Being, who inhabits Eternity, and preserves and supports the World.

In all our Cares, about worldly Treasures, let us steadily bear in Mind, that Riches, possessed by Children who do not truly serve God, are likely to prove Snares that may more grievously entangle them in that Spirit of Selfishness and Exaltation, which stands in Opposition to real Peace and Happiness; and renders them Enemies to the Cross of Christ, who submit to the Influence of it.

To keep a watchful eye towards real Objects of Charity, to visit the Poor in their lonesome Dwelling-places, to comfort them who, through the Dispensations of divine Providence, are in strait and painful Circumstances in this Life, and steadily to endeavour to honour God with our Substance, from a real Sense of the Love of Christ influencing our Minds thereto, is more likely to bring a Blessing to our Children, and will afford more Satisfaction to a Christian favoured with Plenty, than an earnest Desire to collect much Wealth to leave behind us; for "Here we have no continuing City;" may we therefore diligently "seek one that is to come, whose Builder and Maker is God."

"Finally, Brethren, whatsoever Things are true, whatsoever Things are just, whatsoever Things are pure, whatsoever Things are lovely, whatsoever Things are of good Report; if there be any Virtue, if there be any Praise, think on these Things and do them, and the God of Peace shall be with you."

Signed, by Appointment, and on Behalf of our said Meeting, by seven Friends.

On the twenty-eighth Day of the eleventh Month, in the Year 1759, I was at the Quarterly-meeting in Bucks County: This Day being the Meeting of Ministers and Elders, my Heart was enlarged in the Love of Jesus Christ; and the Favour of the Most High was extended to us in that and the ensuing Meeting.

I had Conversation, at my Lodging, with my beloved Friend, Samuel Eastburn; who expressed a Concern to join in a Visit to some Friends, in that County, who had Negroes; and as I had felt a Draught in my Mind to that Work in the said County, came Home and put Things in Order: On the eleventh Day of the twelfth Month following, I went over the River; and on the next Day was at Buckingham Meeting; where, through the Descendings of heavenly Dew, my Mind was comforted, and drawn into a near Unity with the Flock of Jesus Christ.

Entering upon this Visit appeared weighty: And before I left Home my Mind was often sad; under which Exercise I felt, at Times, the Holy Spirit, which helps our Infirmities; through which, in private, my Prayers were, at Times, put up to God, that he would be pleased to purge me from all Selfishness, that I might be strengthened to discharge my Duty faithfully, how hard soever to the natural Part. We proceeded on the Visit in a weighty Frame of Spirit, and went to the Houses of the most active Members, throughout the Country, who had Negroes; and, through the Goodness of the Lord, my Mind was preserved in Resignation in Times of Trial, and, though the Work was hard to Nature, yet through the Strength of that Love which is stronger than Death, Tenderness of Heart was often felt amongst us in our Visits, and we parted from several Families with greater Satisfaction than we expected.

We visited Joseph White's Family, he being in England; and also a Family-sitting at the House of an Elder who bore us Company, and was at Makefield on a First-day: At all which Times my Heart was truly thankful to the Lord, who was graciously pleased to renew his Loving-kindness to us, his poor Servants, uniting us together in his Work.

CHAPTER VII

His Visit, in Company with Samuel Eastburn, to Long-Island, Rhode-Island, Boston, etc. in New-England—Remarks on the Slave-Trade at Newport, and his Exercise on that Account; also on Lotteries—Some Observations on the Island of Nantucket

Having, for some Time past, felt a Sympathy in my Mind with Friends Eastward, I opened my Concern in our Monthly-meeting; and, obtaining a Certificate, set forward on the seventeenth Day of the fourth Month, in the Year 1760, joining in Company, by a previous Agreement, with my beloved Friend, Samuel Eastburn. We had Meetings at Woodbridge, Rahaway, and Plainfield; and were at their Monthly-meeting of Ministers and Elders in Rahaway. We laboured under some Discouragement; but, through the invisible Power of Truth, our Visit was made reviving to the Lowly-minded, with whom I felt a near Unity of Spirit, being much reduced in my Mind. We passed on and visited the chief of the Meetings on Long-Island. It was my Concern, from Day to Day, to say no more nor less than what the Spirit of Truth opened in me; being jealous over myself, lest I should speak any Thing to make my Testimony look agreeable to that Mind in People, which is not in pure Obedience to the Cross of Christ.

The Spring of the Ministry was often low; and, through the subjecting Power of Truth, we were kept low with it; and from Place to Place, such whose Hearts were truly concerned for the Cause of Christ, appeared to be comforted in our Labours; and though it was in general a

Time of Abasement of the Creature, yet, through his Goodness, who is a Helper of the Poor, we had some truly edifying Seasons, both in Meetings, and in Families where we tarried; and sometimes found Strength to labour earnestly with the Unfaithful, especially with those whose Station in Families, or in the Society, was such, that their Example had a powerful Tendency to open the Way for others to go aside from the Purity and Soundness of the blessed Truth. At Jericho, on Long-Island, I wrote Home as follows:

24th of the 4th Month, 1760.

"Dearly beloved Wife,—We are favoured with Health; have been at sundry Meetings in East-Jersey, and on this Island: My Mind hath been much in an inward watchful Frame since I left thee, greatly desiring that our Proceedings may be singly in the Will of our heavenly Father.

"As the present Appearance of Things is not joyous, I have been much shut up from outward Cheerfulness, remembering that Promise, 'Then shalt thou delight thyself in the Lord:'—As this, from Day to Day, has been revived in my Memory, I have considered that his internal Presence on our Minds is a Delight, of all others, the most pure; and that the Honest-hearted not only delight in this, but in the Effect of it upon them. He regards the Helpless and Distressed, and reveals his Love to his Children under Affliction; they delight in beholding his Benevolence, and feeling divine Charity moving upon them: Of this I may speak a little; for though, since I left you, I have often found an engaging Love and Affection toward thee and my Daughter, and Friends about Home, that going out at this Time, when Sickness is so great amongst you, is a Trial upon me; yet I often remember there are many Widows and Fatherless, many who have poor Tutors, many who have evil Examples before them, and many whose Minds are in Captivity, for whose Sake my Heart is, at Times, moved with Compassion; so that I feel my Mind resigned to leave you for a Season, to exercise that Gift which the Lord hath bestowed on me; which though small, compared with some, yet in this I rejoice, that I feel Love unfeigned toward my Fellow-creatures. I recommend you to the Almighty, who, I trust, cares for you; and, under a Sense of his heavenly Love, remain,—Thy loving Husband,

"J. W."

We crossed from the East End of Long-Island to New-London, about thirty Miles, in a large open Boat; while we were out, the Wind rising high, the Waves several Times beat over us, so that to me it appeared dangerous; but my Mind was, at that Time, turned to him, who made and governs the Deep, and my Life was resigned to him: And, as he was mercifully pleased to preserve us, I had fresh Occasion to consider every Day as a Day lent to me; and felt a renewed Engagement to devote my Time, and all I had, to him who gave them.

We had five Meetings in Narraganset; and went thence to Newport on Rhode-Island. Our gracious Father preserved us in an humble Dependence on him through deep Exercises, that were mortifying to the creaturely Will. In several Families in the Country, where we lodged, I felt an Engagement on my Mind to have a Conference with them in private concerning their Slaves; and, through divine Aid, I was favoured to give up thereto: Though, in this Concern, I appeared singular from many, whose Service in

Travelling, I believe, is greater than mine; I do not think hard of them for omitting it; I do not repine at having so unpleasant a Task assigned me, but look with Awfulness to him, who appoints to his Servants their respective Employments, and is good to all who serve him sincerely.

We got to Newport in the Evening, and on the next Day visited two sick Persons, and had comfortable Sittings with them; and in the Afternoon attended the Burial of a Friend.

The next Day we were at Meetings at Newport, in the Forenoon and Afternoon; where the Spring of the Ministry was opened, and Strength given to declare the Word of Life to the People.

The next Day we went on our Journey; but the great Number of Slaves in these Parts, and the Continuance of that Trade from thence to Guinea, made deep Impression on me; and my Cries were often put up to my heavenly Father in secret, that he would enable me to discharge my Duty faithfully, in such Way as he might be pleased to point out to me.

We took Swansea, Freetown, and Tanton, in our Way to Boston; where also we had a Meeting; our Exercise was deep, and the Love of Truth prevailed, for which I bless the Lord. We went Eastward about eighty Miles beyond Boston, taking Meetings, and were in a good Degree preserved in an humble Dependance on that Arm which drew us out; and, though we had some hard Labour with the Disobedient, laying Things home and close to such as were stout against the Truth; yet, through the Goodness of God, we had, at Times, to partake of heavenly Comfort with them who were meek, and were often favoured to part with Friends in the Nearness of true Gospel-fellowship. We returned to Boston, and had another comfortable Opportunity with Friends there; and thence rode back a Day's Journey Eastward of Boston: Our Guide being a heavy Man, and the Weather hot, and my Companion and I considering it, expressed our Freedom to go on without him, to which he consented, and we respectfully took our Leave of him; this we did, as believing the Journey would have been hard to him and his Horse.

We visited the Meetings in those Parts, and were measurably baptized into a feeling of the State of the Society: And in Bowedness of Spirit went to the Yearly-meeting at Newport; where I understood that a large Number of Slaves were imported from Africa into that Town, and then on Sale by a Member of our Society. At this Meeting we met with John Storer from England, Elizabeth Shipley, Ann Gaunt, Hannah Foster, and Mercy Redman, from our Parts, all Ministers of the Gospel, of whose Company I was glad.

At this Time my Appetite failed, and I grew outwardly weak, and had a Feeling of the Condition of Habakkuk as there expressed: "When I heard, my Belly trembled, my Lips quivered, I trembled in myself that I might rest in the Day of Trouble;" I had many Cogitations, and was sorely distressed: And was desirous that Friends might petition the Legislature, to use their Endeavours to discourage the future Importation of Slaves; for I saw that this Trade was a great Evil, and tended to multiply Troubles, and bring Distresses on the People in those parts, for whose Welfare my Heart was deeply concerned.

But I perceived several Difficulties in Regard to petitioning; and such was the Exercise of my Mind, that I had Thought of endeavouring to get an Opportunity to speak a few Words in the House of Assembly, then sitting in Town. This Exercise came upon me in the Afternoon, on the second Day of the Yearly-meeting, and, going to Bed, I got no Sleep till my Mind was wholly resigned therein; and in the Morning I enquired of a Friend how long the Assembly were likely to continue sitting; who told me, they were expected to be prorogued that Day or the next.

As I was desirous to attend the Business of the Meeting, and perceived the Assembly were likely to depart before the Business was over; after considerable Exercise, humbly seeking to the Lord for Instruction, my Mind settled to attend on the Business of the Meeting; on the last Day of which, I had prepared a short Essay of a Petition to be presented to the Legislature, if Way opened: And being informed that there were some appointed, by that Yearly-meeting, to speak with those in Authority, in Cases relating to the Society, I opened my Mind to several of them, and shewed them the Essay I had made; and afterward opened the Case in the Meeting for Business, in Substance as follows:

"I have been under a Concern for some Time, on Account of the great Number of Slaves which are imported in this Colony; I am aware that it is a tender Point to speak to, but apprehend I am not clear in the Sight of Heaven without speaking to it. I have prepared an Essay of a Petition, if Way open, to be presented to the Legislature; and what I have to propose to this Meeting is, that some Friends may be named to withdraw and look over it, and report whether they believe it suitable to be read in the Meeting; if they should think well of reading it, it will remain for the Meeting, after hearing it, to consider, whether to take any farther Notice of it at a Meeting or not." After a short Conference some Friends went out, and, looking over it, expressed their Willingness to have it read; which being done, many expressed their Unity with the Proposal; and some signified, that to have the Subjects of the Petition enlarged upon, and to be signed out of Meeting by such as were free, would be more suitable than to do it there: Though I expected, at first, that if it was done it would be in that Way; yet, such was the Exercise of my Mind, that to move it in the hearing of Friends, when assembled, appeared to me as a Duty; for my Heart yearned toward the Inhabitants of these Parts; believing that by this Trade there had been an Increase of Inquietude amongst them, and a Way made easy for the spreading of a Spirit opposite to that Meekness and Humility, which is a sure Resting-place for the Soul: And that the Continuance of this Trade would not only render their Healing more difficult, but increase their Malady.

Having thus far proceeded, I felt easy to leave the Essay among Friends, for them to proceed in it as they believed best. And now an Exercise revived on my Mind in Relation to Lotteries, which were common in those Parts: I had once moved it in a former Sitting of this Meeting, when Arguments were used in Favour of Friends being held excused who were only concerned in such Lotteries as were agreeable to Law: And now, on moving it again, it was opposed as before; but the Hearts of some solid Friends appeared to be united to discourage the Practice amongst their Members; and the Matter was zealously handled by some on both Sides. In this Debate it appeared very clear to me, that the Spirit of Lotteries was a Spirit of Selfishness, which tended to Confusion and Darkness of Understanding; and that pleading for it in our Meetings, set apart for the Lord's Work, was not right: And, in the Heat of Zeal, I once made Reply to what an ancient Friend said, though when I sat down, I saw that my Words were not enough seasoned with Charity; and, after this, I spake no more on the Subject. At length a Minute was made; a Copy of which was agreed to be sent to their several Quarterly-meetings, inciting Friends to labour to discourage the Practice amongst all professing with us.

Some Time after this Minute was made, I, remaining uneasy with the Manner of my speaking to the ancient Friend, could not see my Way clear to conceal my Uneasiness, but was concerned that I might say nothing to weaken the Cause in which I had laboured; and then, after some close Exercise and hearty Repentance, for that I had not attended closely to the safe Guide, I stood up, and reciting the Passage, acquainted Friends, that, though I durst not go from what I had said as to the Matter, yet I was uneasy with the Manner of my speaking, as believing milder Language would have been better. As this was uttered in some Degree of creaturely Abasement, it appeared to have a good Savour amongst us, after a warm Debate.

The Yearly-meeting being now over, there yet remained on my Mind a secret, though heavy, Exercise in regard to some leading active Members about Newport, being in the Practice of Slave-keeping. This I mentioned to two ancient Friends, who came out of the Country, and proposed to them, if Way opened, to have some Conversation with those Friends: And, thereupon, one of those Country Friends and I consulted one of the most noted Elders who had Slaves; and he, in a respectful Manner, encouraged me to proceed to clear myself of what lay upon me. Now I had, near the Beginning of the Yearly-meeting, a private Conference with this said Elder and his Wife concerning theirs; so that the Way seemed clear to me to advise with him about the Manner of proceeding: I told him, I was free to have a Conference with them all together in a private House; or, if he thought they would take it unkind to be asked to come together, and to be spoke with one in the hearing of another, I was free to spend some Time among them, and visit them all in their own Houses: He expressed his Liking to the first Proposal, not doubting their Willingness to come together: And, as I proposed a Visit to only Ministers, Elders, and Overseers, he named some others, who he desired might be present also: And, as a careful Messenger was wanted to acquaint them in a proper Manner, he offered to go to all their Houses to open the Matter to them; and did so. About the eighth Hour, the next Morning, we met in the Meeting-house Chamber, and the last-mentioned Country Friend, also my Companion, and John Storer, with us; when, after a short Time of Retirement, I acquainted them with the Steps I had taken in procuring that Meeting, and opened the Concern I was under; and so we proceeded to a free Conference upon the Subject. My Exercise was heavy, and I was deeply bowed in Spirit before the Lord, who was pleased to favour us with the seasoning Virtue of Truth, which wrought a Tenderness amongst us; and the Subject was mutually handled in a calm and peaceable Spirit: And, at length, feeling my Mind released from that Burthen which I had been under, I took my Leave of them, in a good Degree of Satisfaction; and, by the Tenderness they manifested in Regard to the Practice, and the Concern several of them expressed in Relation to the Manner of disposing of their Negroes after their Decease, I believed that a good Exercise was spreading amongst them; and I am humbly thankful to God, who supported my Mind, and preserved me in a good Degree of Resignation through these Trials.

Thou, who sometimes travellest in the Work of the Ministry, art made very welcome by thy Friends, and seest many Tokens of their Satisfaction, in having thee for their Guest, it is good for thee to dwell deep, that thou mayst feel and understand the Spirits of People: If we believe Truth points towards a Conference on some Subjects, in a private Way, it is needful for us to take heed that their Kindness, their Freedom, and Affability, do not hinder us from the Lord's Work. I have seen that, in the midst of Kindness and smooth Conduct, to speak close and home to them who entertain us, on Points that relate to their outward Interest, is hard Labour; and sometimes, when I have felt Truth lead toward it, I have found myself disqualified by a superficial Friendship; and as the Sense thereof hath abased me, and my Cries have been to the Lord, so I have been humbled and made content to appear weak, or as a Fool for his Sake; and thus a Door hath opened to enter upon it. To attempt to do the Lord's Work in our own Way, and to speak of that which is the Burthen of the Word in a Way easy to the natural Part, doth not reach the Bottom of the Disorder. To see the Failings of our Friends and think hard of them, without opening that which we ought to open, and still carry a Face of Friendship; this tends to undermine the Foundation of true Unity.

The Office of a Minister of Christ is weighty; and they, who go forth as Watchmen, had need to be steadily on their Guard against the Snares of Prosperity and an outside Friendship.

After the Yearly-meeting, we were at Meetings at New-Town, Cushnet, Long-Plain, Rochester, and Dartmouth: From thence we sailed for Nantucket, in Company with Ann Gaunt and Mercy Redman, and several other Friends: The Wind being slack, we only reached Tarpawling-Cove the first Day; where, going on Shore, we found Room in a Publick-house, and Beds for a few of us, the rest sleeping on the Floor: We went on board again about Break of Day; and, though the Wind was small, we were favoured to come within about four Miles of Nantucket; and then, about ten of us getting into our Boat, we rowed to the Harbour before dark; whereupon a large Boat, going off, brought in the rest of the Passengers about Midnight: The next Day but one was their Yearly-meeting, which held four Days; the last of which was their Monthly-meeting for Business. We had a laborious Time amongst them: Our Minds were closely exercised, and I believe it was a Time of great Searching of Heart: The longer I was on the Island, the more I became sensible that there was a considerable Number of valuable Friends there, though an evil Spirit, tending to Strife, had been at Work amongst them: I was cautious of making any Visits, but as my Mind was particularly drawn to them; and in that Way we had some Sittings in Friends Houses, where the heavenly Wing was, at Times, spread over us, to our mutual Comfort.

My beloved Companion had very acceptable Service on this Island.

When Meeting was over, we all agreed to sail the next Day, if the Weather was suitable and we well; and, being called up the latter Part of the Night, we went on board a Vessel, being in all about fifty; but, the Wind changing, the Seamen thought best to stay in the Harbour till it altered; so we returned on Shore; and, feeling clear as to any farther Visits, I spent my Time in our Chamber chiefly alone; and, after some Hours, my Heart being filled with the Spirit of Supplication, my Prayers and Tears were poured out, before my heavenly Father, for his Help and Instruction in the manifold Difficulties which attended me in Life: And, while I was waiting upon the Lord, there came a Messenger from the Women Friends, who lodged at another House, desiring to confer with us about appointing a Meeting, which to me appeared weighty, as we had been at so many before; but, after a short Conference, and advising with some elderly Friends, a Meeting was appointed, in which the Friend, who first moved it, and who had been much shut up before, was largely opened in the Love of the Gospel: And the next Morning, about Break of Day, going again on board the Vessel, we reached Falmouth on the Main before Night; where our Horses being brought, we proceeded toward Sandwich Quarterly-meeting.

Being two Days in going to Nantucket, and having been there once before, I observed many Shoals in their Bay, which make Sailing more dangerous, especially in stormy Nights; also, that a great Shoal, which encloses their Harbour, prevents their going in with Sloops, except when the Tide is up; waiting without which, for the Rising of the Tide, is sometimes hazardous in Storms; waiting within, they sometimes miss a fair Wind. I took Notice, that on that small Island was a great Number of Inhabitants, and the Soil not very fertile; the Timber so gone, that for Vessels, Fences, and Firewood, they depend chiefly on the buying from the Main; the Cost whereof, with most of their other Expences, they depend principally upon the Whale-fishery to answer. I considered, that as Towns grew larger, and Lands near navigable Waters more cleared, Timber and Wood require more Labour to get it: I understood that the Whales being much hunted, and sometimes wounded and not killed, grew more shy and difficult to come at: I considered that the Formation of the Earth, the Seas, the Islands, Bays, and Rivers, the Motions of the Winds and great Waters, which cause Bars and Shoals in particular Places, were all the Works of him who is perfect Wisdom and Goodness; and, as People attend to his heavenly Instruction, and put their Trust in him, he provides for them in all Parts where he gives them a Being. And as, in this Visit to these People, I felt a strong Desire for their firm Establishment on the sure Foundation, besides what was said more publickly, I was concerned to speak with the Women Friends, in their Monthly-meeting of Business, many being present; and, in the fresh Spring of pure Love, to open before them the Advantage, both inward and outward, of attending singly to the Guidance of the Holy Spirit, and therein to educate their Children in true Humility, and the Disuse of all Superfluities, reminding them of the Difficulties their Husbands and Sons were frequently exposed to at Sea; and that, the more plain and simple their Way of Living was, the less Need of running great Hazards to support them in it; encouraging the young Women in their neat decent Way of attending themselves on the Affairs of the House; shewing, as the Way opened, that, where People were truly humble, used themselves to Business, and were content with a plain Way of Life, it had ever been attended with more true Peace and Calmness of Mind, than they have had who, aspiring to Greatness and outward Shew, have grasped hard for an Income to support themselves in it: And, as I observed they had few or no Slaves amongst them, I had to encourage them to be content without them; making mention of the numerous Troubles and Vexations which frequently attend the Minds of People who depend on Slaves to do their Labour.

We attended the Quarterly-meeting at Sandwich, in Company with Ann Gaunt and Mercy Redman, which was preceded by a Monthly-meeting; and in the whole held three Days: We were various Ways exercised amongst them, in Gospel-love, according to the several Gifts bestowed on us; and were, at Times, overshadowed with the Virtue of Truth, to the Comfort of the Sincere, and stirring up of the Negligent. Here we parted with Ann and

Mercy, and went to Rhode-Island, taking one Meeting in our Way, which was a satisfactory Time; and, reaching Newport the Evening before their Quarterly-meeting, we attended it; and, after that, had a Meeting with our young People, separated from those of other Societies. We went through much Labour in this Town; and now, in taking Leave of it, though I felt close inward Exercise to the last, I found inward Peace; and was, in some Degree, comforted, in a Belief, that a good Number remain in that Place, who retain a Sense of Truth; and that there are some young People attentive to the Voice of the heavenly Shepherd. The last Meeting, in which Friends from the several Parts of the Quarter came together, was a select Meeting; and, through the renewed Manifestation of the Father's Love, the Hearts of the Sincere were united together.

That Poverty of Spirit, and inward Weakness, with which I was much tried the fore Part of this Journey, have of late appeared to me as a Dispensation of Kindness. Appointing Meetings never appeared more weighty to me; and I was led into a deep Search, whether in all Things my Mind was resigned to the Will of God; often querying with myself, what should be the Cause of such inward Poverty; and greatly desired, that no secret Reserve in my Heart might hinder my Access to the divine Fountain. In these humbling Times I was made watchful, and excited to attend the secret Movings of the heavenly Principle in my Mind, which prepared the Way to some Duties, that in more easy and prosperous Times, as to the Outward, I believe I should have been in danger of omitting.

From Newport we went to Greenwich, Shanticut, and Warwick; and were helped to labour amongst Friends in the Love of our gracious Redeemer: And then, accompanied by our Friend, John Casey, from Newport, we rode through Connecticut to Oblong, visited the Meetings of Friends in those Parts, and thence proceeded to the Quarterly-meeting at Ryewoods; and, through the gracious Extendings of divine Help, had some seasoning Opportunities in those Places: So we visited Friends at New York and Flushing; and thence to Rahaway: And here, our Roads parting, I took Leave of my beloved Companion, and true Yoke-mate, Samuel Eastburn; and reached Home on the tenth Day of the eighth Month, 1760, where I found my Family well: And, for the Favours and Protection of the Lord, both inward and outward, extended to me in this Journey, my Heart is humbled in grateful Acknowledgments; and I find renewed Desires to dwell and walk in Resignedness before him.

CHAPTER VIII

His Visits to Pennsylvania, Shrewsbury, and Squan—His publishing the second Part of Considerations on keeping Negroes—His visiting the Families of Friends of Ancocas and Mount-Holly Meetings—His Visits to the Indians at Wehaloosing on the River Susquehannah

Having felt my Mind drawn toward a Visit to a few Meetings in Pennsylvania, I was very desirous to be rightly instructed as to the Time of setting off: And, on the tenth Day of the fifth Month, 1761, being the first Day of the Week, I went to Haddonfield Meeting, concluding to seek for heavenly Instruction, and come Home, or go on, as I might then believe best for me; and there, through the springing up of pure Love, I felt Encouragement, and so crossed the River. In this Visit I was at two Quarterly and three Monthly-meetings; and, in the Love of Truth, felt my Way open to labour with some noted Friends, who kept Negroes: And, as I was favoured to keep to the Root, and endeavoured to discharge what I believed was required of me, I found inward Peace therein, from Time to Time, and Thankfulness of Heart to the Lord, who was graciously pleased to be a Guide to me.

In the eighth Month, 1761, having felt Drawings in my Mind to visit Friends in and about Shrewsbury, I went there, and was at their Monthly-meeting, and their First-day-meeting; and had a Meeting at Squan, and another at Squankum; and, as Way opened, had Conversation with some noted Friends concerning their Slaves: And I returned Home in a thankful Sense of the Goodness of the Lord.

From the Care I felt growing in me some Years, I wrote Considerations on keeping Negroes, Part the Second; which was printed this Year, 1762. When the Overseers of the Press had done with it, they offered to get a Number printed, to be paid for out of the Yearly-meeting Stock, and to be given away; but I being most easy to publish them at my own Expence, and, offering my Reasons, they appeared satisfied.

This Stock is the Contribution of the Members of our religious Society in general; amongst whom are some who keep Negroes; and, being inclined to continue them in Slavery, are not likely to be satisfied with those Books being spread amongst a People where many of the Slaves are taught to read, and especially not at their Expence; and such often, receiving them as a Gift, conceal them: But as they, who make a Purchase, generally buy that which they have a Mind for, I believe it best to sell them; expecting, by that Means, they would more generally be read with Attention. Advertisements being signed by Order of the Overseers of the Press, directed to be read in Monthly-meetings of Business within our own Yearly-meeting, informing where the Books were, and that the Price was no more than the Cost of printing and binding them, many were taken off in our Parts; some I sent to Virginia, some to New-York, and some to Newport, to my Acquaintance there; and some I kept, expecting to give Part of them away, where there appeared a Prospect of Service.

In my Youth I was used to hard Labour; and, though I was middling healthy, yet my Nature was not fitted to endure so much as many others: So that, being often weary, I was prepared to sympathize with those whose Circumstances in Life, as free Men, required constant Labour to answer the Demands of their Creditors, and with others under

Oppression. In the Uneasiness of Body, which I have many Times felt by too much Labour, not as a forced but as a voluntary Oppression, I have often been excited to think on the original Cause of that Oppression, which is imposed on many in the World: And, the latter Part of the Time wherein I laboured on our Plantation, my Heart, through the fresh Visitations of heavenly Love, being often tender, and my leisure Time frequently spent in reading the Life and Doctrines of our blessed Redeemer, the Account of the Sufferings of Martyrs, and the History of the first Rise of our Society, a Belief was gradually settled in my Mind, that if such, as had great Estates, generally lived in that Humility and Plainness which belongs to a Christian Life, and laid much easier Rents and Interests on their Lands and Monies, and thus led the Way to a right Use of Things, so great a Number of People might be employed in Things useful, that Labour, both for Men and other Creatures, would need to be no more than an agreeable Employ; and divers Branches of Business, which serve chiefly to please the natural Inclinations of our Minds, and which, at present, seem necessary to circulate that Wealth which some gather, might, in this Way of pure Wisdom, be discontinued. And, as I have thus considered these Things, a Query, at Times, hath arisen: Do I, in all my Proceedings, keep to that Use of Things which is agreeable to universal Righteousness? And then there hath some Degree of Sadness, at Times, come over me, for that I accustomed myself to some Things, which occasioned more Labour than I believe divine Wisdom intends for us.

From my early Acquaintance with Truth I have often felt an inward Distress, occasioned by the striving of a Spirit in me against the Operation of the heavenly Principle; and in this Circumstance have been affected with a Sense of my own Wretchedness, and in a mourning Condition felt earnest

Longing for that divine Help, which brings the Soul into true Liberty; and sometimes, in this State, retiring into private Places, the Spirit of Supplication hath been given me; and, under a heavenly Covering, I have asked my gracious Father to give me a Heart in all Things resigned to the Direction of his Wisdom.

In visiting People of Note in the Society who had Slaves, and labouring with them in brotherly Love on that Account, I have seen, and the Sight hath affected me, that a Conformity to some Customs, distinguishable from pure Wisdom, has entangled many; and the Desire of Gain, to support these Customs, greatly opposed the Work of Truth: And sometimes, when the Prospect of the Work before me has been such, that in Bowedness of Spirit, I have been drawn into retired Places, and besought the Lord with Tears that he would take me wholly under his Direction, and shew me the Way in which I ought to walk, it hath revived, with Strength of Conviction, that, if I would be his faithful Servant, I must, in all Things, attend to his Wisdom, and be teachable; and so cease from all Customs contrary thereto, however used amongst religious People.

As he is the Perfection of Power, of Wisdom, and of Goodness, so, I believe, he hath provided, that so much Labour shall be necessary for Men's Support, in this World, as would, being rightly divided, be a suitable Employment of their Time; and that we cannot go into Superfluities, or grasp after Wealth in a Way contrary to his Wisdom, without having Connection with some Degree of Oppression, and with that Spirit which leads to Self-exaltation and Strife, and which frequently brings Calamities on Countries, by Parties contending about their Claims.

In the eleventh Month of the Year 1762, feeling an Engagement of Mind to visit some Families in Mansfield. I joined my beloved Friend, Benjamin Jones, and we spent a few Days together in that Service. In the second Month, 1763, I joined in Company with Elizabeth Smith and Mary Noble on a Visit to the Families of Friends at Ancocas; in both which Visits, through the baptizing Power of Truth, the sincere Labourers were often comforted, and the Hearts of Friends opened to receive us. And, in the fourth Month following, I accompanied some Friends in a Visit to the Families of Friends in Mount-Holly, in which my Mind was often drawn into an inward Awfulness, wherein strong Desires were raised for the everlasting Welfare of my Fellow-creatures; and, through the Kindness of our heavenly Father, our Hearts were, at Times, enlarged, and Friends invited, in the Flowings of divine Love, to attend to that which would settle them on the sure Foundation.

Having many Years felt Love in my Heart towards the Natives of this Land, who dwell far back in the Wilderness, whose Ancestors were the Owners and Possessors of the Land where we dwell; and who, for a very small Consideration, assigned their Inheritance to us; and, being at Philadelphia, in the eighth Month, 1761, in a Visit to some Friends who had Slaves, I fell in Company with some of those Natives who lived on the East Branch of the River Susquehannah, at an Indian Town called Wehaloosing, two hundred Miles from Philadelphia, and, in Conversation with them by an Interpreter, as also by Observations on their Countenances and Conduct, I believed some of them were measurably acquainted with that divine Power which subjects the rough and forward Will of the Creature: And, at Times, I felt inward Drawings toward a Visit to that Place, of which I told none except my dear Wife, until it came to some Ripeness; and, then, in the Winter, 1762, I laid it before Friends at our Monthly and Quarterly, and afterwards at our general Spring-meeting; and, having the Unity of Friends, and being thoughtful about an Indian Pilot, there came a Man and three Women from a little beyond that Town to Philadelphia on Business: And I, being informed thereof by Letter, met them in Town in the fifth Month, 1763; and, after some Conversation, finding they were sober People, I, by the Concurrence of Friends in that Place, agreed to join with them as Companions in their Return; and, on the seventh Day of the sixth Month following, we appointed to meet at Samuel Foulk's, at Richland in Bucks County. Now, as this Visit felt weighty, and was performed at a Time when Travelling appeared perilous, so the Dispensations of divine Providence, in preparing my Mind for it, have been memorable; and I believe it good for me to give some Hints thereof.

After I had given up to go, the Thoughts of the Journey were often attended with unusual Sadness; in which Times my Heart was frequently turned to the Lord with inward Breathings for his heavenly Support, that I might not fail to follow him wheresoever he might lead me: And, being at our Youths Meeting at Chesterfield, about a Week before the Time I expected to set off, I was there led to speak on that Prayer of our Redeemer to his Father: "I pray not that thou shouldest take them out of the World, but that thou shouldest keep them from the Evil." And, in attending to the pure Openings of Truth, I had to mention what he elsewhere said to his Father; "I know that thou hearest me at all Times:" So that, as some of his Followers kept their Places, and as his Prayer was granted, it followed necessarily that they were kept from Evil: And, as some of those met with great Hardships and Afflictions in this World, and at last suffered Death by cruel Men, it appears, that whatsoever befals Men while they live in pure

Obedience to God, as it certainly works for their Good, so it may not be considered an Evil as if relates to them. As I spake on this Subject, my Heart was much tendered, and great Awfulness came over me; and then, on the first Day of the next Week, being at our own Afternoon-meeting, and my Heart being enlarged in Love, I was led to speak on the Care and Protection of the Lord over his People, and to make mention of that Passage, where a Band of Assyrians endeavouring to take captive the Prophet, were disappointed; and how the Psalmist said, "The Angel of the Lord encampeth round about them that fear him." And thus, in true Love and Tenderness, I parted from Friends, expecting the next Morning, to proceed on my Journey, and, being weary, went early to Bed; and, after I had been asleep a short Time, I was awaked by a Man calling at my Door; and, arising, was invited to meet some Friends at a Publick-house in our Town, who came from Philadelphia so late, that Friends were generally gone to Bed: These Friends informed me, that an Express arrived the last Morning from Pittsburgh, and brought News that the Indians had taken a Fort from the English Westward, and slain and scalped English People in divers Places, some near the said Pittsburgh; and that some elderly Friends in Philadelphia, knowing the Time of my expecting to set off, had conferred together, and thought good to inform me of these Things, before I left Home, that I might consider them, and proceed as I believed best; so I, going again to Bed, told not my Wife till Morning. My Heart was turned to the Lord for his heavenly Instruction; and it was an humbling Time to me. When I told my dear Wife, she appeared to be deeply concerned about it; but, in a few Hours Time, my Mind became settled in a Belief, that it was my Duty to proceed on my Journey; and she bore it with a good Degree of Resignation. In this Conflict of Spirit, there were great Searchings of Heart, and strong

Cries to the Lord, that no Motion might be, in the least Degree, attended to, but that of the pure Spirit of Truth.

The Subjects before-mentioned, on which I had so lately spoken in publick, were now very fresh before me; and I was brought inwardly to commit myself to the Lord, to be disposed of as he saw best. So I took Leave of my Family and Neighbours, in much Bowedness of Spirit, and went to our Monthly-meeting at Burlington; and, after taking Leave of Friends there, I crossed the River, accompanied by my Friends, Israel and John Pemberton; and, parting the next Morning with Israel, John bore me Company to Samuel Foulk's, where I met the before-mentioned Indians, and we were glad to see each other: Here my Friend, Benjamin Parvin, met me, and proposed joining as a Companion, we having passed some Letters before on the Subject; and now, on his Account, I had a sharp Trial; for, as the Journey appeared perilous, I thought, if he went chiefly to bear me Company, and we should be taken Captive, my having been the Means of drawing him into these Difficulties would add to my own Afflictions: So I told him my Mind freely, and let him know that I was resigned to go alone; but, after all, if he really believed it to be his Duty to go on, I believed his Company would be very comfortable to me: It was indeed a Time of deep Exercise, and Benjamin appeared to be so fastened to the Visit, that he could not be easy to leave me; so we went on, accompanied by our Friends, John Pemberton, and William Lightfoot of Pikeland, and lodged at Bethlehem; and there, parting with John, William and we went forward on the ninth Day of the sixth Month, and got Lodging on the Floor of a House, about five Miles from Fort-Allen: Here we parted with William; and at this Place we met with an Indian Trader, lately come from Wioming; and, in Conversation with him, I perceived that many white People do often sell Rum to the Indians, which, I believe, is a great Evil; first, they being thereby deprived of the Use of their Reason, and their Spirits violently agitated, Quarrels often arise, which end in Mischief; and the Bitterness and Resentments, occasioned hereby, are frequently of long Continuance; Again, their Skins and Furs, gotten through much Fatigue and hard Travels in Hunting, with which they intended to buy Clothing, when they become intoxicated, they often sell at a low Rate for more Rum; and afterward, when they suffer for want of the Necessaries of Life, are angry with those who, for the Sake of Gain, took the Advantage of their Weakness: Of this their Chiefs have often complained, at their Treaties with the English. Where cunning People pass Counterfeits, and impose that on others which is good for nothing, it is considered as a Wickedness; but, to sell that to People which we know does them Harm, and which often works their Ruin, for the Sake of Gain, manifests a hardened and corrupt Heart, and is an Evil, which demands the Care of all true Lovers of Virtue to suppress: And while my Mind, this Evening, was thus employed, I also remembered, that the People on the Frontiers, among whom this Evil is too common, are often poor; who venture to the Outside of a Colony, that they may live more independent on such as are wealthy, who often set high Rents on their Land: Being renewedly confirmed in a Belief, that, if all our Inhabitants lived according to sound Wisdom, labouring to promote universal Love and Righteousness, and ceased from every inordinate Desire after Wealth, and from all Customs which are tinctured with Luxury, the Way would be easy for our Inhabitants, though much more numerous than at present, to live comfortably on honest Employments, without having that Temptation they are often under of being drawn into Schemes to make Settlements on Lands which have not been purchased of the

Indians, or of applying to that wicked Practice of selling Rum to them.

On the tenth Day of the Month we set out early in the Morning, and crossed the Western Branch of Delaware, called the Great Lehie, near Fort-Allen; the Water being high, we went over in a Canoe: Here we met an Indian, and had some friendly Conversation with him, and gave him some Biscuit; and he having killed a Deer, gave the Indians with us some of it: Then, after travelling some Miles, we met several Indian Men and Women with a Cow and Horse, and some Household Goods, who were lately come from their Dwelling at Wioming, and going to settle at another Place; we made them some small Presents, and, some of them understanding English, I told them my Motive in coming into their Country, with which they appeared satisfied: And, one of our Guides talking a While with an ancient Woman concerning us, the poor old Woman came to my Companion and me, and took her Leave of us with an Appearance of sincere Affection. So, going on, we pitched our Tent near the Banks of the same River, having laboured hard in crossing some of those Mountains called the Blue-Ridge; and, by the Roughness of the Stones, and the Cavities between them, and the Steepness of the Hills, it appeared dangerous; but we were preserved in Safety, through the Kindness of him, whose Works in those mountainous Desarts appeared awful: Toward whom my Heart was turned during this Day's Travel.

Near our Tent, on the Sides of large Trees peeled for that Purpose, were various Representations of Men going to, and returning from the Wars, and of some killed in Battle; this being a Path heretofore used by Warriours: And, as I walked about viewing those Indian Histories, which were painted mostly in red, but some in black; and thinking on the innumerable Afflictions which the proud, fierce, Spirit produceth in the World; thinking on the Toils and Fatigues of Warriours, travelling over Mountains and Desarts; thinking on their Miseries and Distresses when wounded far from Home by their Enemies; and of their Bruises and great Weariness in chasing one another over the Rocks and Mountains; and of their restless, unquiet, State of Mind, who live in this Spirit; and of the Hatred which mutually grows up in the Minds of the Children of those Nations engaged in War with each other: During these Meditations, the Desire to cherish the Spirit of Love and Peace amongst these People arose very fresh in me. This was the first Night that we lodged in the Woods; and, being wet with travelling in the Rain, the Ground, our Tent, and the Bushes, which we proposed to lay under our Blankets, being also wet, all looked discouraging; but I believed, that it was the Lord who had thus far brought me forward, and that he would dispose of me as he saw good; and therein I felt easy: So we kindled a Fire, with our Tent open to it; and, with some Bushes next the Ground, and then our Blankets, we made our Bed, and, lying down, got some Sleep; and, in the Morning, feeling a little unwell, I went into the River; the Water was cold, but soon after I felt fresh and well.

The eleventh Day of the sixth Month, the Bushes being wet, we tarried in our Tent till about eight o'Clock; when, going on, we crossed a high Mountain supposed to be upwards of four Miles over; the Steepness on the North Side exceeding all the others. We also crossed two Swamps, and, it raining near Night, we pitched our Tent and lodged.

About Noon, on our Way, we were overtaken by one of the Moravian Brethren, going to Wehaloosing, and an Indian Man with him, who could talk English; and we, being together while our Horses ate Grass, had some friendly Conversation; but they, travelling faster than we, soon left us. This Moravian, I understood, had spent some Time this Spring at Wehaloosing, and was, by some of the Indians, invited to come again.

The twelfth Day of the sixth Month, and first of the Week, it being a rainy Day, we continued in our Tent; and here I was led to think on the Nature of the Exercise which hath attended me: Love was the first Motion, and thence a Concern arose to spend some Time with the Indians, that I might feel and understand their Life, and the Spirit they live in, if haply I might receive some Instruction from them, or they be in any Degree helped forward by my following the Leadings of Truth amongst them: And, as it pleased the Lord to make Way for my going at a Time when the Troubles of War were increasing, and when, by Reason of much wet Weather, Travelling was more difficult than usual at that Season, I looked upon it as a more favourable Opportunity to season my Mind, and bring me into a nearer Sympathy with them: And, as mine Eye was to the great Father of Mercies, humbly desiring to learn what his Will was concerning me, I was made quiet and content.

Our Guide's Horse, though hoppled, went away in the Night; after finding our own, and searching some Time for him, his Footsteps were discovered in the Path going back again, whereupon my kind Companion went off in the Rain, and, about seven Hours after, returned with him: And here we lodged again; tying up our Horses before we went to Bed, and loosing them to feed about Break of Day.

On the thirteenth Day of the sixth Month, the Sun appearing, we set forward; and, as I rode over the barren Hills, my Meditations were on the Alterations of the Circumstances of the Natives of this Land since the Coming in of the English. The Lands near the Sea are conveniently situated for fishing; the Lands near the Rivers, where the Tides flow, and some above, are in many Places fertile, and not mountainous; while the Running of the Tides makes passing up and down easy with any Kind of Traffic. Those Natives have, in some Places, for trifling Considerations, sold their Inheritance so favourably situated; and, in other Places, been driven back by superior Force: So that in many Places, as their Way of clothing themselves is now altered from what it was, and they, far remote from us, have to pass over Mountains, Swamps, and barren Desarts, Travelling is very troublesome, in bringing their Skins and Furs to trade with us.

By the extending of English Settlements, and partly by English Hunters, the wild Beasts, they chiefly depend on for a Subsistance, are not so plenty as they were; and People too often, for the Sake of Gain, open a Door for them to waste their Skins and Furs, in purchasing a Liquor which tends to the Ruin of them and their Families.

My own Will and Desires were now very much broken, and my Heart, with much Earnestness, turned to the Lord, to whom alone I looked for Help in the Dangers before me. I had a Prospect of the English along the Coast, for upwards of nine hundred Miles, where I had travelled; and the favourable Situation of the English, and the Difficulties attending the Natives in many Places, and the Negroes, were open before me; and a weighty and heavenly Care came over my Mind, and Love filled my Heart toward all Mankind, in which I felt a strong Engagement, that we might be obedient to the Lord, while, in tender Mercies, he is yet calling to us; and so attend to pure universal Righteousness, as to give no just Cause of Offence to the Gentiles, who do not profess Christianity, whether the Blacks from Africa, or the native Inhabitants of this Continent: And here I was led into a close laborious Enquiry, whether I, as an Individual, kept clear from all Things which tended to stir up, or were connected with Wars, either in this Land or Africa; and my Heart was deeply concerned, that, in future, I might in all Things keep steadily to the pure Truth, and live and walk in the Plainness and Simplicity of a sincere Follower of Christ. And, in this lonely Journey, I did, this Day, greatly bewail the Spreading of a wrong Spirit, believing, that the prosperous, convenient, Situation of the English, requires a constant Attention to divine Love and Wisdom to guide and support us in a Way answerable to the Will of that good, gracious, and almighty Being, who hath an equal Regard to all Mankind: And, here, Luxury and Covetousness, with the numerous Oppressions, and other Evils attending them, appeared very afflicting to me; and I felt in that which is immutable, that the Seeds of great Calamity and Desolation are sown and growing fast on this Continent: Nor have I Words sufficient to set forth that Longing I then felt, that we, who are placed along the Coast, and have tasted the Love and Goodness of God, might arise in his Strength; and, like faithful Messengers, labour to check the Growth of these Seeds, that they may not ripen to the Ruin of our Posterity.

We reached the Indian Settlement at Wioming; and here we were told, that an Indian Runner had been at that Place a Day or two before us, and brought News of the Indians taking an English Fort westward, and destroying the People, and that they were endeavouring to take another;

and also, that another Indian Runner came there about the Middle of the Night before we got there, who came from a Town about ten Miles above Wehaloosing, and brought News, that some Indian Warriours, from distant Parts, came to that Town with two English Scalps, and told the People, that it was War with the English.

Our Guides took us to the House of a very ancient Man; and, soon after we had put in our Baggage, there came a Man from another Indian House some Distance off; and I, perceiving there was a Man near the Door, went out; and, having a Tomahawk wrapped under his Matchcoat out of Sight, as I approached him, he took it in his Hand; I, however, went forward, and, speaking to him in a friendly Way, perceived he understood some English: My Companion then coming out, we had some Talk with him concerning the Nature of our Visit in these Parts; and then he going into the House with us, and talking with our Guides, soon appeared friendly, and sat down and smoked his Pipe. Though his taking his Hatchet in his Hand, at the Instant I drew near to him, had a disagreeable Appearance, I believe he had no other Intent than to be in Readiness in case any Violence was offered to him.

Hearing the News brought by these Indian Runners, and being told by the Indians where we lodged, that what Indians were about Wioming expected, in a few Days, to move to some larger Towns, I thought that, to all outward Appearance, it was dangerous Travelling at this Time; and was, after a hard Day's Journey, brought into a painful Exercise at Night, in which I had to trace back, and view over the Steps I had taken from my first Moving in the Visit; and though I had to bewail some Weakness which, at Times, had attended me, yet I could not find that I had ever given way to a wilful Disobedience: And then, as I believed

I had, under a Sense of Duty, come thus far, I was now earnest in Spirit, beseeching the Lord to shew me what I ought to do. In this great Distress I grew jealous of myself, lest the Desire of Reputation, as a Man firmly settled to persevere through Dangers, or the Fear of Disgrace arising on my returning without performing the Visit, might have some Place in me: Thus I lay, full of Thoughts, great Part of the Night, while my beloved Companion lay and slept by me; till the Lord, my gracious Father, who saw the Conflicts of my Soul, was pleased to give Quietness: Then I was again strengthened to commit my Life, and all Things relating thereto, into his heavenly Hands; and, getting a little Sleep toward Day, when Morning came we arose.

On the fourteenth Day of the sixth Month, we sought out and visited all the Indians hereabout that we could meet with; they being chiefly in one Place, about a Mile from where we lodged, in all perhaps twenty. Here I expressed the Care I had on my Mind for their Good; and told them, that true Love had made me willing thus to leave my Family to come and see the Indians, and speak with them in their Houses. Some of them appeared kind and friendly. So we took our Leave of these Indians, and went up the River Susquehannah, about three Miles, to the House of an Indian, called Jacob January, who had killed his Hog; and the Women were making store of Bread, and preparing to move up the River. Here our Pilots left their Canoe when they came down in the Spring, which lying dry, was leaky; so that we, being detained some Hours, had a good deal of friendly Conversation with the Family; and, eating Dinner with them, we made them some small Presents. Then, putting our Baggage in the Canoe, some of them pushed slowly up the Stream, and the rest of us rode our Horses; and swimming them over a Creek, called Lahawahamunk, we pitched our Tent a little above it, there being a Shower in the Evening: And, in a Sense of God's Goodness in helping me in my Distress, sustaining me under Trials, and inclining my Heart to trust in him, I lay down in an humble bowed Frame of Mind, and had a comfortable Night's Lodging.

On the fifteenth Day of the sixth Month, we proceeded forward till the Afternoon; when, a Storm appearing, we met our Canoe at an appointed Place; and, the Rain continuing, we stayed all Night, which was so heavy, that it beat through our Tent, and wet us and our Baggage.

On the sixteenth Day, we found, on our Way, abundance of Trees blown down with the Storm the Day before; and had Occasion reverently to consider the kind Dealings of the Lord, who provided a safe Place for us in a Valley, while this Storm continued. By the falling of abundance of Trees across our Path, we were much hindered, and in some Swamps our Way was so stopped, that we got through with extreme Difficulty.

I had this Day often to consider myself as a Sojourner in this World; and a Belief in the All-sufficiency of God to support his People in their Pilgrimage felt comfortable to me; and I was industriously employed to get to a State of perfect Resignation.

We seldom saw our Canoe but at appointed Places, by reason of the Path going off from the River; and, this Afternoon, Job Chilaway, an Indian from Wehaloosing, who talks good English, and is acquainted with several People in and about Philadelphia, met our People on the River; and, understanding where we expected to lodge, pushed back about six Miles, and came to us after Night; and in a While our own Canoe came, it being hard Work pushing up Stream. Job told us, that an Indian came in Haste to their Town yesterday, and told them, that three Warriours, coming from some Distance, lodged in a Town above Wehaloosing a few Nights past; and that these three Men were going against the English at Juniata. Job was going down the River to the Province-store at Shamokin. Though I was so far favoured with Health as to continue travelling, yet, through the various Difficulties in our Journey, and the different Way of living from what I had been used to, I grew sick; and the News of these Warriours being on their March so near us, and not knowing whether we might not fall in with them, was a fresh Trial of my Faith; and though, through the Strength of divine Love, I had several Times been enabled to commit myself to the divine Disposal, I still found the Want of my Strength to be renewed, that I might persevere therein; and my Cries for Help were put up to the Lord, who, in great Mercy, gave me a resigned Heart, in which I found Quietness.

On the seventeenth Day, parting from Job Chilaway, we went on, and reached Wehaloosing about the Middle of the Afternoon, and the first Indian that we saw was a Woman of a modest Countenance, with a Bible, who first spake to our Guide; and then, with a harmonious Voice, expressed her Gladness at seeing us, having before heard of our Coming: Then, by the Direction of our Guide, we sat down on a Log; and he went to the Town, to tell the People we were come. My Companion and I sitting thus together, in a deep inward Stillness, the poor Woman came and sat near us; and, great Awfulness coming over us, we rejoiced in a Sense of God's Love manifested to our poor Souls. After a While, we heard a Conkshell blow several Times, and then came John Curtis, and another Indian Man, who kindly invited us into a House near the Town, where we found, I suppose, about sixty People sitting in Silence; and, after sitting a short Time, I stood up, and in some Tenderness of Spirit acquainted them with the Nature of my Visit, and that a Concern for their Good had made me willing to come thus far to see them; all in a few short Sentences, which some of them understanding interpreted to the others, and there appeared Gladness amongst them. Then I shewed them my Certificate, which was explained to them; and the Moravian, who overtook us on the Way, being now here, bade me welcome.

On the eighteenth Day: We rested ourselves this Forenoon; and the Indians, knowing that the Moravian and I were of different religious Societies, and as some of their People had encouraged him to come and stay a While with them, were, I believe, concerned that no Jarring or Discord might be in their Meetings: And they, I suppose, having conferred together, acquainted me, that the People, at my Request, would, at any Time, come together, and hold Meetings; and also told me, that they expected the Moravian would speak in their settled Meetings, which are commonly held Morning and near Evening. So I found Liberty in my Heart to speak to the Moravian, and told him of the Care I felt on my Mind for the Good of these People; and that I believed no ill Effects would follow it, if I sometimes spake in their Meetings when Love engaged me thereto, without calling them together at Times when they did not meet of course: Whereupon he expressed his Good-will toward my speaking, at any Time, all that I found in my Heart to say: So, near Evening, I was at their Meeting, where the pure Gospel-love was felt, to the tendering some of our Hearts; and the Interpreters, endeavouring to acquaint the People with what I said in short Sentences, found some Difficulty, as none of them were quite perfect in the English and Delaware Tongues; so they helped one another, and we laboured along, divine Love attending: And afterwards, feeling my Mind covered with the Spirit of Prayer, I told the Interpreters that I found it in my Heart to pray to God, and believed, if I prayed aright, he would hear me, and expressed my Willingness for them to omit interpreting; so our Meeting ended with a Degree of divine Love: And, before the People went out, I observed Papunehang (the Man who had been zealous in labouring for a Reformation in that Town, being then very tender) spoke to one of the Interpreters; and I was afterwards told that he said in Substance as follows: "I love to feel where Words come from."

On the nineteenth Day, and first of the Week: This Morning, in the Meeting, the Indian, who came with the Moravian, being also a Member of that Society, prayed; and then the Moravian spake a short Time to the People: And, in the Afternoon, they coming together, and my Heart being filled with a heavenly Care for their Good, I spake to them a While by Interpreters; but none of them being perfect in the Work, and I, feeling the Current of Love run strong, told the Interpreters, that I believed some of the People would understand me, and so I proceeded: In which Exercise I believe the Holy Ghost wrought on some Hearts to Edification, where all the Words were not understood, I looked upon it as a Time of divine Favour, and my Heart was tendered and truly thankful before the Lord; and, after I sat down, one of the Interpreters seemed spirited to give the Indians the Substance of what I had said.

Before our first Meeting, this Morning, I was led to meditate on the manifold Difficulties of these Indians, who, by the Permission of the six Nations, dwell in these Parts; and a near Sympathy with them was raised in me; and, my Heart being enlarged in the Love of Christ, I thought that the affectionate Care of a good Man for his only Brother in Affliction does not exceed what I then felt for that People.

I came to this Place through much Trouble; and though, through the Mercies of God, I believed, that if I died in the Journey, it would be well with me; yet the Thoughts of falling into the Hands of Indian Warriours were, in Times of Weakness, afflicting to me; and, being of a tender Constitution of Body, the Thoughts of Captivity amongst them were, at Times, grievous; as supposing, that they being strong and hardy, might demand Service of me beyond what I could well bear; but the Lord alone was my Keeper; and I believed, if I went into Captivity, it would be for some good End: And thus, from Time to Time, my Mind was centered in Resignation, in which I always found Quietness. And now, this Day, though I had the same dangerous Wilderness between me and Home, I was inwardly joyful that the Lord had strengthened me to come on this Visit, and manifested a fatherly Care over me in my poor lowly Condition, when in mine own Eyes I appeared inferior to many amongst the Indians.

When the last-mentioned Meeting was ended, it being Night, Papunehang went to Bed; and, one of the Interpreters sitting by me, I observed Papunehang spoke with an harmonious Voice, I suppose a Minute or two; and, asking the Interpreter, I was told, that "He was expressing his Thankfulness to God for the Favours he had received that Day; and prayed that he would continue to favour him with that same, which he had experienced in that Meeting." And though Papunehang had before agreed to receive the Moravian, and join with them, he still appeared kind and loving to us.

On the twentieth Day I was at two Meetings, and silent in them.

The twenty-first Day: This Morning, in Meeting, my Heart was enlarged in pure Love amongst them, and, in short plain Sentences, I expressed several Things that rested upon me, which one of the Interpreters gave the People pretty readily; after which, the Meeting ended in Supplication, and I had Cause humbly to acknowledge the Loving-kindness of the Lord towards us; and then I believed that a Door remained open for the faithful Disciples of Jesus Christ to labour amongst these People.

I now feeling my Mind at Liberty to return, took my Leave of them in general, at the Conclusion of what I said in Meeting; and so we prepared to go homeward: But some of their most active Men told us, that, when we were ready to move, the People would choose to come and shake Hands with us; which those who usually come to Meeting did: And, from a secret Draught in my Mind, I went amongst some who did not use to go to Meeting, and took my Leave of them also: And the Moravian and his Indian Interpreter appeared respectful to us at parting. This Town stands on the Bank of Susquehannah, and consists, I believe, of about forty Houses, mostly compact together; some about thirty feet long, and eighteen wide, some bigger, some less; mostly built of split Plank, one End set in the Ground, and the other pinned to a Plate, on which lay Rafters, and covered with Bark. I understand a great Flood last Winter overflowed the chief Part of the Ground where the Town stands; and some were now about moving their Houses to higher Ground.

We expected only two Indians to be our Company; but, when we were ready to go, we found many of them were going to Bethlehem with Skins and Furs, who chose to go in Company with us: So they loaded two Canoes, which they desired us to go in, telling us, that the Waters were so raised with the Rains, that the Horses should be taken by such as were better acquainted with the Fording-places: So we, with several Indians, went in the Canoes, and others went on Horses, there being seven besides ours. And we meeting with the Horsemen once on the Way by Appointment, and that near Night, a little below a Branch called Tankhannah, we lodged there; and some of the young Men going out a little before Dusk with their Guns, brought in a Deer.

On the twenty-second Day, through Diligence, we reached Wioming before Night, and understood the Indians were mostly gone from this Place: Here we went up a small Creek into the Woods with our Canoes, and, pitching our Tent, carried out our Baggage; and before Dark our Horses came to us.

On the twenty-third Day in the Morning their Horses were loaded, and we prepared our Baggage, and so set forward, being in all fourteen; and with diligent Travelling, were favoured to get near half-way to Fort-Allen. The Land on this Road from Wioming to our Frontier being mostly poor, and good Grass scarce, they chose a Piece of low Ground to lodge on, as the best for grazing; and I, having sweated much in Travelling, and being weary, slept sound; I perceived in the Night that I had taken Cold, of which I was favoured to get better soon.

On the twenty-fourth Day we passed Fort-Allen, and lodged near it in the Woods.

Having forded the westerly Branch of Delaware three Times, we thereby had a shorter Way, and missed going over the Top of the Blue Mountains, called the second Ridge. In the second Time fording, where the River cuts through the Mountain, the Waters being rapid, and pretty deep, and my Companion's Mare being a tall, tractable Animal, he sundry Times drove her back through the River, and they loaded her with the Burthens of some small Horses, which they thought not sufficient to come through with their Loads.

The Troubles westward, and the Difficulty for Indians to pass through our Frontier, I apprehend, was one Reason why so many came; as expecting that our being in Company would prevent the outside Inhabitants from being surprised.

On the twenty-fifth Day we reached Bethlehem, taking Care on the Way to keep foremost, and to acquaint People on and near the Road who these Indians were: This we found very needful; for the Frontier Inhabitants were often alarmed at the Report of English being killed by Indians westward.

Amongst our Company were some whom I did not remember to have seen at Meeting, and some of these, at first, were very reserved; but, we being several Days together, and behaving friendly toward them, and making them suitable Returns for the Services they did us, they became more free and social.

On the twenty-sixth Day and first of the Week, having carefully endeavoured to settle all Affairs with the Indians relative to our Journey, we took Leave of them, and I thought they generally parted with us affectionately; so we, getting to Richland, had a very comfortable Meeting amongst our Friends: Here I parted with my kind Friend and Companion, Benjamin Parvin; and, accompanied by my Friend, Samuel Foulk, we rode to John Cadwallader's, from whence I reached Home the next Day, where I found my Family middling well; and they, and my Friends, all along appeared glad to see me return from a Journey which they apprehended dangerous: But my Mind, while I was out, had been so employed in striving for a perfect Resignation, and I had so often been confirmed in a Belief, that whatever the Lord might be pleased to allot for me, would work for Good, I was careful lest I should admit any Degree of Selfishness in being glad over much, and laboured to improve by those Trials in such a Manner as my gracious Father and Protector intends for me. Between the English Inhabitants and Wehaloosing we had only a narrow Path, which in many Places is much grown up with Bushes, and interrupted by abundance of Trees lying across it; these, together with the Mountains, Swamps, and rough Stones, make it a difficult Road to travel; and the more so, for that Rattle-snakes abound there, of which we killed four: People, who have never been in such Places, have but an imperfect Idea of them; but I was not only taught Patience, but also made thankful to God, who thus led me about and instructed me, that I might have a quick and lively Feeling of the Afflictions of my Fellow-creatures, whose Situation in Life is difficult.

CHAPTER IX

His religious Conversation with a Company met to see the Tricks of a Juggler—His Account of John Smith's Advice, and of the Proceedings of a Committee, at the Yearly-meeting in 1764—Contemplations on the Nature of true Wisdom, occasioned by hearing of the Cruelty of the Indians to their Captives—His visiting the Families of Friends at Mount-Holly, Mansfield, and Burlington, in 1764, and the Meetings on the Sea-Coast, from Cape-May, toward Squan, in 1765—His Visit to the lower Counties on Delaware, and the eastern Shore of Maryland, in 1766, in Company with John Sleeper; with some Account of Joseph Nichols and his Followers; and Observations on the different State of the first Settlers in Pennsylvania, who depended on their own Labour, and those of the southern Provinces, who kept Negroes—His visiting the northern Parts of New-Jersey the same Year, and the western Parts of Maryland and Pennsylvania in 1767, and afterwards other Parts of Pennsylvania, and the Families of Friends at Mount-Holly; and again, several Parts of Maryland in 1768—Farther Considerations on keeping Slaves; and his Concern for having formerly, as an Executor, been Party to the Sale of one; and what he did in Consequence of it—Thoughts on Friends exercising Offices in civil Government

The latter Part of the Summer, 1763, there came a Man to Mount-Holly, who had before published, by a printed Advertisement, that, at a certain Publick-house, he would shew many wonderful Operations, which he therein enumerated.

This Man, at the Time appointed, did, by slight of Hand, sundry Things; which, to those gathered, appeared strange.

The next Day, I, hearing of it, and understanding that the Shew was to be continued the next Night, and the People to meet about Sun-set, felt an Exercise on that Account: So I went to the Publick-house in the Evening, and told the Man of the House that I had an Inclination to spend a Part of the Evening there; with which he signified that he was content. Then, sitting down by the Door, I spake to the People as they came together, concerning this Shew; and, more coming and sitting down with us, the Seats of the Door were mostly filled; and I had Conversation with them in the Fear of the Lord, and laboured to convince them that, thus assembling to see those Tricks or Slights of Hand, and bestowing their Money to support Men, who, in that Capacity, were of no Use in the World, was contrary to the Nature of the Christian Religion.

There was one of the Company, who, for a Time, endeavoured, by Arguments, to shew the Reasonableness of their Proceedings herein; but, after considering some Texts of Scripture, and calmly debating the Matter, he gave up the Point. So, having spent about an Hour amongst them, and feeling my Mind easy, I departed.

At our Yearly-meeting at Philadelphia, on the twenty-fifth Day of the ninth Month, 1764, John Smith, of Marlborough, aged upwards of eighty Years, a faithful Minister, though not eloquent, stood up in our Meeting of Ministers and Elders, and, appearing to be under a great Exercise of Spirit, informed Friends in Substance as follows: to wit, "That he had been a Member of the Society upwards of sixty Years, and well remembered, that in those early Times Friends were a plain lowly-minded People; and that there was much Tenderness and Contrition in their Meetings.—That, at twenty Years from that Time, the Society, increasing in Wealth, and in some Degree conforming to the Fashions of the World, true Humility was less apparent, and their Meetings, in general, not so lively and edifying.—That, at the End of forty Years, many of them were grown very rich; that wearing of fine costly Garments, and using of silver (and other) Watches, became customary with them, their Sons and their Daughters, and many of the Society made a specious Appearance in the World; which Marks of outward Wealth and Greatness appeared on some in our Meetings of Ministers and Elders; and as these Things became more prevalent, so the powerful Overshadowings of the Holy Ghost were less manifest in the Society.—That there had been a continued Increase of these Ways of Life even until now; and that the Weakness which hath now overspread the Society, and the Barrenness manifest amongst us, are Matter of much Sorrow." He then mentioned the Uncertainty of his attending these Meetings in future, expecting his Dissolution was now near; and, having tenderly expressed his Concern for us, signified that he had seen in the true Light that the Lord would bring back his People from these Things into which they were thus degenerated; but that his faithful Servants must first go through great and heavy Exercises therein.

On the twenty-ninth Day, the Committee, appointed by the Yearly-meeting to visit the Quarterly and Monthly-meetings, now gave an Account in Writing of their Proceedings in that Service; in which they signified, that, in the Course of it, they had been apprehensive that some Persons holding Offices in Government, inconsistent with our Principles, and others, who kept Slaves, remaining active Members in our Meetings of Discipline, had been one Means of Weakness more and more prevailing in the Management thereof in some Places. After this Report was read, an Exercise revived on my Mind, which, at Times, had attended me several Years, and inward Cries to the Lord were raised in me, that the Fear of Man might not prevent me from doing what he required of me; and standing up, I spake in Substance as follows: "I have felt a Tenderness in my Mind, towards Persons, in two Circumstances mentioned in that Report; that is, toward such active Members as keep Slaves, and such as hold Offices in civil Government; and have desired, that Friends, in all their Conduct, may be kindly affectioned one toward another. Many Friends, who keep Slaves, are under some Exercise on that Account; and, at Times, think about trying them with Freedom; but find many Things in their Way: And the Way of Living, and annual Expences of some of them, are such, that it seems impracticable for them to set their Slaves free, without changing their own Way of Life. It has been my Lot to be often abroad; and I have observed in some Places, at Quarterly and Yearly-meetings, and at some Houses where travelling Friends and their Horses are often entertained, that the yearly Expence of Individuals therein is very considerable: And Friends, in some Places, crouding much on Persons in these Circumstances for Entertainment, hath often rested as a Burthen on my Mind for some Years past; and I now express it in the Fear of the Lord, greatly desiring that Friends now present may duly consider it."

In the Fall of this Year, having hired a Man to work, I perceived, in Conversation, that he had been a Soldier in the late War on this Continent; and, in the Evening, giving a Narrative of his Captivity amongst the Indians, he informed me that he saw two of his Fellow-captives tortured to Death in a very cruel Manner.

This Relation affected me with Sadness, under which I went to Bed; and, the next Morning, soon after I awoke, a fresh and living Sense of divine Love was spread over my Mind; in which I had a renewed Prospect of the Nature of that Wisdom from above, which leads to a right Use of all Gifts, both spiritual and temporal, and gives Content therein: Under a Feeling thereof, I wrote as follows:

"Hath he, who gave me a Being attended with many Wants unknown to Brute-creatures, given me a Capacity superior to theirs; and shewn me, that a moderate Application to Business is proper to my present Condition; and that this, attended with his Blessing, may supply all outward Wants, while they remain within the Bounds he hath fixed; and no imaginary Wants, proceeding from an evil Spirit, have any Place in me? Attend then, O my Soul! to this pure Wisdom, as thy sure Conductor through the manifold Dangers in this World.

"Doth Pride lead to Vanity? Doth Vanity form imaginary Wants? Do these Wants prompt Men to exert their Power in requiring that of others, which they themselves would rather be excused from, were the same required of them?

"Do these Proceedings beget hard Thoughts? Do hard Thoughts, when ripe, become Malice? Does Malice, when ripe, become revengeful; and, in the End, inflict terrible Pains on their Fellow-creatures, and spread Desolation in the World?

"Doth Mankind, walking in Uprightness, delight in each other's Happiness? And do these Creatures, capable of this Attainment, by giving way to an evil Spirit, employ their Wit and Strength to afflict and destroy one another?

"Remember then, O my Soul! the Quietude of those in whom Christ governs, and in all thy Proceedings feel after it.

"Doth he condescend to bless thee with his Presence? To move and influence to Action? To dwell in thee, and walk in thee? Remember then thy Station, as a Being sacred to God; accept of the Strength freely offered thee; and take heed that no Weakness, in conforming to expensive, unwise, and hard-hearted, Customs, gendering to Discord and Strife, be given way to. Doth he claim my Body as his Temple, and graciously grant that I may be sacred to him? O! that I may prize this Favour; and that my whole Life may be conformable to this Character!

"Remember, O my Soul! that the Prince of Peace is thy Lord: That he communicates his unmixed Wisdom to his Family; that they, living in perfect Simplicity, may give no just Cause of Offence to any Creature, but may walk as he walked."

Having felt an Openness in my Heart toward visiting Families in our own Meeting, and especially in the Town of Mount-Holly, the Place of my Abode, I mentioned it in our Monthly-meeting the Fore-part of the Winter, 1764; which being agreed to, and several Friends of our Meeting being united in the Exercise, we proceeded therein; and, through divine Favour, were helped in the Work, so that it appeared to me as a fresh reviving of godly Care amongst Friends: And, the latter Part of the same Winter, I joined my Friend William Jones, in a Visit to Friends Families in Mansfield; in which Labour I had Cause to admire the Goodness of the Lord towards us.

Having felt my Mind drawn toward a Visit to Friends along the Sea-coast from Cape-May to near Squan; and also to visit some People in those Parts, amongst whom there is no settled Worship; I joined with my beloved Friend, Benjamin Jones, in a Visit there, having Friends Unity therein: And, setting off the twenty-fourth Day of the tenth Month, 1765, we had a prosperous and very satisfactory Journey; feeling, at Times, through the Goodness of the heavenly Shepherd, the Gospel to flow freely toward a poor People scattered in those Places: And soon after our Return, I joined my Friends, John Sleeper and Elizabeth Smith, in visiting Friends Families at Burlington, there being at this Time about fifty Families of our Society in that City; and we had Cause humbly to adore our heavenly Father, who baptized us into a Feeling of the State of the People, and strengthened us to labour in true Gospel-love amongst them.

An Exercise having, at Times, for several Years attended me, in regard to paying a religious Visit to Friends on the eastern Shore of Maryland: Such was the Nature of this Exercise, that I believed the Lord moved me to travel on Foot amongst them, that, by so travelling, I might have a more lively Feeling of the Condition of the oppressed Slaves, set an Example of Lowliness before the Eyes of their Masters, and be more out of the Way of Temptation to unprofitable Converse.

The Time now drawing near in which I believed it my Duty to lay my Concern before our Monthly-meeting, I perceived, in Conversation with my beloved Friend, John Sleeper, that he was under a Concern to travel the same Way, and also to travel on Foot in the Form of a Servant amongst them, as he expressed it. This he told me before he knew aught of my Exercise.

We, being thus drawn the same Way, laid our Exercise and the Nature of it before Friends; and, obtaining Certificates, we set off the sixth Day of the fifth Month, 1766; and were at Meetings with Friends at Wilmington, Duck-Creek, Little-Creek, and Motherkill; my Heart being sundry Times tendered under the divine Influence, and enlarged in Love toward the People amongst whom we travelled.

From Motherkill, we crossed the Country about thirty-five Miles to Friends at Tuckahoe in Maryland, and had a Meeting there and at Marshy-Creek.

At these, our three last Meetings, were a considerable Number of People, Followers of one Joseph Nichols, a Preacher; who, I understand, is not in outward Fellowship with any religious Society of People, but professeth nearly the same Principles as our Society doth, and often travels up and down appointing Meetings, to which many People come. I heard some Friends speaking of some of their Neighbours, who had been irreligious People, that were now his Followers, and were become sober well-behaved Men and Women.

Some Irregularities, I hear, have been amongst the People at several of his Meetings; but, from the whole of what I have perceived, I believe the Man and some of his Followers are honestly disposed, but that skilful Fathers are wanting amongst them: From hence we went to Choptank and Third-Haven; and thence to Queen Anne's. The Weather having some Days past been hot and dry, and we, to attend Meetings pursuant to Appointment, having travelled pretty steadily, and had hard Labour in Meetings, I grew weakly, at which I was, for a Time, discouraged; but, looking over our Journey, and thinking how the Lord had supported our Minds and Bodies, so that we got forward much faster than I expected before we came out, I now saw that I had been in Danger of too strongly desiring to get soon through the Journey, and that this bodily Weakness, now attending me, was a Kindness to me; and then, in Contrition of Spirit, I became very thankful to my gracious Father, for this Manifestation of his Love; and, in humble Submission to his Will, my Trust was renewed in him.

On this Part of our Journey, I had many Thoughts on the different Circumstances of Friends, who inhabit Pennsylvania and Jersey, from those who dwell in Maryland, Virginia, and Carolina. Pennsylvania and New-Jersey were settled by many Friends, who were convinced of our Principles in England in Times of Suffering, and, coming over, bought Lands of the Natives, and applied themselves to Husbandry in a peaceable Way; and many of their Children were taught to labour for their Living.

Few Friends, I believe, came from England to settle in any of these southern Provinces; but, by the faithful Labours of travelling Friends in early Times, there were considerable Convincements amongst the Inhabitants of these Parts. Here I remembered my reading of the warlike Disposition of many of the first Settlers in those Provinces, and of their numerous Engagements with the Natives, in which much Blood was shed, even in the Infancy of those Colonies. These People, inhabiting those Places, being grounded in Customs contrary to the pure Truth, when some of them were affected with the powerful preaching of the Word of Life, and joined in Fellowship with our Society, they had a great Work to go through. It is observable, in the History of the Reformation from Popery, that it had a gradual Progress from Age to Age: The Uprightness of the first Reformers, in attending to the Light and Understanding given them, opened the Way for sincere-hearted People to proceed farther afterward; and thus, each one truly fearing God, and labouring in those Works of Righteousness appointed for him in his Day, findeth Acceptance with him: Though, through the Darkness of the Times, and the Corruption of Manners and Customs, some upright Men have had little more for their Day's Work than to attend to the righteous Principle in their Minds, as it related to their own Conduct in Life, without pointing out to others the whole Extent of that, which the same Principle would lead succeeding Ages into. Thus, for Instance, amongst an imperious warlike People, supported by oppressed Slaves, some of these Masters, I suppose, are awakened to feel and see their Error; and. through sincere Repentance, cease from Oppression, and become like Fathers to their Servants; shewing, by their Example, a Pattern of Humility in living, and Moderation in governing, for the Instruction and Admonition of their oppressing Neighbours; those, without carrying the Reformation farther, I believe, have found Acceptance with the Lord. Such was the Beginning; and those who succeeded them, and have faithfully attended to the Nature and Spirit of the Reformation, have seen the Necessity of proceeding forward, and not only to instruct others, by their Example, in governing well, but also to use Means to prevent their Successors from having so much Power to oppress others.

Here I was renewedly confirmed in my Mind, that the Lord (whose tender Mercies are over all his Works, and whose Ear is open to the Cries and Groans of the Oppressed) is graciously moving on the Hearts of People, to draw them off from the Desire of Wealth, and bring them into such an humble, lowly, Way of Living, that they may see their Way clearly, to repair to the Standard of true Righteousness; and not only break the Yoke of Oppression, but know him to be their Strength and Support in a Time of outward Affliction.

We, passing on, crossed Chester-River; and had a Meeting there, and at Cecil and Sassafras. Through my bodily Weakness, joined with a heavy Exercise of Mind, it was to me an humbling Dispensation, and I had a very lively Feeling of the State of the Oppressed; yet I often thought, that what I suffered was little, compared with the Sufferings of the blessed Jesus, and many of his faithful Followers; and may say, with Thankfulness, I was made content.

From Sassafras we went pretty directly Home, where we found our Families well; and, for several Weeks after our Return, I had often to look over our Journey: And though it appeared to me as a small Service, and that some faithful Messengers will yet have more bitter Cups to drink in those southern Provinces, for Christ's Sake, than we had; yet I found Peace in that I had been helped to walk in Sincerity, according to the Understanding and Strength given me.

On the thirteenth Day of the eleventh Month, 1766, with the Unity of Friends at our Monthly-meeting, in Company with my beloved Friend, Benjamin Jones, I set out on a Visit to Friends in the upper Part of this Province, having had Drawings of Love in my Heart that Way a considerable Time: We travelled as far as Hardwick; and I had inward Peace in my Labours of Love amongst them.

Through the humbling Dispensations of divine Providence, my Mind hath been brought into a farther Feeling of the Difficulties of Friends and their Servants south-westward; and being often engaged in Spirit on their Account, I believed it my Duty to walk into some Parts of the western

Shore of Maryland, on a religious Visit; and, having obtained a Certificate from Friends of our Monthly-meeting, I took my Leave of my Family under the heart-tendering Operation of Truth; and, on the twentieth Day of the fourth Month, 1767, I rode to the Ferry opposite to Philadelphia, and from thence walked to William Horne's, at Derby, that Evening; and next Day pursued my journey alone, and reached Concord week-day Meeting.

Discouragements and a Weight of Distress had, at Times, attended me in this lonesome Walk; through which Afflictions I was mercifully preserved: And now, sitting down with Friends, my Mind was turned toward the Lord, to wait for his holy Leadings; who, in infinite Love, was pleased to soften my Heart into an humble Contrition, and did renewedly strengthen me to go forward; so that to me it was a Time of heavenly Refreshment in a silent Meeting.

The next Day I came to New-Garden week-day Meeting, in which I sat with Bowedness of Spirit; and, being baptized into a Feeling of the State of some present, the Lord gave us a heart-tendering Season; to his Name be the Praise.

I passed on, and was at Nottingham Monthly-meeting; and at a Meeting at Little-Britain on First-day: And in the Afternoon several Friends came to the House where I lodged, and we had a little Afternoon-meeting; and, through the humbling Power of Truth, I had to admire the Loving-kindness of the Lord manifested to us!

On the twenty-sixth Day, I crossed Susquehannah; and coming amongst People in outward Ease and Greatness, chiefly on the Labour of Slaves, my Heart was much affected; and, in awful Retiredness, my Mind was gathered inward to the Lord, being humbly engaged that in true

Resignation I might receive Instruction from him, respecting my Duty amongst this People.

Though travelling on Foot was wearisome to my Body; yet thus travelling was agreeable to the State of my Mind.

I went gently on, being weakly; and was covered with Sorrow and Heaviness, on Account of the spreading prevailing Spirit of this World, introducing Customs grievous and oppressive on one Hand, and cherishing Pride and Wantonness on the other. In this lonely Walk, and State of Abasement and Humiliation, the State of the Church in these Parts was opened before me; and I may truly say with the Prophet, "I was bowed down at the hearing of it; I was dismayed at the seeing of it." Under this Exercise, I attended the Quarterly-meeting at Gunpowder; and, in Bowedness of Spirit, I had to open, with much Plainness, what I felt respecting Friends living in Fullness, on the Labours of the poor oppressed Negroes; and that Promise of the Most High was now revived: "I will gather all Nations and Tongues; and they shall come and see my Glory."—Here the Sufferings of Christ, and his tasting Death for every Man, and the Travels, Sufferings, and Martyrdoms, of the Apostles and primitive Christians, in labouring for the Conversion of the Gentiles, were livingly revived in me; and, according to the Measure of Strength afforded, I laboured in some Tenderness of Spirit, being deeply affected amongst them: And thus the Difference, between the present Treatment which these Gentiles, the Negroes, receive at our Hands, and the Labours of the primitive Christians for the Conversion of the Gentiles was pressed home, and the Power of Truth came over us; under a Feeling of which, my Mind was united to a tender-hearted People in those Parts; and the Meeting concluded in a

Sense of God's Goodness toward his humble dependent Children.

The next Day was a general Meeting for Worship, much crouded; in which I was deeply engaged in inward Cries to the Lord for Help, that I might stand wholly resigned, and move only as he might be pleased to lead me: And I was mercifully helped to labour honestly and fervently amongst them, in which I found inward Peace; and the Sincere were comforted.

From hence I turned toward Pipe-Creek, and passed on to the Red-Lands; and had several Meetings amongst Friends in those Parts. My Heart was often tenderly affected, under a Sense of the Lord's Goodness, in sanctifying my Troubles and Exercises, turning them to my Comfort, and, I believe, to the Benefit of many others; for, I may say, with Thankfulness, that in this Visit, it appeared like a fresh tendering Visitation in most Places.

I passed on to the western Quarterly-meeting in Pennsylvania; during the several Days of this Meeting, I was mercifully preserved in an inward feeling after the Mind of Truth, and my publick Labours tended to my Humiliation, with which I was content: And, after the Quarterly-meeting of Worship ended, I felt Drawings to go to the Women's Meeting of Business; which was very full: And here the Humility of Jesus Christ, as a Pattern for us to walk by, was livingly opened before me; and in treating on it my Heart was enlarged; and it was a baptizing Time. From hence I went on; and was at Meetings at Concord, Middletown, Providence, and Haddonfield, and so Home; where I found my Family well. A sense of the Lord's merciful Preservation, in this my Journey, excites reverent Thankfulness to him.

On the second Day of the ninth Month, 1767, with the Unity of Friends, I set off on a Visit to Friends in the upper Part of Berks and Philadelphia Counties; was at eleven Meetings in about two Weeks; and have renewed Cause to bow in Reverence before the Lord, who, by the powerful Extendings of his humbling Goodness, opened my Way amongst Friends, and made the Meetings (I trust) profitable to us. And, the Winter following, I joined Friends on a Visit to Friends Families, in some Part of our Meeting; in which Exercise, the pure Influence of divine Love made our Visits reviving.

On the fifth Day of the fifth Month, 1768, I left Home under the humbling Hand of the Lord, having obtained a Certificate, in order to visit some Meetings in Maryland; and to proceed without a Horse looked clearest to me. I was at the Quarterly-meetings at Philadelphia and Concord; and then went on to Chester-River; and, crossing the Bay with Friends, was at the Yearly-meeting at West-River; thence back to Chester-River; and, taking a few Meetings in my Way, proceeded Home. It was a Journey of much inward Waiting; and, as my Eye was to the Lord, Way was, several Times, opened to my humbling Admiration, when Things had appeared very difficult.

In my Return, I felt a Relief of Mind, very comfortable to me; having, through divine Help, laboured in much Plainness, both with Friends selected, and in the more publick Meetings; so that (I trust) the pure Witness, in many Minds, was reached.

The eleventh Day of the sixth Month, 1769. Sundry Cases have happened, of late Years, within the Limits of our Monthly-meeting, respecting that of exercising pure Righteousness toward the Negroes; in which I have lived under a Labour of Heart, that Equity might be steadily kept to. On this Account, I have had some close Exercises amongst Friends; in which, I may thankfully say, I find Peace: And, as my Meditations have been on universal Love, my own Conduct in Time past became of late very grievous to me.

As Persons, setting Negroes free in our Province, are bound by Law to maintain them, in case they have Need of Relief, some, who scrupled keeping Slaves for Term of Life, in the Time of my Youth, were wont to detain their young Negroes in their Service till thirty Years of Age, without Wages, on that Account; and with this Custom I so far agreed, that I, being joined to another Friend, in executing the Will of a deceased Friend, once sold a Negro Lad till he might attain the Age of thirty Years, and applied the Money to the Use of the Estate.

With Abasement of Heart, I may now say, that sometimes, as I have sat in a Meeting, with my Heart exercised toward that awful Being, who respecteth not Persons nor Colours, and have looked upon this Lad, I have felt that all was not clear in my Mind respecting him; and as I have attended to this Exercise, and fervently sought the Lord, it hath appeared to me, that I should make some Restitution, but in what Way I saw not till lately; when, being under some Concern that I may be resigned to go on a Visit to some Part of the West-Indies, and under close Engagement of Spirit, seeking to the Lord for Counsel herein, that of my joining in the Sale aforesaid, came heavily upon me; and my Mind, for a Time, was covered with Darkness and Sorrow; and, under this sore Affliction, my Heart was softened to receive Instruction: And here I first saw, that, as I had been one of the two Executors, who had sold this Lad nine Years longer than is common for our own Children to serve, so I should now offer a Part of my Substance to redeem the last Half of that nine Years; but, as the Time was not yet come, I executed a Bond, binding me and my Executors to pay to the Man, he was sold to, what, to candid Men, might appear equitable for the last four Years and a Half of his Time, in case the said Youth should be living, and in a Condition likely to provide comfortably for himself.

The ninth Day of the tenth Month, 1769. My Heart hath often been deeply afflicted under a Feeling I have had, that the Standard of pure Righteousness is not lifted up to the People by us, as a Society, in that Clearness which it might have been, had we been so faithful to the Teachings of Christ as we ought to have been: And, as my Mind hath been inward to the Lord, the Purity of Christ's Government hath been opened in my Understanding; and, under this Exercise, that of Friends being active in civil Society, in putting Laws in force which are not agreeable to the Purity of Righteousness, hath, for several Years, been an increasing Burthen upon me; having felt, in the Openings of universal Love, that where a People, convinced of the Truth of the inward Teachings of Christ, are active in putting Laws in Execution which are not consistent with pure Wisdom, it hath a necessary Tendency to bring Dimness over their Minds: And, as my Heart hath been thus exercised, and a tender Sympathy in me toward my Fellow-members, I have, within a few Months past, in several Meetings for Discipline, expressed my Concern on this Subject.

CHAPTER X

His preparing to visit Friends in England—His embarking at Chester, in Company with Samuel Emlen, in a Ship bound to London—His deep Exercise, in observing the Difficulties and Hardships the common Sailors are exposed to—Considerations on the Dangers to which Youth are exposed, in being trained to a sea-faring Life; and its Inconsistency with a pious Education—His Thoughts in a Storm at Sea: With many instructive Contemplations on the Voyage—And his Arrival at London

Having been some Time under a religious Concern to prepare for crossing the Seas, in order to visit Friends in the northern Parts of England, and more particularly Yorkshire; after weighty Consideration, I thought it expedient to inform Friends, at our Monthly-meeting at Burlington, of it; who, having Unity with me therein, gave me a Certificate; and I afterward communicated the same to our Quarterly-meeting, and they likewise certified their Concurrence therewith. Some Time after which, at the general Spring-meeting of Ministers and Elders, I thought it my Duty to acquaint them of the religious Exercise which attended my Mind; with which they likewise signified their Unity by a Certificate, dated the twenty-fourth Day of the third Month, 1772, directed to Friends in Great-Britain.

In the fourth Month following, I thought the Time was come for me to make some Enquiry for a suitable Conveyance; being apprehensive that, as my Concern was principally toward the northern Parts of England, it would be most proper to go in a Vessel bound to Liverpool or

Whitehaven: And, while I was at Philadelphia, deliberating on this Occasion, I was informed, that my beloved Friend, Samuel Emlen, jun., intending to go to London, and having taken a Passage for himself in the Cabbin of a Ship, called Mary and Elizabeth, of which James Sparks was Master, and John Head, of the City of Philadelphia, one of the Owners; and I feeling a Draught in my Mind toward the Steerage of the same Ship, went first and opened to Samuel the Feeling I had concerning it.

My beloved Friend appeared glad that I had Thoughts of going in the Vessel with him, though my Prospect was toward the Steerage; and he, offering to go with me, we went on board, first in the Cabbin, a commodious Room, and then into the Steerage; where we sat down on a Chest, the Sailors being busy about us: Then the Owner of the Ship came, and sat down with us.

Here my Mind was turned toward Christ, the heavenly Counsellor; and I feeling, at this Time, my own Will subjected, my Heart was contrite before him.

A Motion was made, by the Owner, to go and sit in the Cabbin, as a Place more retired; but I felt easy to leave the Ship, and made no Agreement as to a Passage in her; but told the Owner, if I took a Passage in the Ship, I believed it would be in the Steerage; but did not say much as to my Exercise in that Case.

I went to my Lodgings, and soon after went to Bed, and my Mind was under a deep Exercise before the Lord; whose helping Hand was manifested to me as I slept that Night, and his Love strengthened my Heart. In the Morning I went with two Friends on board the Vessel again; and, after a short Time spent therein, I went, with Samuel Emlen, to the

House of the Owner; to whom, in the Hearing of Samuel only, I opened my Exercise, in relation to a Scruple with regard to a Passage in the Cabbin.

After this I agreed for a Passage in the Steerage; and, hearing in Town that Joseph White had a Desire to see me, I felt the Reviving of a Desire to see him, and went then to his House, and next Day Home; where I tarried two Nights; and then, early in the Morning, I parted with my Family, under a Sense of the humbling Hand of God upon me; and going to Philadelphia, had Opportunity with several of my beloved Friends; who appeared to be concerned for me, on Account of the unpleasant Situation of that Part of the Vessel where I was likely to lodge.

Having stayed two Nights in Philadelphia, I went the next Day to Derby Monthly-meeting; where, through the Strength of divine Love, my Heart was enlarged toward the Youth then present; under which I was helped to labour in some Tenderness of Spirit. Then, lodging at William Horne's, I, with one Friend, went to Chester; where, meeting with Samuel Emlen, we went on board, the first Day of the fifth Month, 1772; and, as I sat down alone, on a Seat on the Deck, I felt a satisfactory Evidence that my Proceedings were not in my own Will, but under the Power of the Cross of Christ.

Seventh Day of the fifth Month. We have had rough Weather mostly since I came on board; and the Passengers, James Reynolds, John Till-Adams, Sarah Logan and her hired Maid, and John Bispham, were all sea-sick, more or less, at Times; from which Sickness, through the tender Mercies of my heavenly Father, I have been preserved; my Afflictions now being of another Kind.

There appeared an Openness in the Minds of the Master of the Ship and of the Cabbin-Passengers toward me: We were often together on the Deck, and sometimes in the Cabbin.

My Mind, through the merciful Help of the Lord, hath been preserved in a good Degree, watchful and inward; and I have, this Day, great Cause to be thankful, in that I remain to feel Quietness of Mind.

As my lodging in the Steerage, now near a Week, hath afforded me sundry Opportunities of seeing, hearing, and feeling, with respect to the Life and Spirit of many poor Sailors, an inward Exercise of Soul hath attended me, in regard to placing our Children and Youth where they may be likely to be exampled and instructed in the pure Fear of the Lord; and I, being much amongst the Seamen, have, from a Motion of Love, sundry Times taken Opportunities, with one of them at a Time alone, and in a free Conversation laboured to turn their Minds toward the Fear of the Lord: And this Day we had a Meeting in the Cabbin, where my Heart was contrite under a Feeling of divine Love.

Now, concerning Lads being trained up as Seamen; I believe a Communication from one Part of the World to some other Parts of it, by Sea, is, at Times, consistent with the Will of our heavenly Father; and to educate some Youth in the Practice of sailing, I believe, may be right: But how lamentable is the present Corruption of the World! how impure are the Channels through which Trade hath a Conveyance! how great is that Danger, to which poor Lads are now exposed, when placed on shipboard to learn the Art of sailing!

O! that all may take Heed and beware of Covetousness! O that all may learn of Christ, who was meek and low of Heart! Then, in faithfully following him, he will teach us to be content with Food and Raiment, without respect to the Customs or Honours of this World.

Men, thus redeemed, will feel a tender Concern for their Fellow-creatures, and a Desire that those in the lowest Stations may be assisted and encouraged; and, where Owners of Ships attain to the perfect Law of Liberty, and are Doers of the Word, these will be blessed in their Deeds.

Rising to work in the Night is not commonly pleasant in any case; but, in dark rainy Nights, it is very disagreeable, even though each Man were furnished with all Conveniences: But, if Men must go out at Midnight, to help manage the Ship in the Rain, and, having small Room to sleep and lay their Garments in, are often beset to furnish themselves for the Watch, their Garments or something relating to their Business being wanting and not easily found, when, from the Urgency occasioned by high Winds, they are hastened and called up suddenly, here is a Trial of Patience on the poor Sailors and the poor Lads their Companions.

If, after they have been on Deck several Hours in the Night, and come down into the Steerage soaking wet, and are so close stowed that proper Convenience for change of Garment is not easily come at, but for Want of proper Room, their wet Garments are thrown in Heaps, and sometimes, through much crouding, are trodden under Foot in going to their Lodgings and getting out of them, and they have great Difficulties, at Times, each one to find his own, here are Trials on the poor Sailors.

Now, as I have been with them in my Lodge, my Heart hath often yearned for them, and tender Desires have been raised in me, that all Owners and Masters of Vessels may dwell in the Love of God, and therein act uprightly; and, by seeking less for Gain, and looking carefully to their Ways, may earnestly labour to remove all Cause of Provocation from the poor Seamen, either to fret or use Excess of Strong-drink; for, indeed, the poor Creatures, at Times, in the Wet and Cold, seem to apply to Strong-drink to supply the Want of other Convenience.

Great Reformation in the World is wanting; and the Necessity of it, amongst these who do Business on great Waters, hath, at this Time, been abundantly opened before me.

The eighth Day of the fifth Month. This Morning the Clouds gathered, the Wind blew strong from South-eastward, and before Noon increased to that Degree that Sailing appeared dangerous. The Seamen then bound up some of their Sails, and took down some; and, the Storm increasing, they put the Dead-lights, so called, into the Cabbin-Windows, and lighted a Lamp as at Night.

The Wind now blew vehemently, and the Sea wrought to that Degree, that an awful Seriousness prevailed in the Cabbin, in which I spent, I believe, about seventeen Hours; for I believed the poor wet toiling Seamen had Need of all the Room in the crouded Steerage, and the Cabbin-Passengers had given me frequent Invitations.

They ceased now from Sailing, and put the Vessel in the Posture called, lying-to.

My Mind, in this Tempest, through the gracious Assistance
of the Lord, was preserved in a good Degree of
Resignation; and I felt, at Times, a few Words in his Love
to my Ship-mates, in regard to the All-sufficiency of him
who formed the great Deep, and whose Care is so
extensive, that a Sparrow falls not without his Notice; and
thus, in a tender Frame of Mind, spake to them of the
Necessity of our yielding, in true Obedience, to the
Instructions of our heavenly Father, who sometimes,
through Adversities, intendeth our Refinement.

About eleven at Night I went out on the Deck, when the
Sea wrought exceedingly, and the high-foaming Waves, all
round about, had in some Sort the Appearance of Fire, but
did not give much, if any, Light.

The Sailor, then at the Helm, said he lately saw a Corposant
at the Head of the Mast.

About this Time I observed the Master of the Ship ordered
the Carpenter to keep on the Deck; and, though he said
little, I apprehended his Care was, that the Carpenter, with
his axe, might be in Readiness, in case of any Extremity.

Soon after this, the Vehemency of the Wind abated; and,
before Morning, they again put the Ship under Sail.

The tenth Day of the Month, and first of the Week, it being
fine Weather, we had a Meeting in the Cabbin, at which
most of the Seamen were present: This Meeting to me was
a strengthening Time.

The thirteenth Day of the Month. As I continue to lodge in
the Steerage, I feel an Openness this Morning, to express
something farther of the State of my Mind, in Respect to

poor Lads bound Apprentice to learn the Art of Sailing. As I believe Sailing is of some Use in the World, a Labour of Soul attends me, that the pure Counsel of Truth may be humbly waited for in this Case, by all concerned in the Business of the Seas.

A pious Father, whose Mind is exercised for the everlasting Welfare of his Child, may not, with a peaceable Mind, place him out to an Employment amongst a People, whose common Course of Life is manifestly corrupt and prophane; so great is the present Defect amongst Seafaring Men, in regard to Piety and Virtue: And, through an abundant Traffic, and many Ships of War, so many People are employed on the Sea, that this Subject of placing Lads to the Employment appears very weighty.

Prophane Examples are very corrupting, and very forcible. And as my Mind, Day after Day, and Night after Night, hath been affected with a sympathizing Tenderness toward poor Children, put to the Employment of Sailors, I have sometimes had weighty Conversation with the Sailors in the Steerage, who were mostly respectful to me, and more and more so the longer I was with them: They mostly appeared to take kindly what I said to them; but their Minds have appeared to be so deeply impressed with that almost universal Depravity amongst Sailors, that the poor Creatures, in their Answers to me on this Subject, have revived in my Remembrance that of the degenerate Jews a little before the Captivity, as repeated by Jeremiah the Prophet, "There is no Hope."

Now, under this Exercise, a Sense of the Desire of outward Gain prevailing amongst us hath felt grievous, and a strong Call to the professed Followers of Christ hath been raised in me, that all may take Heed, lest, through loving this present World, they be found in a continued Neglect of Duty, with respect to a faithful Labour for a Reformation.

Silence, as to every Motion proceeding from the Love of Money, and an humble Waiting upon God to know his Will concerning us, has now appeared necessary: He alone is able to strengthen us to dig deep, to remove all which lies between us and the safe Foundation, and so direct us in our outward Employments, that pure universal Love may shine forth in our Proceedings.

Desires arising from the Spirit of Truth are pure Desires; and when a Mind, divinely opened toward a young Generation, is made sensible of corrupting Examples, powerfully working, and extensively spreading amongst them, how moving is the Prospect!

The sixteenth Day of the Month. Wind for several Days past often high, what the Sailors call squally, rough Sea and frequent Rains. This last Night a very trying Night to the poor Seamen: The Water, chief Part of the Night, running over the main Deck, and sometimes Breaking-waves came on the Quarter-deck. The latter Part of the Night, as I lay in Bed, my Mind was humbled under the Power of divine Love; and Resignedness to the great Creator of the Earth and Seas, renewedly wrought in me; whose fatherly Care over his Children felt precious to my Soul: And Desires were now renewed in me, to embrace every Opportunity of being inwardly acquainted with the Hardships and Difficulties of my Fellow-creatures, and to labour in his Love for the spreading of pure universal Righteousness on the Earth. The Opportunities were frequent of hearing Conversation amongst the Sailors, in respect to the Voyages to Africa, and the Manner of bringing the deeply-oppressed Slaves into our Islands. The Thoughts of their

Condition, frequently in Chains and Fetters on board the Vessels, with Hearts loaded with Grief, under the Apprehensions of miserable Slavery; my Mind was frequently opened to meditate on these Things.

On the seventeenth Day of the Month, and first of the Week, we had a Meeting in the Cabbin; to which the Seamen generally came. My Spirit was contrite before the Lord; whose Love, at this Time, affected my Heart.

This Afternoon I felt a tender Sympathy of Soul with my poor Wife and Family left behind; in which State, my Heart was enlarged in Desires that they may walk in that humble Obedience wherein the everlasting Father may be their Guide and Support, through all the Difficulties in this World; and a Sense of that gracious Assistance, through which my Mind hath been strengthened to take up the Cross and leave them, to travel in the Love of Truth, hath begotten Thankfulness in my Heart to our great Helper.

On the twenty-fourth Day of the Month, and first of the Week, a clear pleasant Morning: And, as I sat on Deck, I felt a Reviving in my Nature; which, through much rainy Weather and high Winds, being shut up in a close unhealthy Air, was weakened.

Several Nights of late I felt Breathing difficult; so that a little after the rising of the second Watch (which is about Midnight) I got up, and stood, I believe, near an Hour, with my Face near the Hatchway, to get the fresh Air at the small Vacancy under the Hatch-door; which is commonly shut down, partly to keep out Rain, and sometimes to keep the Breaking-waves from dashing into the Steerage.

I may, with Thankfulness to the Father of Mercies, acknowledge, that, in my present weak State, my Mind hath been supported to bear the Affliction with Patience; and have looked at the present Dispensation as a Kindness from the great Father of Mankind, who, in this my floating Pilgrimage, is in some Degree bringing me to feel that, which many thousands of my Fellow-creatures often suffer in a greater Degree.

My Appetite failing, the Trial hath been the heavier; and I have felt tender Breathings in my Soul after God, the Fountain of Comfort, whose inward Help hath supplied, at Times, the Want of outward Convenience: And strong Desires have attended me, that his Family, who are acquainted with the Movings of his holy Spirit, may be so redeemed from the Love of Money, and from that Spirit in which Men seek Honour one of another, that in all Business, by Sea or Land, we may constantly keep in View the coming of his Kingdom on Earth, as it is in Heaven; and, by faithfully following this safe Guide, shew forth Examples, tending to lead out of that under which the Creation groans!

This Day we had a Meeting in the Cabbin; in which I was favoured in some Degree to experience the fulfilling of that Saying of the Prophet, "The Lord hath been a Strength to the Poor, a Strength to the Needy in their Distress;" for which, my Heart is bowed in Thankfulness before him!

The twenty-eighth Day of the Month.—Wet Weather of late, small Winds inclining to Calms: Our Seamen have cast a Lead, I suppose about one hundred Fathoms, but find no Bottom: Foggy Weather this Morning.

Through the Kindness of the great Preserver of Men my Mind remains quiet; and a Degree of Exercise, from Day to Day, attends me, that the pure peaceable Government of Christ may spread and prevail amongst Mankind.

The leading on of a young Generation in that pure Way in which the Wisdom of this World hath no Place; where Parents and Tutors, humbly waiting for the heavenly Counsellor, may example them in the Truth, as it is in Jesus;—this, for several Days, hath been the Exercise of my Mind. O! how safe, how quiet, is that State, where the Soul stands in pure Obedience to the Voice of Christ, and a watchful Care is maintained not to follow the Voice of the Stranger!

Here Christ is felt to be our Shepherd, and, under his Leading, People are brought to a Stability; and, where he doth not lead forward, we are bound, in the Bonds of pure Love, to stand still and wait upon him. In the Love of Money, and in the Wisdom of this World, Business is proposed; then the Urgency of Affairs pushes forward; nor can the Mind in this State, discern the good and perfect Will of God concerning us.

The Love of God is manifested in graciously calling us to come out of that which stands in Confusion: But, if we bow not in the Name of Jesus; if we give not up those Prospects of Gain, which, in the Wisdom of this World, are open before us, but say, in our Hearts, I must needs go on, and, in going on, I hope to keep as near to the Purity of Truth as the Business before me will admit of; here the Mind remains entangled, and the Shining of the Light of Life into the Soul is obstructed.

In an entire Subjection of our Wills the Lord graciously opens a Way for his People, where all their Wants are bounded by his Wisdom; and here we experience the Substance of what Moses the Prophet figured out in the Water of Separation, as a Purification from Sin.

Esau is mentioned as a Child red all over, like a hairy Garment: In Esau is represented the natural Will of Man. In preparing the Water of Separation, a red Heifer, without Blemish, on which there had been no Yoke, was to be slain, and her Blood sprinkled by the Priest seven Times toward the Tabernacle of the Congregation; then her Skin, her Flesh, and all pertaining to her, were to be burnt without the Camp; and of her Ashes the Water was prepared. Thus the crucifying the old Man, or natural Will, is represented; and hence comes a Separation from that carnal Mind, which is Death.

"He who toucheth the dead Body of a Man, and purifieth not himself with the Water of Separation, he defileth the Tabernacle of the Lord; he is unclean." Numb. xix. 13.

If any, through the Love of Gain, go forth into Business, wherein they dwell as amongst the Tombs, and touch the Bodies of those who are dead; if these, through the infinite Love of God feel the Power of the Cross of Christ to crucify them to the World, and therein learn humbly to follow the divine Leader;—here is the Judgment of this World;—here the Prince of this World is cast out.

The Water of Separation is felt; and, though we have been amongst the Slain, and, through the Desire of Gain, have touched the dead Body of a Man, yet, in the purifying Love of Christ, we are washed in the Water of Separation; are brought off from that Business, from that Gain, and from that Fellowship, which was not agreeable to his holy Will: And I have felt a renewed Confirmation, in the Time of this Voyage, that the Lord, in his infinite Love, is calling to his visited Children, so to give up all outward Possessions and Means of getting Treasures, that his holy Spirit may have free Course in their Hearts, and direct them in all their Proceedings.

To feel the Substance pointed at in this Figure, Man must know Death, as to his own Will.

"No Man can see God, and live." This was spoken by the Almighty to Moses the Prophet, and opened by our blessed Redeemer.

As Death comes on our own Wills, and a new Life is formed in us, the Heart is purified and prepared to understand clearly. "Blessed are the Pure in Heart; for they shall see God." In Purity of Heart the Mind is divinely opened to behold the Nature of universal Righteousness, or the Righteousness of the Kingdom of God. "No Man hath seen the Father, save he that is of God; he hath seen the Father."

The natural Mind is active about the Things of this Life; and, in this natural Activity, Business is proposed, and a Will in us to go forward in it. As long as this natural Will remains unsubjected, so long there remains an Obstruction against the Clearness of divine Light operating in us; but when we love God with all our Heart, and with all our Strength, then in this Love, we love our Neighbours as ourselves; and a Tenderness of Heart is felt toward all People for whom Christ died, even such who, as to outward Circumstances, may be to us as the Jews were to the

Samaritans. Who is my Neighbour? See this Question answered by our Saviour, Luke x. 30.

In this Love we can say, that Jesus is the Lord; and the Reformation in our Souls is manifested in a full Reformation of our Lives, wherein all Things are new, and all Things are of God; 2 Cor. v. 18. in this the Desire of Gain is subjected.

When Employment is honestly followed in the Light of Truth, and People become diligent in Business, "fervent in Spirit, serving the Lord;" Rom. xii. 11. here the Name is opened: "This is the Name by which he shall be called, THE LORD OUR RIGHTEOUSNESS." Jerem. xxiii. 6. O! how precious is this Name! it is like Ointment poured out. The chaste Virgins are in Love with the Redeemer; and, for the promoting his peaceable Kingdom in the World, are content to endure Hardness, like good Soldiers; and are so separated in Spirit from the Desire of Riches, that in their Employments they become extensively careful to give none Offence, neither to Jews nor Heathen, nor the Church of Christ.

On the thirty-first Day of the Month, and first of the Week, we had a Meeting in the Cabbin, with near all the Ship's Company; the Whole being near thirty. In this Meeting, the Lord, in Mercy, favoured us with the Extendings of his Love.

The second Day of the sixth Month. Last Evening the Seamen found Bottom at about seventy Fathoms.

This Morning, fair Wind, and pleasant. As I sat on Deck, my Heart was overcome with the Love of Christ, and melted into Contrition before him; and, in this State, the

Prospect of that Work, to which I have felt my Mind drawn when in my native Land, being in some Degree opened before me, I felt like a little Child: and my Cries were put up to my heavenly Father for Preservation, that, in a humble Dependence on him, my Soul might be strengthened in his Love, and kept inwardly waiting for his Counsel.

This Afternoon we saw that Part of England called the Lizard.

Some Dunghill-fowls yet remained of those the Passengers took for their Sea-store; I believe about fourteen perished in the Storms at Sea, by the Waves breaking over the Quarter-deck; and a considerable Number with Sickness, at different Times. I observed the Cocks crew, coming down the Delaware, and while we were near the Land; but afterward I think I did not hear one of them crow till we came near the Land in England, when they again crowed a few Times.

In observing their dull Appearance at Sea, and the pining Sickness of some of them, I often remembered the Fountain of Goodness, who gave Being to all Creatures, and whose Love extends to that of caring for the Sparrows; and believe, where the Love of God is verily perfected, and the true Spirit of Government watchfully attended to, a Tenderness toward all Creatures made subject to us will be experienced, and a Care felt in us, that we do not lessen that Sweetness of Life, in the animal Creation, which the great Creator intends for them in our Government.

The fourth Day of the Month. About Noon a Pilot came off from Dover; where my beloved Friend, Samuel Emlen, went on Shore, and thence to London; but I felt easy in staying in the Ship.

The seventh Day of the Month, and first of the Week. Clear Morning; we lay at Anchor for the Tide, and had a Parting-meeting with the Ship's Company; in which my Heart was enlarged in a fervent Concern for them, that they may come to experience Salvation through Christ. We had a Head-Wind up the Thames; lay sometimes at Anchor; saw many Ships passing, and some at Anchor near; and had large Opportunity of feeling the Spirit in which the poor bewildered Sailors too generally live.—That lamentable Degeneracy, which so much prevails on the People employed on the Seas, so affected my Heart, that I cannot easily convey the Feeling I have had to another.

CHAPTER XI

His attending the Yearly-meeting in London; and, after it, proceeding towards Yorkshire, visiting several Quarterly and other Meetings in the Counties of Hertford, Warwick, Oxford, Nottingham, York, and Westmoreland; and thence again into Yorkshire, and to the City of York; with some instructive Thoughts and Observations, and Letters on divers Subjects—His hearing of the Decease of William Hunt; and some Account of him—His Sickness at York; and End of his Pilgrimage there

On the eighth Day of the sixth Month, 1772, we landed at London; and I went straightway to the Yearly-meeting of Ministers and Elders, which had been gathered (I suppose) about half an Hour.

In this Meeting my Mind was humbly contrite: In the Afternoon the Meeting of Business opened; which, by Adjournments, held near a Week. In these Meetings I often felt a living Concern for the Establishment of Friends in the pure Life of Truth; and my Heart was enlarged in the Meeting of Ministers, Meeting of Business, and in several Meetings of publick Worship; and I felt my Mind united in true Love to the faithful Labourers now gathered at this Yearly-meeting.

On the fifteenth Day of the Month, I left London, and went to a Quarterly-meeting at Hertford.

The first Day of the seventh Month. I have been at Quarterly-meetings at Sherrington, Northampton, Banbury, and Shipston; and had sundry Meetings between: My Mind hath been bowed under a Sense of divine Goodness manifested amongst us; my Heart hath been often enlarged in true Love, both amongst Ministers and Elders, and in publick Meetings; that through the Lord's Goodness, I believe it hath been a fresh Visitation to many, in particular to the Youth.

The seventeenth Day of the Month. Was this Day at Birmingham: Have been at Meetings at Coventry, Warwick, in Oxfordshire, and sundry other Places; have felt the humbling Hand of the Lord upon me; and through his tender Mercies find Peace in the Labours I have gone through.

The twenty-sixth Day of the Month. I have continued travelling northward, visiting Meetings: Was this Day at Nottingham; which, in the Forenoon especially, was, through divine Love, a Heart-tendering Season: Next Day had a Meeting in a Friend's House with Friends Children and some Friends; this, through the strengthening Arm of the Lord, was a Time to be thankfully remembered.

The second Day of the eighth Month, and first of the Week. Was this Day at Sheffield, a large inland Town: Have been at sundry Meetings last Week; and feel inward Thankfulness for that divine Support, which hath been graciously extended to me.

The ninth Day of the Month, and first of the Week, was at Rushworth: Have lately passed through some painful Labour; but have been comforted, under a Sense of that divine Visitation, which I feel extended toward many young People.

The sixteenth Day of the Month, and first of the Week, I was at Settle: It hath of late been a Time of inward Poverty; under which my Mind hath been preserved in a watchful tender State, feeling for the Mind of the holy Leader, and I find Peace in the Labours I have passed through.

I have felt great Distress of Mind, since I came on this Island, on Account of the Members of our Society being mixed with the World in various Sorts of Business and Traffick, carried on in impure Channels. Great is the Trade to Africa for Slaves! and, in loading these Ships, abundance of People are employed in the Factories; amongst whom are many of our Society. Friends, in early Times, refused, on a religious Principle, to make, or trade in, Superfluities; of which we have many large Testimonies on Record; but, for Want of Faithfulness, some gave way; even some, whose Examples were of Note in our Society; and from thence others took more Liberty. Members of our Society worked in Superfluities, and bought and sold them; and thus Dimness of Sight came over many: At length, Friends got into the Use of some Superfluities in Dress, and in the Furniture of their Houses; and this hath spread from less to more, till Superfluity of some Kinds is common amongst us.

In this declining State, many look at the Example one of another, and too much neglect the pure Feeling of Truth. Of late Years, a deep Exercise hath attended my Mind, that Friends may dig deep, may carefully cast forth the loose Matter, and get down to the Rock, the sure Foundation, and there hearken to that divine Voice which gives a clear and certain Sound; and I have felt in that which doth not deceive, that if Friends, who have known the Truth, keep in that Tenderness of Heart, where all Views of outward Gain are given up, and their Trust is only on the Lord, he will graciously lead some to be Patterns of deep Self-denial in Things relating to Trade and Handicraft-labour; and that some, who have plenty of the Treasures of this World, will example in a plain frugal Life, and pay Wages, to such as they may hire, more liberally than is now customary in some Places.

The twenty-third Day of the Month. Was this Day at Preston-Patrick, and had a comfortable Meeting. I have, several Times, been entertained at the Houses of Friends, who had sundry Things about them which had the Appearance of outward Greatness; and, as I have kept inward, Way hath opened for Conversation with such in private, in which Divine Goodness hath favoured us together with heart-tendering Times.

I rested a few Days, in Body and Mind, with our Friend Jane Crosfield; who was once in America: Was, on the sixth Day of the Week, at Kendal in Westmoreland; and at Greyrig Meeting the thirtieth Day of the Month, and first of the Week.

I have known Poverty of late, and been graciously supported to keep in the Patience; and am thankful, under a Sense of the Goodness of the Lord toward those that are of a contrite Spirit.

The sixth Day of the ninth Month, and first of the Week. Was this Day at Counterside, a large Meeting-house, and very full; and, through the Opening of pure Love, it was a strengthening Time to me, and (I believe) to many more.

The thirteenth Day of the Month. Was this Day at Richmond, a small Meeting; but, the Town's People coming in, the House was crowded: It was a Time of heavy Labour; and (I believe) was a profitable Meeting.

At this Place I heard that my Kinsman William Hunt, from North-Carolina, who was on a religious Visit to Friends in England, departed this Life on the ninth Day of the ninth Month, Instant, of the Small-pox, at Newcastle.—He appeared in the Ministry when a Youth; and his Labours therein were of good Savour. He travelled much in that Work in America. I once heard him say, in publick Testimony, that his Concern was (in that Visit) to be devoted to the Service of Christ so fully, that he might not spend one Minute in pleasing himself: Which Words, joined with his Example, were a Means of stirring up the pure Mind in me.

On this Visit to England I have felt some Instructions sealed on my Mind, which I am concerned to leave in Writing, for the Use of such as are called to the Station of a Minister of Christ.

Christ being the Prince of Peace, and we being no more than Ministers, I find it necessary for us, not only to feel a Concern in our first going forth, but to experience the renewing thereof, in the Appointment of Meetings.

I felt a Concern, in America, to prepare for this Voyage; and, being, through the Mercy of God, brought safe here, my Heart was like a Vessel that wanted Vent; and for several Weeks, at first, when my Mouth was opened in Meetings, it often felt like the raising of a Gate in a Watercourse, where a Weight of Water lay upon it; and in these Labours there appeared a fresh Visitation to many, especially the Youth; but sometimes, after this, I felt empty and poor, and yet felt a Necessity to appoint Meetings.

In this State I was exercised to abide in the pure Life of Truth, and in all my Labours to watch diligently against the Motions of Self in my own Mind.

I have frequently felt a Necessity to stand up, when the Spring of the Ministry was low; and to speak from the Necessity, in that which subjecteth the Will of the Creature; and herein I was united with the suffering Seed, and found inward Sweetness with these mortifying Labours.

As I have been preserved in a watchful Attention to the divine Leader, under these Dispensations, Enlargement at Times hath followed, and the Power of Truth hath risen higher, in some Meetings, than I ever knew it before through me.

Thus I have been more and more instructed, as to the Necessity of depending, not upon a Concern which I felt in America, to come on a Visit to England, but upon the fresh Instructions of Christ, the Prince of Peace, from Day to Day.

Now, of late, I felt a Stop in the Appointment of Meetings, not wholly, but in Part; and I do not feel Liberty to appoint them so quick one after another as I have heretofore.

The Work of the Ministry being a Work of divine Love, I feel that the Openings thereof are to be waited for, in all our Appointments.

O! how deep is divine Wisdom! Christ puts forth his Ministers, and goeth before them: And O! how great is the Danger of departing from the pure Feeling of that which leadeth safely!

Christ knoweth the State of the People; and, in the pure Feeling of the Gospel-Ministry, their States are opened to his Servants.

Christ knoweth when the Fruit-bearing Branches themselves have Need of purging.

O! that these Lessons may be remembered by me! and that all who appoint Meetings may proceed in the pure Feeling of Duty.

I have sometimes felt a Necessity to stand up; but that Spirit which is of the World hath so much prevailed in many, and the pure Life of Truth been so pressed down, that I have gone forward, not as one travelling in a Road cast up and well prepared, but as a Man walking through a Miry place, in which are Stones here and there, safe to step on, but so situated, that, one Step being taken, Time is necessary to see where to step next.

Now I find that, in the pure Obedience, the Mind learns Contentment, in appearing weak and foolish to that Wisdom which is of the World; and in these lowly Labours, they who stand in a low Place, rightly exercised under the Cross, will find Nourishment.

The Gift is pure; and, while the Eye is single in attending thereto, the Understanding is preserved clear: Self is kept out. We rejoice in filling up that which remains of the Afflictions of Christ, for his Body's Sake, which is the Church.

The natural Man loveth Eloquence, and many love to hear eloquent Orations; and, if there is not a careful Attention to the Gift, Men who have once laboured in the pure Gospel-ministry, growing weary of Suffering, and ashamed of appearing weak, may kindle a Fire, compass themselves about with Sparks, and walk in the Light; not of Christ who is under Suffering; but of that Fire which they, going from the Gift, have kindled; and that in Hearers, which is gone from the meek suffering State, into the worldly Wisdom, may be warmed with this Fire, and speak highly of these Labours. That which is of God gathers to God; and that which is of the World is owned by the World.

In this Journey a Labour hath attended my Mind, that the Ministers amongst us may be preserved in the meek feeling Life of Truth, where we may have no Desire but to follow Christ and be with him; that, when he is under Suffering, we may suffer with him, and never desire to rise up in Dominion, but as he, by the Virtue of his own Spirit, may raise us.

A few Days after writing these Considerations, our dear Friend, in the Course of his religious Visits, came to the City of York, and attended most of the Sittings of the Quarterly-meeting there; but, before it was over, was taken ill of the Small-pox. Our Friend, Thomas Priestman, and others who attended him, preserved the following Minutes of his Expressions in the Time of his Sickness and of his Decease.

First-day, the twenty-seventh of the ninth Month, 1772. His Disorder appeared to be the Small-pox.

Second-day. He said he felt the Disorder to affect his Head, so that he could think little, and but as a Child.

Third-day he uttered the following Prayer.—O Lord my God! the amazing Horrors of Darkness were gathered around me and covered me all over, and I saw no Way to go forth; I felt the Depth and Extent of the Misery of my Fellow-creatures separated from the divine Harmony, and it was heavier than I could bear, and I was crushed down under it; I lifted up my Hand, I stretched out my Arm, but there was none to help me; I looked round about and was amazed; in the Depths of Misery, O Lord! I remembered that thou art omnipotent, that I had called thee Father, and I felt that I loved thee, and I was made quiet in thy Will, and I waited for Deliverance from thee; thou hadst Pity upon me when no Man could help me: I saw that Meekness under Suffering was shewed to us in the most affecting Example of thy Son, and thou taughtest me to follow him, and I said, "Thy Will, O Father! be done."

Fourth-day-morning, being asked how he felt himself, he meekly answered, I do not know that I have slept this Night, I feel the Disorder making its Progress, but my Mind is mercifully preserved in Stillness and Peace: Sometime after he said he was sensible the Pains of Death must be hard to bear; but, if he escaped them now, he must sometime pass through them, and he did not know that he could be better prepared, but had no Will in it. He said he had settled his outward Affairs to his Mind, had taken Leave of his Wife and Family as never to return, leaving them to the divine Protection; adding, and though I feel them near to me at this Time, yet I freely give them up, having a Hope that they will be provided for. And a little after said, This Trial is made easier than I could have thought, my Will being wholly taken away; for if I were anxious for the Event, it would have been harder; but I am not, and my Mind enjoys a perfect Calm.

In the Night a young Woman having given him something to drink, he said, My Child, thou seemest very kind to me, a poor Creature, the Lord will reward thee for it. A While after he cried out with great Earnestness of Spirit, O my Father! my Father! and soon after he said, O my Father! my Father! how comfortable art thou to my Soul in this trying Season! Being asked if he could take a little Nourishment; after some Pause he replied, my Child, I cannot tell what to say to it; I seem nearly arrived where my Soul shall have Rest from all its Troubles. After giving in something to be inserted in his Journal, he said, I believe the Lord will now excuse me from Exercises of this Kind; and I see no Work but one, which is to be the last wrought by me in this World; the Messenger will come that will release me from all these Troubles; but it must be in the Lord's Time, which I am waiting for. He said he had laboured to do whatever was required, according to the Ability received, in the Remembrance of which he had Peace; and, though the Disorder was strong at Times, and would like a Whirlwind come over his Mind, yet it had hitherto been kept steady, and centered in everlasting Love; adding, and if that be mercifully continued, I ask nor desire no more. Another Time he said, he had long had a view of visiting this Nation, and, sometime before he came, had a Dream, in which he saw himself in the northern Parts of it, and that the Spring of the Gospel was opened in him much as in the Beginning of Friends, such as George Fox and William Dewsberry, and he saw the different States of the People, as clear as he had ever seen Flowers in a Garden; but in his going along he was suddenly stopt, though he could not see for what End; but, looking towards Home, fell into a Flood of Tears which waked him.

At another Time he said, My Draught seemed strongest towards the North, and I mentioned, in my own Monthly-meeting, that attending the Quarterly-meeting at York, and being there, looked like Home to me.

Fifth-day-night, having repeatedly consented to take Medicine with a View to settle his Stomach, but without Effect, the Friend, then waiting on him, said, through Distress, What shall I do now? He answered with great Composure, Rejoice evermore, and in every Thing give Thanks; but added a little after, this is sometimes hard to come at.

Sixth-day-morning, he broke forth early in Supplication on this wise: O Lord! it was thy Power that enabled me to forsake Sin in my Youth, and I have felt thy Bruises for Disobedience; but, as I bowed under them, thou didst heal me, continuing a Father and a Friend: I feel thy Power now, and I beg that, in the approaching trying Moment, thou wilt keep my Heart stedfast unto thee.——Upon his giving Directions to a Friend concerning some little Things, she said, I will take Care, but hope thou wilt live to order them thyself. He replied, My Hope is in Christ; and, though I may seem a little better, a Change in the Disorder may soon happen, and my little Strength be dissolved; and, if it so happen, I shall be gathered to my everlasting Rest. On her saying she did not doubt that, but could not help mourning to see so many faithful Servants removed at so low a Time, he said, All Good cometh from the Lord, whose Power is the same, and can work as he sees best. The same Day he had given Directions about wrapping his Corpse, perceiving a Friend to weep, he said, I would rather thou wouldst guard against weeping for me, my Sister; I sorrow not, though I have had some painful Conflicts; but now they seem over, and Matters well settled, and I look at the Face of my dear Redeemer; for sweet is his Voice, and his Countenance is comely.

First-day, fourth of the tenth Month, being very weak, and in general difficult to be understood, he uttered a few

Words in Commemoration of the Lord's Goodness, and added, How tenderly have I been waited on in this Time of Affliction! in which I may say, in JOB'S Words, Tedious Days and wearisome Nights are appointed unto me: And how many are spending their Time and Money in Vanity and Superfluities, while thousands and tens of thousands want the Necessaries of Life, who might be relieved by them, and their Distresses, at such a Time as this, in some degree softened, by the administering suitable Things!

Second-day-morning, the Apothecary, who appeared very anxious to assist him, being present, he queried about the Probability of such a Load of Matter being thrown off his weak Body; and, the Apothecary making some Remarks implying he thought it might, he spoke with an audible Voice on this wise:—My Dependance is on the Lord Jesus, who, I trust, will forgive my Sins, which is all I hope for; and, if it be his Will to raise up this Body again, I am content; and, if to die, I am resigned; and, if thou canst not be easy without trying to assist Nature, I submit. After which his Throat was so much affected, that it was very difficult for him to speak so as to be understood; and he frequently wrote when he wanted any Thing. About the second Hour, on Fourth-day Morning, he asked for Pen and Ink, and, at several Times, with much Difficulty, wrote thus: I believe my being here is in the Wisdom of Christ; I know not as to Life or Death.

About a Quarter before six, the same Morning, he seemed to fall into an easy Sleep, which continued about Half an Hour; when, seeming to awake, he breathed a few Times with more Difficulty, and expired, without Sigh, Groan, or Struggle!

End of the Journal

THE LAST EPISTLE & OTHER WRITINGS OF JOHN WOOLMAN

THE INTRODUCTION

My Mind hath often been affected with Sorrow, on Account of the prevailing of that Spirit, which leads from an humble waiting on the inward Teaching of Christ, to pursue Ways of Living, attended with unnecessary Labour, and which draws forth the Minds of many People to seek after outward Power, and to strive for Riches, which frequently introduce Oppression, and bring forth Wars and grievous Calamities.

It is with Reverence that I acknowledge the Mercies of our Heavenly Father, who, in Infinite Love, did visit me in my Youth, and wrought a Belief in me, that through true Obedience a State of inward Purity may be known in this Life, in which we may love Mankind in the same Love with which our Redeemer loveth us, and therein learn Resignation to endure Hardships, for the real Good of others.

While the Eye is single, the whole Body is full of Light, Mat. vi. 22. but for want of this, selfish Desires, and an imaginary Superiority, darken the Mind; hence Injustice frequently proceeds; and where this is the Case, to convince the Judgment, is the most effectual Remedy.

Where violent Measures are pursued in opposing Injustice, the Passions, and Resentments, of the Injured, frequently operate in the Prosecution of their Designs; and after Conflicts productive of very great Calamities, the Minds of contending Parties often remain as little acquainted with the pure Principle of Divine Love, as they were before; but where People walk in that pure Light in which all their Works are wrought in God, John iii. 21. and under Oppression persevere in the meek Spirit, and abide firm in the Cause of Truth, without actively complying with oppressive Demands, through those the Lord hath often manifested his Power, in opening the Understandings of others, to the promoting Righteousness in the Earth.

A Time, I believe, is coming, wherein this Divine Work will so spread and prevail, that Nation shall not lift up Sword against Nation, nor learn War any more, Isaiah ii. 4. And as we, through the tender Mercies of God, do feel that this precious Work is begun, I am concerned to encourage my Brethren and Sisters in a Holy Care and Diligence, that each of us may so live, under the sanctifying Power of Truth, as to be redeemed from all unnecessary Cares; that our Eye being single to him, no Customs, however prevalent, which are contrary to the Wisdom from above, may hinder us from faithfully following his Holy Leadings, in whatsoever he may graciously appoint for us.

CONSIDERATIONS ON PURE WISDOM AND HUMAN POLICY

To have our Trust settled in the Lord, and not to seek after, nor desire outward Treasures, any further than his Holy Spirit leads us therein, is a happy State, as saith the Prophet, Blessed is the Man that trusteth in the Lord, and whose Hope the Lord is.

Pure Wisdom leads People into Lowliness of Mind, in which they learn Resignation to the Divine Will, and Contentment in suffering for his Cause, when they cannot keep a clear Conscience without suffering.

In this pure Wisdom the Mind is attentive to the Root, and original Spring of Motions and Desires; and as we know the Lord to be our Refuge, and find no Safety but in humbly walking before him, we feel an Holy Engagement, that every Desire which leads therefrom may be brought to Judgment.

While we proceed in this precious Way, and find ardent Longings for a full Deliverance from every thing which defiles, all Prospects of Gain, that are not consistent with the Wisdom from above, are considered as Snares, and an inward Concern is felt, that we may live under the Cross, and faithfully attend to that Holy Spirit, which is sufficient to preserve out of them.

When I have considered that Saying of Christ, Mat. vi. 19, Lay not up for yourselves Treasures upon Earth, his Omnipotence hath often occurred to my Mind.

While we believe that he is every where present with his People, and that perfect Goodness, Wisdom and Power are united in him, how comfortable is the Consideration.

Our Wants may be great, but his Power is greater. We may be oppressed and despised, but he is able to turn our patient Sufferings into Profit to ourselves, and to the Advancement of his Work on Earth. His People, who feel the Power of his Cross, to crucify all that is selfish in them, who are engaged in outward Concerns, from a Convincement that it is their Duty, and resign themselves, and their Treasures, to him; these feel that it is dangerous to give way to that in us, which craves Riches and Greatness in this World.

As the Heart truly contrite, earnestly desires to know Christ, and the Fellowship of his Sufferings, Phil. iii. 10. so far as the Lord for gracious Ends may lead into them; as such feel that it is their Interest to put their Trust in God, and to seek no Gain but that which he, by his Holy Spirit, leads into; so, on the contrary, they who do not reverently wait for this Divine Teacher, and are not humbly concerned, according to their Measure, to fill up that which is behind of the Afflictions of Christ, Col. i. 24. in patiently suffering for the promoting Righteousness in the Earth; but have an Eye toward the Power of Men, and the outward Advantage of Wealth, these are often attentive to those Employments which appear profitable, even though the Gains arise from such Trade and Business which proceeds from the Workings of that Spirit, which is estranged from the self-denying Life of an humble contrite Christian.

While I write on this Subject, I feel my Mind tenderly affected toward those honestly disposed People, who have been brought up in Employments attended with those Difficulties.

To such I may say, in the feeling of our Heavenly Father's Love, and number myself with you, O that our Eyes may be single to the Lord! May we reverently wait on him for Strength, to lay aside all unnecessary Expence of every Kind, and learn Contentment, in a plain simple Life.

May we, in Lowliness, submit to the Leadings of his Spirit, and enter upon any outward Employ which he graciously points out to us, and then whatever Difficulties arise, in Consequence of our Faithfulness, I trust they will work for our Good.

Small Treasure to a resigned Mind is sufficient. How happy is it to be content with a little, to live in Humility, and feel that in us, which breathes out this Language, Abba! Father.

If that, called the Wisdom of this World, had no Resemblance of true Wisdom, the Name of Wisdom, I suppose, had not been given to it.

As wasting outward Substance, to gratify vain Desires, on one hand; so Slothfulness and Neglect, on the other, do often involve Men and their Families in Trouble, and reduce them to Want and Distress; to shun both these opposite Vices, is good in itself, and hath a Resemblance of Wisdom; but while People thus provident, have it principally in View to get Riches, and Power, and the Friendship of this World, and do not humbly wait for the Spirit of Truth to lead them into Purity; these, through an anxious Care to obtain the End desired, reach forth for Gain in worldly Wisdom, and, in regard to their inward State, fall into divers Temptations and Snares. And though such may think of applying Wealth to good Purposes, and to use their Power to prevent Oppression, yet Wealth and Power is often applied otherwise; nor can we depart from the Leadings of our Holy Shepherd, without going into Confusion.

Great Wealth is frequently attended with Power, which nothing but Divine Love can qualify the Mind to use rightly; and as to the Humility, and Uprightness of our Children after us, how great is the Uncertainty! If, in acquiring Wealth, we take hold on the Wisdom which is from beneath, and depart from the Leadings of Truth, and Example our Children herein, we have great Cause to apprehend, that Wealth may be a Snare to them; and prove an Injury to others, over whom their Wealth may give them Power.

To be redeemed from that Wisdom which is from beneath, and walk in the Light of the Lord, is a precious Situation; thus his People are brought to put their Trust in him; and in this humble Confidence in his Wisdom, Goodness and Power, the Righteous find a Refuge in Adversities, superior to the greatest outward Helps, and a Comfort more certain than any worldly Advantages can afford.

ON LABOUR

Having from my Childhood been used to Bodily Labour for a Living, I may express my Experience therein.

Right Exercise affords an innocent Pleasure in the Time of it, and prepares us to enjoy the Sweetness of Rest; but from the Extremes each Way, arise Inconveniences.

Moderate Exercise opens the Pores, gives the Blood a lively Circulation, and the better enables us to judge rightly respecting that Portion of Labour which is the true Medium.

The Fowls of the Air sow not, nor gather into Barns, yet our Heavenly Father feedeth them, Mat. vi. 26. nor do I believe that Infinite Goodness and Power would have allotted Labour to us, had he not seen that Labour was proper for us in this Life.

The original Design, and true Medium of Labour, is a Subject that, to me, appears worthy of our serious Consideration.

Idle Men are often a Burden to themselves, neglect the Duty they owe to their Families, and become burdensome to others also.

As outward Labour, directed by the Wisdom from above, tends to our Health, and adds to our Happiness in this Life; so, on the contrary, entering upon it in a selfish Spirit, and pursuing it too long, or too hard, hath a contrary Effect.

I have observed, that too much Labour not only makes the Understanding dull, but so intrudes upon the Harmony of the Body, that after ceasing from our Toil, we have another to pass through, before we can be so composed as to enjoy the Sweetness of Rest.

From too much Labour in the Heat, frequently proceeds immoderate Sweats, which do often, I believe, open the Way for Disorders, and impair our Constitutions.

When we go beyond the true Medium, and feel Weariness approaching, but think Business may suffer if we cease, at such a Time spirituous Liquors are frequently taken, with a View to support Nature under these Fatigues.

I have found that too much Labour in the Summer heats the Blood, that taking strong Drink to support the Body under such Labour, increaseth that Heat, and though a Person may be so far temperate as not to manifest the least Disorder, yet the Mind, in such a Circumstance, doth not retain that Calmness and Serenity which we should endeavour to live in.

Thus toiling in the Heat, and drinking strong Liquor, makes Men more resolute, and less considerate, and tends very much to disqualify from successfully following him who is meek and low of Heart.

As laying out Business, more than is consistent with pure Wisdom, is an Evil, so this Evil frequently leads into more. Too much Business leads to Hurry. In the Hurry and Toil too much strong Drink is often used, and hereby many proceed to Noise and Wantonness, and some, though more considerate, do often suffer Loss, as to a true Composedness of Mind.

I feel sincere Desires in my Heart that no Rent, nor Interest, might be laid so high as to be a Snare to Tenants. That no Desires of Gain may draw any too far in Business. That no Cares to support Customs, which have not their Foundation in pure Wisdom, may have Place in our Minds, but that we may build on the sure Foundation, and feel our Holy Shepherd to lead us, who alone is able to preserve us, and bring forth from every Thing which defiles.

Having several Times, in my Travels, had Opportunity to observe the Labour and Manner of Life of great Numbers of Slaves, it appears to me that the true Medium is lamentably neglected by many, who assign them their Portion of Labour.

Without saying much at this Time, concerning buying and selling Men for Term of Life, who have as just a Right to Liberty as we have; nor about the great Miseries, and Effusion of Blood, consequent to promoting the Slave-trade, and to speak as favourably as may be, with regard to continuing those in Bondage who are amongst us, we cannot say there is no Partiality in it; for whatever Tenderness may be manifested by Individuals in their Life-time towards them, yet for People to be transmitted from a Man to his Posterity, in the helpless Condition of Slaves, appears inconsistent with the Nature of the Gospel Spirit. From such Proceedings it often follows, that Persons in the Decline of Life, are deprived of Monies equitably due to them, and committed to the Care, and subjected to the absolute Power of young unexperienced Men, who know but little about the Weakness of old Age, nor understand the Language of declining Life.

Where Parents give their Estates to their Children, and then depend on them for a Maintainance, they sometimes meet with great Inconveniences; but if the Power of Possession, thus obtained, doth often reverse the Obligations of Gratitude and filial Duty, and makes manifest, that Youth are often ignorant of the Language of old Age, how hard is the Case of ancient Negroes, who, deprived of the Wages equitably due to them, are left to young People, who have been used to look upon them as their Inferiors.

For Men to behold the Fruits of their Labour withheld from them, and possessed by others, and in old Age find themselves destitute of those comfortable Accommodations, and that tender Regard which their Time of Life requires:

When they feel Pains and Stiffness in their Joints and Limbs, Weakness of Appetite, and that a little Labour is wearisome, and still behold themselves in the neglected uncomfortable Condition of a Slave, and oftentimes to a young unsympathising Man:

For Men to be thus treated from one Generation to another, who, besides their own Distresses, think on the Slavery entailed on their Posterity, and are grieved: What disagreeable Thoughts must they have of the professed Followers of Jesus! And how must their Groans ascend to that Almighty Being, who will be a Refuge for the Oppressed, Psalm ix. 9.

ON SCHOOLS

Suffer the little Children to come unto me, and forbid them not, for of such is the Kingdom of God, Mark x. 14.

To encourage Children to do Things with a View to get Praise of Men, to me appears an Obstruction to their being inwardly acquainted with the Spirit of Truth. For it is the Work of the Holy Spirit to direct the Mind of God, that in all our Proceedings we may have a single Eye to him. To give Alms in secret, to fast in secret, and labour to keep clear of that Disposition reproved by our Saviour, All their Works which they do is for to be seen of Men, Mat. xxiii. 5.

That Divine Light which enlightens all Men, I believe, does often shine in the Minds of Children very early, and to humbly wait for Wisdom, that our Conduct toward them may tend to forward their Acquaintance with it, and strengthen them in Obedience thereto, appears to me to be a Duty on all of us.

By cherishing the Spirit of Pride, and the Love of Praise in them, I believe they may sometimes improve faster in Learning, than otherwise they would; but to take Measures to forward Children in Learning, which naturally tend to divert their Minds from true Humility, appears to me to savour of the Wisdom of this World.

If Tutors are not acquainted with Sanctification of Spirit, nor experienced in an humble waiting for the Leadings of Truth, but follow the Maxims of the Wisdom of this World, such Children who are under their Tuition, appear to me to be in Danger of imbibing Thoughts, and Apprehensions, reverse to that Meekness, and Lowliness of Heart, which is necessary for all the true Followers of Christ.

Children at an Age fit for Schools, are in a Time of Life which requires the patient Attention of pious People, and if we commit them to the Tuition of such, whose Minds we believe are not rightly prepared to train them up in the Nurture and Admonition of the Lord, we are in Danger of not acting the Part of faithful Parents toward them; for our Heavenly Father doth not require us to do Evil, that Good may come of it; and it is needful that we deeply examine ourselves, lest we get entangled in the Wisdom of this World, and, through wrong Apprehensions, take such Methods in Education, as may prove a great Injury to the Minds of our Children.

It is a lovely Sight to behold innocent Children; and when they are sent to such Schools where their tender Minds are in imminent Danger of being led astray by Tutors, who do not live a self-denying Life, or by the Conversation of such Children who do not live in Innocence, it is a Case much to be lamented.

While a pious Tutor hath the Charge of no more Children than he can take due Care of, and keeps his Authority in the Truth, the good Spirit in which he leads and governs, works on the Minds of such who are not hardened, and his Labours not only tend to bring them forward in outward Learning, but to open their Understandings with respect to the true Christian Life; but where a Person hath Charge of too many, and his Thoughts and Time are so much employed in the outward Affairs of his School, that he does not so weightily attend to the Spirit and Conduct of each Individual, as to be enabled to administer rightly to all in due Season; through such Omission he not only suffers, as to the State of his own Mind, but the Minds of the Children are in Danger of suffering also.

To watch the Spirit of Children, to nurture them in Gospel Love, and labour to help them against that which would mar the Beauty of their Minds, is a Debt we owe them; and a faithful Performance of our Duty, not only tends to their lasting Benefit, and our own Peace, but also to render their Company agreeable to us.

Instruction, thus administered, reaches the pure Witness in the Minds of such Children who are not hardened, and begets Love in them toward those who thus lead them on; but where too great a Number are committed to a Tutor, and he, through much Cumber, omits a careful Attention to the Minds of Children, there is Danger of Disorders gradually increasing amongst them, till the Effects thereof appear in their Conduct, too strong to be easily remedied.

A Care hath lived on my Mind, that more Time might be employed by Parents at Home, and by Tutors at School, in weightily attending to the Spirit and Inclinations of Children, and that we may so lead, instruct, and govern them, in this tender Part of Life, that nothing may be omitted in our Power, to help them on their Way to become the Children of our Father, who is in Heaven.

Meditating on the Situation of Schools in our Provinces, my Mind hath, at Times, been affected with Sorrow, and under these Exercises it hath appeared to me, that if those who have large Estates, were faithful Stewards, and laid no Rent, nor Interest, nor other Demands, higher than is consistent with universal Love; and those in lower Circumstances would, under a moderate Employ, shun unnecessary Expence, even to the smallest Article; and all unite in humbly seeking to the Lord, he would graciously instruct us, and strengthen us, to relieve the Youth from various Snares, in which many of them are entangled.

ON THE RIGHT USE OF THE LORD'S OUTWARD GIFTS

As our Understandings are opened by the pure Light, we experience that, through an inward approaching to God, the Mind is strengthened in Obedience; and that by gratifying those Desires which are not of his begetting, those Approaches to him are obstructed, and the deceivable Spirit gains Strength.

These Truths, being as it were engraven upon our Hearts, and our everlasting Interest in Christ evidently concerned herein, we become fervently engaged, that nothing may be nourished which tends to feed Pride or Self-love in us. Thus in pure Obedience, we are not only instructed in our Duty to God, but also in the Affairs which necessarily relate to this Life, and the Spirit of Truth which guides into all Truth, leavens the Mind with a pious Concern, that whatsoever we do in Word or Deed, may be done in his Name, Col. iii. 17.

Hence such Buildings, Furniture, Food, and Raiment, as best answer our Necessities, and are the least likely to feed that selfish Spirit which is our Enemy, are the most acceptable to us.

In this State the Mind is tender, and inwardly watchful, that the Love of Gain draw us not into any Business, which may weaken our Love to our Heavenly Father, or bring unnecessary Trouble to any of his Creatures.

Thus the Way gradually opens to cease from that Spirit which craves Riches and Things fetched far, which so mixeth with the Customs of this World, and so intrudes upon the true Harmony of Life, that the right Medium of Labour is very much departed from. And as the Minds of People are settled in a steady Concern, not to hold nor possess any Thing but what may be held consistent with the Wisdom from above, they consider what they possess as the Gift of God, and are inwardly exercised, that in all Parts of their Conduct they may act agreeable to the Nature of the peaceable Government of Christ.

A little supports such a Life; and in a State truly resigned to the Lord, the Eye is single, to see what outward Employ he leads into, as a Means of our Subsistence, and a lively Care is maintained to hold to that without launching further.

There is a Harmony in the several Parts of this Divine Work in the Hearts of People; he who leads them to cease from those gainful Employments, carried on in that Wisdom which is from beneath, delivers also from the Desire after worldly Greatness, and reconciles the Mind to a Life so plain, that a little doth suffice.

Here the real Comforts of Life are not lessened. Moderate Exercise, in the Way of true Wisdom, is pleasant both to Mind and Body.

Food and Raiment sufficient, though in the greatest Simplicity, is accepted with Content and Gratitude.

The mutual Love, subsisting between the faithful Followers of Christ, is more pure than that Friendship which is not seasoned with Humility, how specious soever the Appearance.

Where People depart from pure Wisdom in one Case, it is often an Introduction to depart from it in many more; and thus a Spirit which seeks for outward Greatness, and leads into worldly Wisdom to attain it, and support it, gets Possession of the Mind.

In beholding the customary Departure from the true Medium of Labour, and that unnecessary Toil which many go through, in supporting outward Greatness, and procuring Delicacies.

In beholding how the true Calmness of Life is changed into Hurry, and that many, by eagerly pursuing outward Treasure, are in great Danger of withering as to the inward State of the Mind.

In meditating on the Works of this Spirit, and on the Desolations it makes amongst the Professors of Christianity, I may thankfully acknowledge, that I often feel pure Love beget Longings in my Heart, for the Exaltation of the peaceable Kingdom of Christ, and an Engagement to labour according to the Gift bestowed on me, for the promoting an humble, plain, temperate Way of living. A Life where no unnecessary Care, nor Expences, may incumber our Minds, nor lessen our Ability to do Good; where no Desires after Riches, or Greatness, may lead into hard Dealing; where no Connections with worldly-minded Men, may abate our Love to God, nor weaken a true Zeal for Righteousness. A Life wherein we may diligently labour for Resignedness to do, and suffer, whatever our Heavenly Father may allot for us, in reconciling the World to himself.

When the Prophet Isaiah had uttered his Vision, and declared that a Time was coming wherein Swords should be beat into Plowshares, and Spears into pruning Hooks, and that Nation shall not lift up Sword against Nation, nor learn War any more; he immediately directs the Minds of People to the Divine Teacher, in this remarkable Language; O House of Jacob! come ye, and let us walk in the Light of the Lord, Isaiah ii. 5.

To wait for the Direction of this Light, in all temporal as well as spiritual Concerns, appears necessary; for if in any Case we enter lightly into temporal Affairs, without feeling this Spirit of Truth to open our Way therein, and through the Love of this World proceed on, and seek for Gain by that Business or Traffick, which is not of the Father, but of the World, 1 John ii. 16 we fail in our Testimony to the Purity and Peace of his Government, and get into that which is for Chastisement.

This Matter hath lain heavy on my Mind, it being evident, that a Life less humble, less simple and plain, than that which Christ leads his Sheep into, does necessarily require a Support, which pure Wisdom does not provide for; hence there is no Probability of our being a peculiar People, so zealous of good Works, as to have no Fellowship with Works of Darkness, Titus ii. 14. Ephes. v. 11. while we have Wants to supply which have their Foundation in Custom, and do not come within the Meaning of those Expressions, your Heavenly Father knoweth that ye have need of all these Things, Mat. vi. 32.

These Things which he beholds necessary for his People, he fails not to give them in his own Way and Time; but as his Ways are above our Ways, and his Thoughts above our Thoughts, so imaginary Wants are different from these Things which he knoweth that we have need of.

As my Meditations have been on these Things, Compassion hath filled my Heart toward my Fellow Creatures, involved in Customs, grown up in the Wisdom of this World, which is Foolishness with God, 1 Cor. iii. 19. And O that the Youth may be so thoroughly experienced in an humble Walking before the Lord, that they may be his Children, and know him to be their Refuge, their safe unfailing Refuge, through the various Dangers attending this uncertain State of Being!

If those whose Minds are redeemed from the Love of Wealth, and who are content with a plain, simple Way of living, do yet find that to conduct the Affairs of a Family, without giving Countenance to unrighteous Proceedings, or having Fellowship with Works of Darkness, the most diligent Care is necessary.

If Customs, distinguishable from universal Righteousness, and opposite to the true Self-denying Life, are now prevalent, and so mixed with Trade, and with almost every Employ, that it is only through humble waiting on the inward Guidance of Truth, that we may reasonably hope to walk safely, and support an uniform Testimony to the peaceable Government of Christ:

If this be the Case, how lamentably do they expose themselves to Temptations, who give way to the Love of Riches, conform to expensive Living, and reach forth for Gain, to support Customs, which our Holy Shepherd leads not into.

CONSIDERATIONS ON THE TRUE HARMONY OF MANKIND, AND

How it is to be maintained.

By JOHN WOOLMAN

And the Remnant of Jacob shall be in the midst of many People, as the Dew from the Lord, as the Showers upon the Grass, that tarrieth not for Man, nor waiteth for the Sons of Men, Micah v. 7.

LONDON:

Re-printed by Mary Hinde.

THE INTRODUCTION

As Mankind from one Parent are divided into many Families, and as Trading to Sea is greatly increased within a few Ages past; amidst this extended Commerce how necessary is it that the professed Followers of Christ keep sacred his Holy Name, and be employed about Trade and Traffick no farther than Justice and Equity evidently accompanies? That we may give no just Cause of Offence to any, however distant, or unable to plead their own Cause; and may continually keep in View the Spreading of the true and saving Knowledge of God, and his Son Jesus Christ, amongst our Fellow Creatures, which through his infinite Love some feel to be more precious than any other Treasure.

CONSIDERATIONS ON THE TRUE HARMONY OF MANKIND &c.

CHAPTER I

On serving the Lord in our outward Employments

Under the humbling Dispensations of the Father of Mercies, I have felt an inward Labour for the Good of my Fellow Creatures, and a Concern that the Holy Spirit, which alone can restore Mankind to a State of true Harmony, may with Singleness of Heart be waited for and followed.

I trust there are many under that Visitation, which if faithfully attended to, will make them quick of Understanding in the Fear of the Lord, and qualify with Firmness to be true Patterns of the Christian Life, who in Living and Walking may hold forth an Invitation to others, to come out of the Entanglements of the Spirit of this World.

And that which I feel first to express is, a Care for those who are in Circumstances, which appear difficult, with respect to supporting their Families in a Way answerable to pure Wisdom, that they may not be discouraged, but remember that in humbly obeying the Leadings of Christ, he owneth us as his Friends, Ye are my Friends if ye do whatsoever I command you; and to be a Friend to Christ, is to be united to him, who hath all Power in Heaven and in Earth; and though a Woman may forget her sucking Child, yet will he not forget his faithful Ones.

The Condition of many who dwell in Cities hath often affected me with a Brotherly Sympathy, attended with a Desire that Resignation may be laboured for; and where the Holy Leader directeth to a Country Life, or some Change of Employ, he may be faithfully followed; for, under the refining Hand of the Lord, I have seen that the Inhabitants of some Cities are greatly increased through some Branches of Business which the Holy Spirit doth not lead into, and that being entangled in these Things, tends to bring a Cloud over the Minds of People convinced of the Leadings of this Holy Leader, and obstructs the coming of the Kingdom of Christ on Earth as it is in Heaven.

Now if we indulge a Desire to imitate our Neighbours in those Things which harmonise not with the true Christian Walking, these Entanglements may hold fast to us, and some, who in an awakening Time, feel tender Scruples, with respect to their Manner of Life, may look on the Example of others more noted in the Church, who yet may not be refined from every Degree of Dross; and by looking on these Examples, and desiring to support their Families in a Way pleasant to the natural Mind, there may be Danger of the Worldly Wisdom gaining Strength in them, and of their Departure from that pure Feeling of Truth, which if faithfully attended to, would teach Contentment in the Divine Will, even in a very low Estate.

One formerly speaking on the Profitableness of true Humility saith, "He that troubles not himself with anxious Thoughts for more than is necessary, lives little less than the Life of Angels, whilst by a Mind content with little, he imitates their want of nothing." Cave's Prim. Christi. Page 31.

"It is not enough," says Tertullian, "that a Christian be chaste and modest, but he must appear to be so: A Virtue of which he should have so great a Store, that it should flow from his Mind upon his Habit, and break from the Retirements of his Conscience, into the Superficies of his Life." Same Book, Page 43.

"The Garments we wear," says Clemens, "ought to be mean and frugal—that is true Simplicity of Habit, which takes away what is vain and superfluous, that the best and most solid Garment, which is the farthest from Curiosity." Page 49.

Though the Change from Day to Night, is by a Motion so gradual as scarcely to be perceived, yet when Night is come we behold it very different from the Day; and thus as People become wise in their own Eyes, and prudent in their own Sight, Customs rise up from the Spirit of this World, and spread by little, and little, till a Departure from the Simplicity that there is in Christ becomes as distinguishable as Light from Darkness, to such who are crucified to the World.

Our Holy Shepherd, to encourage his Flock in Firmness and Perseverance, reminds them of his Love for them; As the Father hath loved me, so have I loved you; continue ye in my Love. And in another Place graciously points out the Danger of departing therefrom, by going into unsuitable Employments; this he represents in the Similitude of Offence from that useful active Member, the Hand; and to fix the Instruction the deeper, names the right Hand; If thy right Hand offend thee, cut it off and cast it from thee—If thou feelest Offence in thy Employment, humbly follow him who leads into all Truth, and is a strong and faithful Friend to those who are resigned to him.

Again, he points out those Things which appearing pleasant to the natural Mind, are not best for us, in the Similitude of Offence from the Eye; If thy right Eye offend thee, pluck it out and cast it from thee. To pluck out the Eye, or cut off the Hand, is attended with sharp Pain; and how precious is the Instruction which our Redeemer thus opens to us, that we may not faint under the most painful Trial, but put our Trust in him, even in him who sent an Angel to feed Elijah in the Wilderness; who fed a Multitude with a few Barley Loaves, and is now as attentive to the Wants of his People as ever.

The Prophet Isaiah represents the unrighteous Doings of the Israelites toward the Poor, as the Fruits of an effeminate Life; As for my People, Children are their Oppressors, and Women rule over them: What mean ye, that ye beat my People to pieces, and grind the Faces of the Poor? saith the Lord God. Then he mentions the Haughtiness of the Daughters of Sion, and enumerates many Ornaments, as Instances of their Vanity; to uphold which, the Poor were so hardly dealt with, that he sets forth their Poverty, their Leanness and Inability to help themselves, in the Similitude of a Man maimed by Violence, or beaten to pieces, and forced to endure the painful Operation of having his Face gradually worn away in the manner of grinding.

And I may here add, that at Times, when I have felt true Love open my Heart towards my Fellow Creatures, and being engaged in weighty Conversation in the Cause of Righteousness, the Instructions I have received under these Exercises, in Regard to the true Use of the outward Gifts of God, have made deep and lasting Impressions on my Mind.

I have here beheld, how the Desire to provide Wealth, and to uphold a delicate Life, hath grievously entangled many, and been like Snares to their Offspring; and tho' some have been affected with a Sense of their Difficulties, and appeared desirous, at Times, to be helped out of them; yet for want of abiding under the humbling Power of Truth, they have continued in these Entanglements; for in remaining conformable to this World, and giving Way to a delicate Life, this expensive Way of living, in Parents, and in Children, hath called for a large Supply, and in answering this Call the Faces of the Poor have been ground away, and made thin through hard Dealing.

There is Balm, there is a Physician; and O what Longings do I feel! that we may embrace the Means appointed for our Healing, know that removed which now ministers Cause for the Cries of many People to ascend to Heaven against their Oppressors, and that we may see the true Harmony restored.

Behold how good and how pleasant it is, for Brethren to dwell together in Unity. The Nature of this Unity is thus opened by the Apostle; If we walk in the Light, as Christ is in the Light, we shall have Fellowship one with another, and the Blood of Christ will cleanse us from all Sin.

The Land may be polluted with innocent Blood, which like the Blood of Abel may cry to the Almighty; but those who walk in the Light, as Christ is in the Light, they know the Lamb of God, who taketh away Sin.

Walking is a Phrase frequently used in Scripture, to represent our Journey thro' Life, and appears to comprehend the various Affairs and Transactions properly relating to our being in this World.

Christ being the Light, dwells always in the Light; and if our walking be thus, and in every Affair and Concern we faithfully follow this Divine Leader, he preserves from giving just Cause for any to quarrel with us: And where this Foundation is laid, and mutually kept to, by Families conversant with each other, the Way is open for these Comforts in Society, which our Heavenly Father intends as a Part of our Happiness in this World; and then we may experience the Goodness, and Pleasantness of dwelling together in Unity; but where Ways of Living take place, which tend to Oppression, and in the Pursuit of Wealth, People do that to others which they know would not be acceptable to themselves, either in exercising an absolute Power over them, or otherwise laying on them unequitable Burdens; here a Fear lest that Measure should be meted to them, which they have measured to others, incites a Care to support that by Craft and cunning Devices which stands not on the firm Foundation of Righteousness: Thus the Harmony of Society is broken, and from hence Commotions and Wars do frequently arise in the World.

Come out of Babylon my People, that ye be not Partakers of her Sins, and that ye receive not of her Plagues. Rev. xv. 3, 4. This Babel, or Babylon, was built in the Spirit of Self-exaltation: Let us build us a City and a Tower, whose Top may reach to Heaven, and let us make us a Name. Gen. xi. 4. In departing from an humble Trust in God, and following a selfish Spirit, People have Intentions to get the upperhand of their Fellow Creatures, privately meditate on Means to obtain their Ends, have a Language in their Hearts which is hard to understand. In Babel the Language is confounded.

This City is represented as a Place of Business, and those employed in it, as Merchants of the Earth: The Merchants of the Earth are waxed rich through the Abundance of her Delicacies. Rev. xviii. 3.

And it is remarkable in this Call, that the Language from the Father of Mercies is, my People, Come out of Babylon my People. Thus his tender Mercies are toward us in an imperfect State; and as we faithfully attend to the Call, the Path of Righteousness is more and more opened; Cravings, which have not their Foundation in pure Wisdom, more and more cease; and in an inward Purity of Heart, we experience a Restoration of that which was lost at Babel, represented by the inspired Prophet in the returning of a pure Language. Zeph. iii. 9.

Happy for them who humbly attend to the Call, Come out of Babylon my People. For though in going forth we may meet with Trials, which for a Time may be painful, yet as we bow in true Humility, and continue in it, an Evidence is felt that God only is wise; and that in weaning us from all that is selfish he prepares the Way to a quiet Habitation, where all our Desires are bounded by his Wisdom. And an Exercise of Spirit attends me, that we who are convinced of the pure Leadings of Truth, may bow in the deepest Reverence, and so watchfully regard this Leader, that many who are grievously entangled in a Wilderness of vain Customs, may look upon us and be instructed. And O that such who have Plenty of this World's Goods, may be faithful in that with which they are entrusted! and Example others in the true Christian Walking.

Our blessed Saviour, speaking on Worldly Greatness, compares himself to one waiting and attending on a Company at Dinner; Whether is greater, he that sitteth at Meat or he that serveth? Is not he that sitteth at Meat? But I am amongst you as he that serveth. Luke xxii. 27.

Thus in a World greatly disordered, where Men aspiring to outward Greatness were wont to oppress others to support their Designs, he who was of the highest Descent, being the Son of God, and greater than any amongst the greatest Families of Men, by his Example and Doctrines foreclosed his Followers from claiming any Shew of outward Greatness, from any supposed Superiority in themselves, or derived from their Ancestors.

He who was greater than Earthly Princes, was not only meek and low of Heart, but his outward Appearance was plain and lowly, and free from every Stain of the Spirit of this World.

Such was the Example of our blessed Redeemer, of whom the beloved Disciple said, He that saith he abideth in him, ought also to walk even as he walked.

John Bradford, who suffered Martyrdom under Queen Mary, wrote a Letter to his Friends out of Prison, a short Time before he was burnt, in which are these Expressions; "Consider your Dignity as Children of God, and Temples of the Holy Ghost, and Members of Christ, be ashamed therefore to think, speak, or do any Thing unseemly, for God's Children, and the Members of Christ." Fox's Acts and Mon. Page 1177.

CHAPTER II

On the Example of CHRIST

As my Mind hath been brought into a Brotherly Feeling with the Poor, as to the Things of this Life, who are under Trials in regard to getting a Living in a Way answerable to the Purity of Truth; a Labour of Heart hath attended me, that their Way may not be made difficult through the Love of Money in those who are tried with plentiful Estates, but that they with Tenderness of Heart may sympathize with them.

It was the Saying of our blessed Redeemer, Ye cannot serve God and Mammon. There is a deep Feeling of the Way of Purity, a Way in which the Wisdom of the World hath no Part, but is opened by the Spirit of Truth, and is called the Way of Holiness; a Way in which the Traveller is employed in watching unto Prayer; and the outward Gain we get in this Journey is considered as a Trust committed to us, by him who formed and supports the World; and is the rightful Director of the Use and Application of the Product of it.

Now except the Mind be preserved chaste, there is no Safety for us; but in an Estrangement from true Resignation, the Spirit of the World casts up a Way, in which Gain is many Times principally attended to, and in which there is a selfish Application of outward Treasures.

How agreeable to the true Harmony of Society, is that Exhortation of the Apostle? Look not every Man on his own Things, but every Man also on the Things of others. Let this Mind be in you which was also in Christ Jesus.

A Person in outward Prosperity may have the Power of obtaining Riches, but the same Mind being in him which is in Christ Jesus, he may feel a Tenderness of Heart towards those of low Degree; and instead of setting himself above them, may look upon it as an unmerited Favour, that his Way through Life is more easy than the Way of many others; may improve every Opportunity of leading forth out of those Customs which have entangled the Family; employ his Time in looking into the Wants of the poor Members, and hold forth such a perfect Example of Humiliation, that the pure Witness may be reached in many Minds; and the Way opened for a harmonious walking together.

Jesus Christ, in promoting the Happiness of others, was not deficient in looking for the Helpless, who lay in Obscurity, nor did he save any Thing to render himself honourable amongst Men, which might have been of more Use to the weak Members in his Father's Family; of whose Compassion towards us I may now speak a little. He who was perfectly happy in himself, moved with infinite Love, took not upon him the Nature of Angels, but our imperfect Natures, and therein wrestled with the Temptations which attend us in this Life; and being the Son of him who is greater than Earthly Princes, yet became a Companion to poor, sincere-hearted Men; and though he gave the clearest Evidence that Divine Power attended him, yet the most unfavourable Constructions were framed by a self-righteous People; those Miracles represented as the Effect of a diabolical Power, and Endeavours used to render him hateful, as having his Mission from the Prince of Darkness; nor did their Envy cease till they took him like a Criminal, and brought him to Trial. Though some may affect to carry the Appearance of being unmoved at the Apprehension of Distress, our dear Redeemer, who was perfectly sincere, having the same human Nature which we have, and feeling, a little before he was apprehended, the Weight of that Work upon him, for which he came into the World, was sorrowful even unto Death; here the human Nature struggled to be excused from a Cup so bitter; but his Prayers centered in Resignation, Not my Will but thine be done. In this Conflict, so great was his Agony, that Sweat like Drops of Blood fell from him to the Ground.

Behold now, as foretold by the Prophet, he is in a judicial Manner numbered with the Transgressors! Behold him as some poor Man of no Reputation, standing before the High Priest and Elders, and before Herod and Pilate, where Witnesses appear against him, and he mindful of the most gracious Design of his Coming, declineth to plead in his own Defence, but as a Sheep that is dumb before the Shearer, so under many Accusations, Revilings, and Buffetings, remained silent. And though he signified to Peter, that he had Access to Power sufficient to overthrow all their outward Forces; yet retaining a Resignation to suffer for the Sins of Mankind, he exerted not that Power, but permitted them to go on in their malicious Designs, and pronounce him to be worthy of Death, even him who was perfect in Goodness; thus in his Humiliation his Judgment was taken away, and he, like some vile Criminal, led as a Lamb to the Slaughter. Under these heavy Trials (tho' poor unstable Pilate was convinced of his Innocence, yet) the People generally looked upon him as a Deceiver, a Blasphemer, and the approaching Punishment as a just Judgment upon him; They esteemed him smitten of God and afflicted. So great had been the Surprize of his Disciples, at his being taken by armed Men, that they forsook him, and fled; thus they hid their Faces from him, he was despised, and by their Conduct it appeared as though they esteemed him not.

But contrary to that Opinion, of his being smitten of God and afflicted, it was for our Sakes that he was put to Grief; he was wounded for our Transgressions; he was bruised for our Iniquities; and under the Weight of them manifesting the deepest Compassion for the Instruments of his Misery, laboured as their Advocate, and in the Deeps of Affliction, with an unconquerable Patience, cried out, Father, forgive them, they know not what they do!

Now this Mind being in us, which was in Christ Jesus, it removes from our Hearts the Desire of Superiority, Worldly Honour, or Greatness; a deep Attention is felt to the Divine Counsellor, and an ardent Engagement to promote, as far as we may be enabled, the Happiness of Mankind universally: This State, where every Motion from a selfish Spirit yieldeth to pure Love, I may, with Gratitude to the Father of Mercies acknowledge, is often opened before me as a Pearl to dig after; attended with a living Concern, that amongst the many Nations and Families on the Earth, those who believe in the Messiah, that he was manifested to destroy the Works of the Devil, and thus to take away the Sins of the World, may experience the Will of our Heavenly Father, may be done on Earth as it is in Heaven. Strong are the Desires I often feel, that this Holy Profession may remain unpolluted, and the Believers in Christ may so abide in the pure inward Feeling of his Spirit, that the Wisdom from above may shine forth in their Living, as a Light by which others may be instrumentally helped on their Way, in the true harmonious Walking.

CHAPTER III

On Merchandizing

Where the Treasures of pure Love are opened, and we obediently follow him who is the Light of Life, the Mind becomes chaste; and a Care is felt, that the Unction from the Holy One may be our Leader in every Undertaking.

In being crucified to the World, broken off from that Friendship which is Enmity with God, and dead to the Customs and Fashions which have not their Foundation in the Truth; the Way is prepared to Lowliness in outward Living, and to a Disentanglement from those Snares which attends the Love of Money; and where the faithful Friends of Christ are so situated that Merchandize appears to be their Duty, they feel a Restraint from proceeding farther than he owns their Proceeding; being convinced that we are not our own, but are bought with a Price, that none of us may live to ourselves, but to him who died for us, 2 Cor. v. 15. Thus they are taught, not only to keep to a moderate Advance and Uprightness in their Dealings; but to consider the Tendency of their Proceeding; to do nothing which they know would operate against the Cause of universal Righteousness; and to keep continually in View the Spreading of the peaceable Kingdom of Christ amongst Mankind.

The Prophet Isaiah spake of the gathered Church, in the Similitude of a City, where many being employed were all preserved in Purity; They shall call them the Holy People, the Redeemed of the Lord, and thou shalt be called sought out, a City not forsaken, Isa. lxiii. 10. And the Apostle, after mentioning the Mystery of Christ's Sufferings, exhorts, Be ye Holy in all Manner of Conversation, 1 Pet. i. 15. There is a Conversation necessary in Trade; and there is a Conversation so foreign from the Nature of Christ's Kingdom, that it is represented in the Similitude of one Man pushing another with a warlike Weapon; There is that speaketh like the Piercings of a Sword, Prov. xii. 18. Now in all our Concerns it is necessary that the Leading of the Spirit of Christ be humbly waited for, and faithfully followed, as the only Means of being preserved chaste as an Holy People, who in all Things are circumspect, Exod. xxiii. 13, that nothing we do may carry the Appearance of Approbation of the Works of Wickedness, make the Unrighteous more at Ease in Unrighteousness, or occasion the Injuries committed against the Oppressed to be more lightly looked over.

Where Morality is kept to, and supported by the Inhabitants of a Country, there is a certain Reproach attends those Individuals amongst them, who manifestly deviate therefrom. But where Iniquity is committed openly, and the Authors of it are not brought to Justice, nor put to Shame, their Hands grow strong. Thus the general Corruption of the Jews shortly before their State was broke up by the Chaldeans, is described by their Boldness in Impiety; for as their Leaders were connected together in Wickedness they strengthened one another, and grew confident; Were they ashamed when they had committed Abominations? Nay, they were not at all ashamed, neither could they blush, Jer. vi. 15, on which Account the Lord thus expostulates with them, What hath my Beloved to do in my House, seeing she hath wrought Lewdness with many, and the Holy Flesh is passed from thee; when thou doest Evil, then thou rejoicest, Jer. xi. 15.

Now the faithful Friends of Christ, who hunger and thirst after Righteousness, and inwardly breathe that his Kingdom may come on Earth as it is in Heaven, he teacheth them to be quick of Understanding in his Fear, and to be very attentive to the Means he may appoint for promoting pure Righteousness in the Earth; and as Shame is due to those whose works manifestly operate against the gracious Design of his Sufferings for us, a Care lives on their Minds that no wrong Customs however supported may bias their Judgments, but that they may humbly abide under the Cross, and be preserved in a Conduct which may not contribute to strengthen the Hands of the Wicked in their Wickedness, or to remove Shame from those to whom it is justly due. The Coming of that Day is precious, in which we experience the Truth of this Expression, The Lord our Righteousness, Jer. xiii. 6, and feel him to be made unto us Wisdom and Sanctification.

The Example of a righteous Man is often looked at with Attention. Where righteous Men join in Business, their Company gives Encouragement to others; and as one Grain of Incense deliberately offered to the Prince of this World, renders an Offering to God in that State unacceptable; and from those esteemed Leaders of the People may be injurious to the Weak; it requires deep Humility of Heart, to follow him faithfully, who alone gives sound Wisdom, and the Spirit of true Discerning; and O how necessary it is, to consider the Weight of a Holy Profession!

The Conduct of some formerly gave Occasion of Complaint against them; Thou hast defiled thy Sanctuaries by the Multitude of thine Iniquities, by the Iniquity of thy Traffick, Ezek. xxviii. 18, and in several Places it is charged against Israel, that they had polluted the Holy Name.

The Prophet Isaiah represents inward Sanctification in the Similitude of being purged from that which is Fuel for Fire; and particularly describes the outward Fruits, brought forth by those who dwell in this inward Holiness; They walk righteously, and speak uprightly. By walking he represents the Journey through Life, as a righteous Journey; and by speaking uprightly, seems to point at that which Moses appears to have had in View, when he thus express'd himself; Thou shall not follow a Multitude to do Evil, nor speak in a Cause to decline after many to wrest Judgment, Exod. xxiii. 2.

He goes on to shew their Firmness in Equity; representing them as Persons superior to all the Arts of getting Money, which have not Righteousness for their Foundation; They despise the Gain of Oppressions: And further shews how careful they are that no Prospects of Gain may induce them to become partial in Judgment respecting an Injury; They shake their Hands from holding Bribes.

Again, where any Interest is so connected with shedding Blood, that the Cry of innocent Blood goes also with it; he points out their Care to keep innocent Blood from crying against them, in the Similitude of a Man's stopping his Ears to prevent a Sound from entering his Head; They stop their Ears from hearing Blood: And where they know that Wickedness is committed, he points out with Care, that they do not by an unguarded Friendship with the Authors of it, appear like unconcerned Lookers on, but as People so deeply affected with Sorrow, that they cannot endure to stand by and behold it; this he represents in the Similitude of a Man shutting his Eyes from seeing Evil.

Who amongst us shall dwell with devouring Fire? Who amongst us shall dwell with everlasting Burnings? He that walketh righteously and speaketh uprightly. He that despiseth the Gain of Oppressions, that shaketh his Hands from holding of Bribes, that stoppeth his Ears from hearing of Blood, and shutteth his Eyes from seeing Evil, Isa. xxxiii. 15.

He proceeds in the Spirit of Prophecy to shew how the Faithful, being supported under Temptations, would be preserved from that Defilement that there is in the Love of Money; that as they who in a reverent Waiting on God, feel their Strength renewed, are said to mount upward; so here their Preservation from the Snare of unrighteous Gain, is represented in the Likeness of a Man, borne up above all crafty, artful Means of getting the Advantage of another; They shall dwell on high; and points out the Stability and Firmness of their Condition; His Place of Defence shall be the Munition of Rocks; and that under all the outward Appearances of Loss, in denying himself of gainful Profits for Righteousness Sake, yet through the Care of him who provides for the Sparrows, he should have a Supply answerable to his infinite Wisdom; Bread shall be given him, his Waters shall be sure. And as our Saviour mentions the Sight of God to be attainable by the Pure in Heart, so here the Prophet pointed out, how in true Sanctification the Understanding is opened, to behold the peaceable harmonious Nature of his Kingdom; thine Eyes shall see the King in his Beauty: And that looking beyond all the Afflictions which attend the Righteous, to a Habitation eternal in the Heavens, they with an eye divinely open shall behold the Land that is very far off.

He shall dwell on high, his Place of Defence shall be the Munition of Rocks, Bread shall be given him, his Waters shall be sure. Thine Eyes shall see the King in his Beauty;

they shall behold the Land that is very far off, Isa. xxxiii. 16.

I often remember, and to me the Subject is awful, that the great Judge of all the Earth doeth that which is right, and that he, before whom the Nations are as the Drop of a Bucket, is no Respecter of Persons. Happy for them, who like the inspired Prophet, in the Way of his Judgments wait for him, Isa. xxvi. 8.

When we feel him to sit as a Refiner with Fire, and know a Resignedness wrought in us, to that which he appoints for us, his Blessing in a very low Estate, is found to be more precious than much outward Treasure in those Ways of Life, where the Leadings of his Spirit are not followed.

The Prophet in a Sight of a divine Work amongst many People, declared in the Name of the Lord, I will gather all Nations and Tongues, and they shall come and see my Glory, Isa. lxvi. 18. And again, from the rising of the Sun to the going down of the same, my Name shall be great amongst the Gentiles, and in every Place Incense shall be offered to my Name, and a pure Offering, Malachi i. 11.

Behold here how the Prophets had an inward Sense of the Spreading of the Kingdom of Christ; and how he was spoken of as one who should take the Heathen for his Inheritance, and the utmost Parts of the Earth for his Possession, Psal. ii. 8. That he was given for a Light to the Gentiles; and for Salvation to the Ends of the Earth, Isa. xlix. 6.

When we meditate on this divine Work, as a Work of Ages; a Work that the Prophets felt long before Christ appeared visibly on Earth, and remember the bitter Agonies he endured when he poured out his Soul unto Death, that the Heathen Nations, as well as others, might come to the Knowledge of the Truth and be saved.

When we contemplate on this marvellous Work, as that which the Angels desire to look into, 1 Pet. i. 12. And behold People amongst whom this Light hath eminently broken forth, and who have received many Favours from the bountiful Hand of our Heavenly Father; not only indifferent with respect to publishing the glad Tidings amongst the Gentiles, as yet sitting in Darkness and entangled with many Superstitions; but aspiring after Wealth and worldly Honours, take hold of Means to obtain their Ends, tending to stir up Wrath and Indignation, and to beget an Abhorrence in them to the Name of Christianity. When these Things are weightily attended to, how mournful is the Subject?

It is worthy of Remembrance, that People in different Ages, deeply baptized into the Nature of that Work for which Christ suffered, have joyfully offered up their Liberty and Lives for the promoting of it in the Earth.

Policarp, who was reputed a Disciple of the Apostle John, having attained to great Age, was at length sentenced to die for his Religion; and being brought to the Fire, prayed nearly as follows, "Thou God and Father of our Lord Jesus Christ, by whom I have received the Knowledge of thee! O God of the Angels and Powers, and of every living Creature, and of all Sorts of just Men which live in thy Presence. I thank thee, that thou hast graciously vouchsafed this Day and this Hour to allot me a Portion among the Number of Martyrs, among the People of Christ, unto the Resurrection of everlasting Life; among whom I shall be received in thy Sight, this Day, as a fruitful and acceptable

Sacrifice; wherefore for all this, I praise thee, I bless thee, I glorify thee through the everlasting High Priest, Jesus Christ, thy well-beloved Son; to whom, with thee and the Holy Ghost, be all Glory, World without End. Amen."

Bishop Latimer, when Sentence of Death by Fire was pronounced against him, on Account of his Firmness in the Cause of Religion, he said, "I thank God most heartily, that he hath prolonged my Life to this End; that I may in this Case glorify him by this Kind of Death." Fox's Acts and Mon. 936.

William Dewsbury, who had suffered much for his Religion, in his last Sickness, encouraging his Friends to Faithfulness, made mention, like good old Jacob, of the Loving kindness of God to him in the Course of his Life, and that through the Power of Divine Love, he, for Christ's Sake, had joyfully entered Prisons. See Introduction to his Works.

I mention these as a few Examples, out of many of the powerful Operations of the Spirit of Christ, where People are fully devoted to it, and of the ardent Longings in their Minds for the Spreading of his Kingdom amongst Mankind. Now to those, in the present Age, who truly know Christ, and feel the Nature of his peaceable Government opened in their Understandings, how loud is that Call wherewith we are called to Faithfulness; that in following this pure Light of Life, we, as Workers together with him, may labour in that great Work for which he was offered as a Sacrifice on the Cross; and that his peaceable Doctrines may shine through us in their real Harmony, at a Time when the Name of Christianity is become hateful to many of the Heathen.

When Gehazi had obtained Treasures which the Prophet under divine Direction had refused, and was returned from the Business; the Prophet troubled at his Conduct, queried if it was a Time thus to prepare for a specious Living.

Is it a Time to receive Money and Garments, Men Servants and Maid Servants? The Leprosy therefore of Naaman shall cleave to thee, and to thy Seed for ever, 2 Kings v. 26. And O that we may lay to Heart the Condition of the present Time, and humbly follow his Counsel, who alone is able to prepare the Way for a true harmonious Walking amongst Mankind.

CHAPTER IV

On Divine Admonitions

Such are the Perfections of our Heavenly Father, that in all the Dispensations of his Providence, it is our Duty, in every Thing, to give Thanks. Though from the first Settlement of this Part of America, he hath not extended his Judgments to the Degree of Famine, yet Worms at Times have come forth beyond numbering, and laid waste Fields of Grain and Grass, where they have appeared; another Kind, in great Multitudes, working out of Sight, in Grass Ground, have so eat the Roots, that the Surface, being loosened from the Soil beneath, might be taken off in great Sheets.

These Kind of devouring Creatures appearing seldom, and coming in such Multitudes, their Generation appears different from most other Reptiles, and by the Prophet were call'd God's Army sent amongst the People, Joel ii. 25.

There have been Tempests of Hail, which have very much destroyed the Grain where they extended. Through long Drought in Summer, Grain in some Places hath been less than half the usual Quantity; [1] and in the Continuance thereof, I have beheld with Attention, from Week to Week, how Dryness from the Top of the Earth, hath extended deeper and deeper, while the Corn and Plants have languished; and with Reverence my Mind hath been turned towards him, who being perfect in Goodness, in Wisdom and Power, doeth all Things right. And after long Drought, when the Sky hath grown dark with a Collection of Matter, and Clouds like Lakes of Water hung over our Heads, from whence the thirsty Land hath been soaked; I have at Times, with Awfulness, beheld the vehement Operation of

Lightning, made sometimes to accompany these Blessings, as a Messenger from him who created all Things, to remind us of our Duty in a right Use of those Benefits, and give striking Admonitions, that we do not misapply those Gifts, in which an Almighty Power is exerted, in bestowing them upon us.

When I have considered that many of our Fellow Creatures suffer much in some Places, for want of the Necessaries of Life, whilst those who rule over them are too much given to Luxury, and divers Vanities; and behold the apparent Deviation from pure Wisdom amongst us, in the Use of the outward Gifts of God; those Marks of Famine have appeared like humbling Admonitions from him, that we might be instructed by gentle Chastisements, and might seriously consider our Ways; remembering that the outward Supply of Life is a Gift from our Heavenly Father, and no more venture to use, or apply his Gifts, in a Way contrary to pure Wisdom.

Should we continue to reject those merciful Admonitions, and use his Gifts at Home, contrary to the gracious Design of the Giver, or send them Abroad in a Way of Trade, which the Spirit of Truth doth not lead into; and should he whose Eyes are upon all our Ways, extend his Chastisements so far as to reduce us to much greater Distress than hath yet been felt by these Provinces; with what sorrow of Heart might we meditate on that Subject, Hast thou not procured this unto thyself, in that thou hast forsaken the Lord thy God, when he led thee by the Way? Thine own Wickedness shall correct thee, and thy Backslidings shall reprove thee; know therefore, and see that it is an evil Thing and bitter, that thou hast forsaken the Lord thy God, and that my Fear is not in thee, saith the Lord of Hosts, Jer. ii. 17, 19.

My Mind hath often been affected with Sorrow, in beholding a wrong Application of the Gifts of our Heavenly Father; and those Expressions concerning the Defilement of the Earth have been opened to my Understanding; The Earth was corrupt before God, and the Earth was filled with Violence, Gen. vi. 11. Again, Isaiah xxiv. 5. The Earth also is defiled under the Inhabitants thereof.

The Earth being the Work of a Divine Power, may not as such be accounted unclean; but when Violence is committed thereon, and the Channel of Righteousness so obstructed, that in our Skirts are found the Blood of the Souls of poor Innocents; not by a secret Search, but upon all these, [2] Jer. ii. 34.

When Blood shed unrighteously remains unatoned for, and the Inhabitants are not effectually purged from it, when they do not wash their Hands in Innocency, as was figured in the Law, in the Case of one being found slain; but seek for Gain arising from Scenes of Violence and Oppression, here the Land is polluted with Blood, Deut. xxi. 6.

Moreover, when the Earth is planted and tilled, and the Fruits brought forth are applied to support unrighteous Purposes; here the gracious Design of infinite Goodness, in these his Gifts being perverted, the Earth is defiled; and the Complaint formerly uttered becomes applicable; Thou hast made me to serve with thy Sins; thou hast wearied me with thine Iniquities, Isaiah xliii. 24.

AN EPISTLE TO THE QUARTERLY AND MONTHLY MEETINGS OF FRIENDS.

By JOHN WOOLMAN.

LONDON:

Re-printed by Mary Hinde.

AN EPISTLE, &c.

Beloved Friends,—Feeling at this Time a renewed Concern that the pure Principle of Light and Life, and the righteous Fruits thereof may spread and prevail amongst Mankind, there is an Engagement on my Heart to labour with my Brethren in religious Profession, that none of us may be a Stumbling-block in the Way of others; but may so walk that our Conduct may reach the pure Witness in the Hearts of such who are not in Profession with us.

And, dear Friends, while we publickly own that the Holy Spirit is our Leader, the Profession is in itself weighty, and the Weightiness thereof increaseth in Proportion as we are noted among the Professors of Truth, and active in dealing with such who walk disorderly.

Many under our Profession, for Want of due Attention, and a perfect Resignation, to this Divine Teacher, have in some Things manifested a Deviation from the Purity of our religious Principles, and these Deviations having crept in amongst us by little and little, and increasing from less to greater, have been so far unnoticed, that some living in them, have been active in putting Discipline in Practice with relation to others, whose Conduct hath appeared more dishonourable in the World.

Now as my Mind hath been exercised before the Lord, I have seen, that the Discipline of the Church of Christ standeth in that which is pure; that it is the Wisdom from above which gives Authority to Discipline, and that the Weightiness thereof standeth not in any outward Circumstances, but in the Authority of Christ who is the Author of it; and where any walk after the Flesh, and not according to the Purity of Truth, and at the same Time are active in putting Discipline in Practice, a Veil is gradually drawn over the Purity of Discipline, and over that Holiness of Life, which Christ leads those into, in whom, the Love of God is verily perfected, 1 John ii. 5.

When we labour in true Love with Offenders, and they remain obstinate, it sometimes is necessary to proceed as far as our Lord directed; Let him be to thee as an heathen Man, or a Publican, Mat. xviii. 17.

Now when such are disowned, and they who act therein feel Christ made unto them Wisdom, and are preserved in his meek, restoring Spirit, there is no just Cause of Offence ministered to any; but when such who are active in dealing with Offenders, indulge themselves in Things which are contrary to the Purity of Truth, and yet judge others whose Conduct appears more dishonourable than theirs, here the pure Authority of Discipline ceaseth as to such Offenders, and a Temptation is laid in their Way to wrangle and contend;—Judge not, said our Lord, that ye be not Judged. Now this forbidding alludes to Man's Judgment, and points out the Necessity of our humbly attending to that sanctifying Power, under which the Faithful experience the Lord to be a Spirit of Judgment to them, Isa. xxviii. 6. And as we feel his Holy Spirit to mortify the Deeds of the Body in us, and can say, It is no more I that live, but Christ that liveth in me, here right Judgment is known.

And while Divine Love prevails in our Hearts, and Self in us is brought under Judgment, a Preparation is felt to labour in a right Manner with Offenders; but if we abide not in this Love, our outward Performance in dealing with others, degenerates into Formality; for this is the Love of God, that we keep his Commandments, John i. 3.

How weighty are those Instructions of our Redeemer concerning religious Duties, when he points out, that they who pray, should be so obedient to the Teachings of the Holy Spirit, that humbly confiding in his Help, they may say, Thy Name, O Father I be hallowed. Thy Kingdom come. Thy Will be done on Earth, as it is in Heaven.—In this awful State of Mind is felt that Worship which stands in doing the Will of God on Earth, as it is done in Heaven, and keeping the Holy Name sacred: To take a Holy Profession upon us is awful, nor can we keep his Holy Name sacred, but by humbly abiding under the Cross of Christ. The Apostle laid a heavy Complaint against some who prophaned this Holy Name by their Manner of Living, Through you, he says, the Name of God is blasphemed among the Gentiles, Rom. ii. 24.

Some of our Ancestors, through many Tribulations, were gathered into the State of true Worshippers, and had Fellowship in that which is pure; and as one was inwardly moved to kneel down in their Assemblies, and publickly call on the Name of the Lord, those in the Harmony of united Exercise then present, joined in the Prayer: I mention this, in order that we of the present Age, may look unto the Rock from whence we were hewn, and remember that to unite in Worship, is an Union in Prayer, and that Prayer acceptable to the Father, is only in a Mind truly sanctified, where the sacred Name is kept Holy, and the Heart resigned to do his Will on Earth, as it is done in Heaven; If ye abide in me, saith Christ, and my Words abide in you, ye shall ask what ye will in my Name, and it shall be done unto you.—Now we know not what to pray for as we ought, but as the Holy Spirit doth open and direct our Minds, and as we faithfully yield to its Influences, our Prayers are in the Will of our Heavenly Father, who fails not to grant that which his own Spirit, through his Children, asketh;—thus Preservation from Sin is known, and the Fruits of Righteousness are brought forth by such who inwardly unite in Prayer.

How weighty are our solemn Meetings when the Name of Christ is kept Holy!

"How precious is that State in which the Children of the Lord are so redeemed from the Love of this World, that they are accepted and blessed in all that they do!" R. Barclay's Apology, Page 404.

How necessary is it that we who profess these Principles, and are outwardly active in supporting them, should faithfully abide in Divine Strength, that as he who has called us, is Holy, so we may be Holy in all manner of Conversation, 1 Pet. i. 15.

If one professing to be influenced by the Spirit of Christ, propose to unite in a Labour to promote Righteousness in the Earth, and in Time past he hath manifestly deviated from the Paths of Equity, then to act consistent with this Principle, his first Work is to make Restitution so far as he may be enabled; for if he attempts to contribute toward a Work intended to promote Righteousness, while it appears that he neglecteth, or refuseth to act righteously himself, his Conduct has a Tendency to entangle the Minds of those who are weak in the Faith, who behold these Things, and to draw a Veil over the Purity of Righteousness, by carrying an Appearance as though that was Righteousness which is not.

Again, if I propose to assist in supporting those Doctrines wherein that Purity of Life is held forth, in which Customs proceeding from the Spirit of this World have no Place, and at the same Time strengthen others in those Customs by my Example; the first Step then in an orderly Proceeding, is to cease from those Customs myself, and afterwards to labour, as I may be enabled, to promote the like Disposition and Conduct in others.

To be convinced of the pure Principle of Truth, and diligently exercised in walking answerable thereto, is necessary before I can consistently recommend this Principle to others.—I often feel a Labour in Spirit, that we who are active Members in religious Society, may experience in ourselves the Truth of those Expressions of the Holy One; I will be sanctified in them that come nigh me, Lev. x. 3.——In this Case, my Mind hath been often exercised when alone, Year after Year, for many Years, and in the Renewings of Divine Love, a tender Care hath been incited in me, that we who profess the inward Principle of Light to be our Teacher, may be a Family united in that Purity of Worship, which comprehends a Holy Life, and ministers Instruction to others.

My Mind is often drawn towards Children in the Truth, who having a small Share of the Things of this Life, and coming to have Families, may be inwardly exercised before the Lord to support them in a Way agreeable to the Purity of Truth, in which they may feel his Blessing upon them in their Labours; the Thoughts of such being entangled with Customs, contrary to pure Wisdom, conveyed to them through our Hands, doth often very tenderly, and movingly affect my Heart, and when I look towards, and think on the succeeding Generation, fervent Desires are raised in me, that we by yielding to that Holy Spirit which leads into all Truth, may not do the Work of the Lord deceitfully, may not live contrary to the Purity of the Divine Principle we profess; but that as faithful Labourers in our Age, we may be instrumental in removing Stumbling-blocks out of the Way of those who may succeed us.

So great was the Love of Christ, that he gave himself for the Church, that he might sanctify and cleanse it, that it should be Holy, and without Blemish, not having Spot or Wrinkle, or any such Thing, Eph. v. 25. and where any take the Name of Christ upon them, professing to be Members of his Church, and led by his Holy Spirit, and yet manifestly deviate from the Purity of Truth, they herein act against the gracious Design of his giving himself for them, and minister Cause for the Continuance of his Afflictions, viz. in his Body the Church.

Christ suffered Afflictions in a Body of Flesh prepared by the Father, but the Afflictions of his mystical Body are yet unfinished; for they who are baptized into Christ are baptized into his Death; and as we humbly abide under his sanctifying Power, and are brought forth into Newness of Life, we feel Christ to live in us, who being the same Yesterday, To-day, and forever, and always at Unity with himself, his Spirit in the Hearts of his People leads to an inward Exercise for the Salvation of Mankind; and when under a Travail of Spirit, we behold a visited People entangled by the Spirit of the World with its Wickedness and Customs, and thereby rendered incapable of being faithful Examples to others, Sorrow and Heaviness under a Sense of these Things, is often experienced, and thus in some Measure is filled up that which remains of the Afflictions of Christ.

Our blessed Saviour speaking concerning Gifts offered in Divine Service, says, If thou bring thy Gift to the Altar, and there remembrest that thy Brother hath ought against thee, leave there thy Gift before the Altar, and go thy Way, first be reconciled to thy Brother, and then come and offer thy Gift, Mat. v. 23, 24. Now there is no true Unity, but in that wherein the Father and the Son are united, nor can there be a perfect Reconciliation but in ceasing from that which ministers Cause for the Continuation of the Afflictions of Christ; and if any professing to bring their Gift to the Altar, do remember the customary Contradiction which some of their Fruits bear to the pure spiritual Worship, here it appears necessary to lay to Heart this Command, Leave thy Gift by the Altar.

Christ graciously calls his People Brethren; Whosoever shall do the Will of God, the same is my Brother, Mark iii. 35. Now if we walk contrary to the Truth as it is in Jesus, while we continue to profess it, we offend against Christ, and if under this Offence we bring our Gift to the Altar, our Redeemer doth not direct us to take back our Gift, he doth not discourage our proceeding in a good Work; but graciously points out the necessary Means by which the Gift may be rendered acceptable, Leave, saith he, thy Gift by the Altar, first go and be reconciled to thy Brother, cease from that which grieves the Holy Spirit, cease from that which is against the Truth, as it is in Jesus, and then come and offer thy Gift.

I feel, while I am writing, a Tenderness to those who through Divine Favour are preserved in a lively Sense of the State of the Churches, and at Times may be under Discouragements with regard to proceeding in that pure Way which Christ by his Holy Spirit leads into: The Depth of Disorder and Weakness, which so much prevails, being opened, Doubtings are apt to arise as to the Possibility of proceeding as an Assembly of the Lord's People in the pure Council of Truth; and here I feel a Concern to express in Uprightness, that which hath been opened in my Mind, under the Power of the Cross of Christ, relating to a visible gathered Church, the Members whereof are guided by the Holy Spirit.

The Church is called the Body of Christ, Col. i. 24.

Christ is called the Head of the Church, Eph. i. 22.

The Church is called the Pillar, and Ground of Truth, 1 Tim. iii. 15.

Thus the Church hath a Name that is sacred, and the Necessity of keeping this Name Holy, appears evident; for where a Number of People unite in a Profession of being led by the Spirit of Christ, and publish their Principles to the World, the Acts and Proceedings of that People may in some Measure be considered as such which Christ is the Author of.

Now while we stand in this Station, if the pure Light of Life is not followed and regarded in our Proceedings, we are in the Way of prophaning the Holy Name, and of going back toward that Wilderness of Sufferings and Persecution, out of which, through the tender Mercies of God, a Church hath been gathered; Christ liveth in sanctified Vessels, Gal. ii. 20. and where they behold his Holy Name prophaned, and the pure Gospel Light eclipsed, through the Unfaithfulness of any who by their Station appear to be Standard-bearers under the Prince of Peace, the living Members in the Body of Christ in beholding these Things, do in some degree experience the Fellowship of his Sufferings; and as the Wisdom of the World more and more takes Place in conducting the Affairs of this visible gathered Church, and the pure Leadings of the Holy Spirit less waited for and followed, so the true Suffering Seed is more and more oppressed.

My Mind is often affected with a Sense of the Condition of sincere-hearted People in some Kingdoms, where Liberty of Conscience is not allowed, many of whom being burthened in their Minds with prevailing Superstition joined with Oppressions, are often under Sorrow; and where such have attended to that pure Light which hath in some degree opened their Understandings, and for their Faithfulness thereto, have been brought to Examination and Trial, how heavy are the Persecutions which in divers Parts of the World are exercised upon them! How mighty, as to the outward, is that Power by which they are borne down, and oppressed!

How deeply affecting is the Condition of many upright-hearted People who are taken into the Papal Inquisition! What lamentable Cruelties, in deep Vaults, in a private Way, are exercised on many of them! And how lingering is that Death by a small slow Fire, which they have frequently indured, who have been faithful to the End!

How many tender spirited Protestants have been sentenced to spend the Remainder of their Lives in a Galley chained to Oars, under hard-hearted Masters, while their young Children are placed out for Education, and taught Principles so contrary to the Conscience of the Parents, that by dissenting from them, they have hazarded their Liberty, Lives, and all that was dear to them of the Things of this World!

There have been in Time past severe Persecutions under the English Government, and many sincere-hearted People have suffered Death for the Testimony of a good Conscience, whose Faithfulness in their Day hath ministred Encouragement to others, and been a Blessing to many who have succeeded them; thus from Age to Age, the Darkness being more and more removed, a Channel at length, through the tender Mercies of God, hath been opened for the Exercise of the pure Gift of the Gospel Ministry, without Interruption from outward Power, a Work, the like of which is rare, and unknown in many Parts of the World.

As these Things are often fresh in my Mind, and this great Work of God going on in the Earth has been open before me, that Liberty of Conscience with which we are favoured, hath appeared not as a light Matter.

A Trust is committed to us, a great and weighty Trust, to which our diligent Attention is necessary, wherever the active Members of this visible gathered Church use themselves to that which is contrary to the Purity of our Principles, it appears to be a Breach of this Trust, and one Step back toward the Wilderness, one Step towards undoing what God in infinite Love hath done through his faithful Servants, in a Work of several Ages, and like laying the Foundation for future Sufferings.

I feel a living Invitation in my Mind to such who are active in our religious Society, that we may lay to Heart this Matter, and consider the Station in which we stand; a Place of outward Liberty under the free Exercise of our Conscience toward God, not obtained but through great and manifold Afflictions of those who lived before us. There is Gratitude due from us to our Heavenly Father, and Justice to our Posterity; can our Hearts endure, or our Hands be strong, if we desert a Cause so precious, if we turn aside from a Work, under which so many have patiently laboured?

May the deep Sufferings of our Saviour be so dear to us, that we may never trample under Foot the adorable Son of God, nor count the Blood of the Covenant unholy!

May the Faithfulness of the Martyrs when the Prospect of Death by Fire was before them, be remembred. And may the patient constant Sufferings of the upright-hearted Servants of God in latter Ages be revived in our Minds. And may we so follow on to know the Lord, that neither the Faithful in this Age, nor those in Ages to come, may ever be brought under Suffering, through our sliding back from the Work of Reformation in the World.

While the active Members in the visible gathered Church stand upright, and the Affairs thereof are carried on under the Leadings of the Holy Spirit, although Disorders may arise among us, and cause many Exercises to those who feel the Care of the Churches upon them; yet while these continue under the Weight of the Work, and labour in the Meekness of Wisdom for the Help of others, the Name of Christ in the visible gathered Church may be kept sacred; but while they who are active in the Affairs of this Church, continue in a manifest Opposition to the Purity of our

Principles, this, as the Prophet Isaiah x. 18. expresseth it, is like as when a Standard-bearer fainteth; and thus the Way opens to great and prevailing Degeneracy, and to Sufferings for such who through the Power of Divine Love, are separated to the Gospel of Christ, and cannot unite with any Thing which stands in Opposition to the Purity of it.

The Necessity of an inward Stillness, hath under these Exercises appeared clear to my Mind; in true Silence Strength is renewed, the Mind herein is weaned from all Things, but as they may be enjoyed in the Divine Will, and a Lowliness in outward Living opposite to Worldly Honour, becomes truly acceptable to us;—in the Desire after outward Gain, the Mind is prevented from a perfect Attention to the Voice of Christ, but being weaned from all Things, but as they may be enjoyed in the Divine Will, the pure Light shines into the Soul, and where the Fruits of that Spirit which is of the World, are brought forth by many who profess to be led by the Spirit of Truth, and Cloudiness is felt to be gathering over the visible gathered Church, the Sincere in Heart who abide in true Stillness, and are exercised therein before the Lord for his Name's Sake, have a Knowledge of Christ in the Fellowship of his Sufferings, and inward Thankfulness is felt at Times, that through Divine Love, our own Wisdom is cast out, and that forward active Part in us subjected, which would rise and do something in the visible gathered Church, without, the pure Leadings of the Spirit of Christ.

While aught remains in us different from a perfect Resignation of our Wills, it is like a Seal to a Book wherein is written, that good, and acceptable, and perfect Will of God concerning us, Rom. xii. 2. but when our Minds entirely yield to Christ, that Silence is known, which followeth the opening of the last of the Seals, Rev. viii. 1.

In this Silence we learn abiding in the Divine Will, and there feel, that we have no Cause to promote but that only in which the Light of Life directs us in our Proceedings, and that the alone Way to be useful in the Church of Christ, is to abide faithfully under the Leadings of his Holy Spirit in all Cases, and being preserved thereby in Purity of Heart, and Holiness of Conversation, a Testimony to the Purity of his Government may be held forth through us, to others.

As my Mind hath been thus exercised, I have seen that to be active and busy in the visible gathered Church, without the Leadings of the Holy Spirit, is not only unprofitable, but tends to increase Dimness; and where Way is not opened to proceed in the Light of Truth, a Stop is felt by those who humbly attend to the Divine Leader, a Stop which in relation to good Order in the visible gathered Church, is of the greatest Consequence to be observed; thus Robert Barclay in his Treatise on Discipline holds forth, Page 65, 68, 84. "That the Judgment or Conclusion of the Church or Congregation, is no further effectual as to the true End and Design thereof, but as such Judgment or Conclusion proceeds from the Spirit of God operating on their Minds who are sanctified in Christ Jesus."

Now in this Stop I have learned the Necessity of waiting on the Lord in Humility, that the Works of all may be brought to the Light, and those to Judgment which are wrought in the Wisdom of this World; and have also seen, that in a Mind thoroughly subjected to the Power of the Cross, there is a Savour of Life to be felt, which evidently tends to gather Souls to God, while the greatest Works in the visible gathered Church brought forth in Man's Wisdom, remain to be unprofitable.

Where People are divinely gathered into a Holy Fellowship, and faithfully abide under the Influence of that Spirit which leads into all Truth, they are the Light of the World, Mat. v. 14. Now holding this Profession, to me hath appeared weighty, even beyond what I can fully express, and what our blessed Lord seemed to have in View, when he proposed the Necessity of counting the Cost, before we begin to build.

I trust there are many who at Times, under Divine Visitation, feel an inward Enquiry after God; and when such in the Simplicity of their Hearts mark the Lives of a People, who profess to walk by the Leadings of his Spirit, of what great Concernment is it that our Lights shine clear, that nothing of our Conduct carry a Contradiction to the Truth as it is in Jesus, or be a Means of prophaning his Holy Name, and be a Stumbling-block in the Way of those sincere Enquirers!

When such Seekers, who wearied with empty Forms, look toward uniting with us as a People, and behold active Members among us depart in their customary Way of Living, from that Purity of Life, which under humbling Exercises hath been opened before them, as the Way of the Lord's People, how mournful and discouraging is the Prospect! And how strongly doth such Unfaithfulness operate against the Spreading of the peaceable, harmonious Principle, and Testimony of Truth amongst Mankind!

In entering into that Life, which is hid with Christ in God, we behold his peaceable Government, where the whole Family are governed by the same Spirit, and the doing to others as we would they should do unto us, groweth up as good Fruit from a good Tree; the Peace, Quietness, and harmonious Walking in this Government is beheld with humble Reverence to him who is the Author of it; and in partaking of the Spirit of Christ, we partake of that which labours, and suffers for the Increase of this peaceable Government among the Inhabitants of the World; and I have felt a Labour of long Continuance, that we, who profess this peaceable Principle, may be faithful Standard-bearers under the Prince of Peace, and that nothing of a defiling Nature, tending to Discord and Wars, may remain among us.

May each of us query with ourselves, have the Treasures I possess been gathered in that Wisdom which is from above, so far as hath appeared to me?

Have none of my Fellow Creatures an equitable Right to any Part which is called mine?

Have the Gifts, and Possessions received by me from others, been conveyed in a Way free from all Unrighteousness, so far as I have seen?

The Principle of Peace in which our Trust is only in the Lord, and our Minds weaned from a Dependance on the Strength of Armies, hath appeared to me very precious, and I often feel strong Desires, that we who profess this Principle, may so walk, as to give just Cause for none of our Fellow Creatures to be offended at us; that our Lives may evidently manifest, that we are redeemed from that Spirit in which Wars are. Our blessed Saviour in pointing out the Danger of so leaning on Man, as to neglect the Leadings of his Holy Spirit, said, Call no Man your Father upon the Earth; for one is your Father which is in Heaven, Mat. xxiii. 9. Where the Wisdom from above is faithfully followed, and therein we are entrusted with Substance, it is a Treasure committed to our Care in the Nature of an

Inheritance, as an Inheritance from him, who formed, and supports the World. Now in this Condition the true Enjoyment of the good Things of this Life is understood, and that Blessing felt, in which is real Safety; this is what I apprehend our blessed Lord had in View, when he pronounced, Blessed are the Meek, for they shall inherit the Earth.

Selfish Worldly-minded Men may hold Lands in the selfish Spirit, and depending on the Strength of the outward Power, be perplexed with secret Uneasiness, lest the Injured should sometime overpower them, and that Measure meted to them, which they measure to others. Thus selfish Men may possess the Earth; but it is the Meek who inherit it, and enjoy it as an Inheritance from the Heavenly Father, free from all the Defilements, and Perplexities of Unrighteousness.

Where Proceedings have been in that Wisdom which is from beneath, and inequitable Gain gathered by a Man, and left as a Gift to his Children, who being entangled by the same Worldly Spirit, have not attained to that Clearness of Light in which the Channels of Righteousness are opened, and Justice done to those who remain silent under Injuries: Here I have seen under humbling Exercise of Mind, that the Sins of the Fathers are embraced by the Children, and become their Sins, and thus of the Days of Tribulation, the Iniquities in the Fathers are visited upon these Children, who take hold of the Unrighteousness of their Fathers, and live in that Spirit in which those Iniquities were committed; to which agreeth the Prophecy of Moses, concerning a rebellious People; They that are left of you shall pine away in their Iniquities, in your Enemy's Land, and in the Iniquities of their Fathers shall they pine away, Lev. xxvi. 39. and our blessed Lord in beholding the Hardness of

Heart in that Generation, and feeling in himself, that they lived in the same Spirit in which the Prophets had been persecuted unto Death, signified, That the Blood of all the Prophets which was shed from the Foundation of the World, should be required of that Generation, from the Blood of Abel, unto the Blood of Zacharias, who perished between the Altar and the Temple, Luke xi. 51.

Tender Compassion fills my Heart towards my Fellow Creatures estranged from the harmonious Government of the Prince of Peace, and a Labour attends me, that they may be gathered to this peaceable Habitation.

In being inwardly prepared to suffer Adversity for Christ's Sake, and weaned from a Dependance on the Arm of Flesh, we feel, that there is a Rest for the People of God, and that it stands in a perfect Resignation of ourselves to his Holy Will; in this Condition, all our Wants and Desires are bounded by pure Wisdom, and our Minds wholly attentive to the Counsel of Christ inwardly communicated, which hath appeared to me as a Habitation of Safety for the Lord's People, in Times of outward Commotion and Trouble, and Desires from the Fountain of pure Love, are opened in me, to invite my Brethren and Fellow Creatures to feel for, and seek after that which gathers the Mind into it.

John Woolman.

Mount-Holly, New-Jersey,

4th Month 1772.

REMARKS ON SUNDRY SUBJECTS.

By JOHN WOOLMAN.

LONDON:

Printed by Mary Hinde.

REMARKS &c.

CHAPTER I

On loving our Neighbours as ourselves

When we love the Lord with all our Hearts, and his Creatures in his Love, we are then preserv'd in Tenderness both toward Mankind and the Animal Creation; but if another Spirit gets Room in our Minds, and we follow it in our Proceedings, we are then in the Way of disordering the Affairs of Society.

If a Man successful in Business expends Part of his Income in Things of no real Use, while the Poor employed by him pass through great Difficulties in getting the Necessaries of Life, this requires his serious Attention.

If several principal Men in Business unite in setting the Wages of those who work for Hire, and therein have Regard to a Profit to themselves answerable to unnecessary Expence in their Families, while the Wages of the other on a moderate Industry will not afford a comfortable Living for their Families, and a proper Education for their

Children, this is like laying a Temptation in the Way of some to strive for a Place higher than they are in, when they have not Stock sufficient for it.

Now I feel a Concern in the Spring of pure Love, that all who have Plenty of outward Substance, may Example others in the right Use of Things; may carefully look into the Condition of poor People, and beware of exacting on them with Regard to their Wages.

While hired Labourers, by moderate Industry, through the Divine Blessing, may live comfortably, raise up Families, and give them suitable Education, it appears reasonable for them to be content with their Wages.

If they who have Plenty love their Fellow Creatures in that Love which is Divine, and in all their Proceedings have an equal Regard to the Good of Mankind universally, their Place in Society is a Place of Care, an Office requiring Attention, and the more we possess, the greater is our Trust, and with an Increase of Treasure, an Increase of Care becomes necessary.

When our Will is subject to the Will of God, and in relation to the Things of this World, we have nothing in View, but a comfortable Living equally with the rest of our Fellow Creatures, then outward Treasures are no farther desirable than as we feel a Gift in our Minds equal to the Trust, and Strength to act as dutiful Children in his Service, who hath formed all Mankind, and appointed a Subsistence for us in this World.

A Desire for Treasures on any other Motive, appears to be against that Command of our blessed Saviour, Lay not up for yourselves Treasures here on Earth, Mat. vi. 19.

He forbids not laying up in the Summer against the Wants of Winter; nor doth he teach us to be slothful in that which properly relates to our being in this World; but in this Prohibition he puts in yourselves, Lay not up for yourselves Treasures here on Earth.

Now in the pure Light, this Language is understood, for in the Love of Christ there is no Respect of Persons; and while we abide in his Love, we live not to ourselves, but to him who died for us. And as we are thus united in Spirit to Christ, we are engaged to labour in promoting that Work in the Earth for which he suffer'd.

In this State of Mind our Desires are, that every honest Member in Society may have a Portion of Treasure, and Share of Trust, answerable to that Gift, with which our Heavenly Father hath gifted us.

In great Treasure, there is a great Trust. A great Trust requireth great Care. But the laborious Mind wants Rest.

A pious Man is content to do a Share of Business in Society, answerable to the Gifts with which he is endowed, while the Channels of Business are free from Unrighteousness, but is careful lest at any Time his Heart be over-charg'd.

In the harmonious Spirit of Society Christ is all in all, Col. iii. 11.

Here it is that old Things are past away, all Things are new, all Things are of God, 2 Cor. v. 17, 18, and the Desire for outward Riches is at an End.

They of low Degree who have small Gifts, enjoy their Help who have large Gifts; those with their small Gifts, have a small degree of Care, while these with their large Gifts, have a large degree of Care: And thus to abide in the Love of Christ, and enjoy a comfortable Living in this World is all that is aimed at by those Members in Society, to whom Christ is made Wisdom and Righteousness.

But when they who have much Treasure, are not faithful Stewards of the Gifts of God, great Difficulties attend it.

Now this Matter hath deeply affected my Mind. The Lord, through merciful Chastisements, hath given me a Feeling of that Love, in which the Harmony of Society standeth, and a Sight of the Growth of that Seed which bringeth forth Wars and great Calamities in the World, and a Labour attends me to open it to others.

Now to act with Integrity, according to that Strength of Mind and Body with which our Creator hath endowed each of us, appears necessary for all, and he who thus stands in the lowest Station, appears to be entitled to as comfortable and convenient a Living, as he whose Gifts of Mind are greater, and whose Cares are more extensive.

If some endowed with strong Understandings as Men, abide not in the harmonious State, in which we love our Neighbours as ourselves, but walk in that Spirit in which the Children of this World are wise in their Generation; these by the Strength of Contrivance may sometimes gather great Treasure, but the Wisdom of this World is Foolishness with God; and if we gather Treasures in Worldly Wisdom, we lay up Treasures for ourselves; and great Treasures managed in any other Spirit, than the Spirit of Truth, disordereth the Affairs of Society, for hereby the good Gifts of God in this outward Creation are turned into the Channels of Worldly Honour, and frequently applied to support Luxury, while the Wages of poor Labourers are such, that with moderate Industry and Frugality they may not live comfortably, raise up Families, and give them suitable Education, but through the Streightness of their Condition, are often drawn on to labour under Weariness, to toil through Hardships themselves, and frequently to oppress those useful Animals with which we are intrusted.

From Age to Age, throughout all Ages, Divine Love is that alone, in which Dominion has been, is, and will be rightly conducted.

In this the Endowments of Men are so employed, that the Friend and the Governor are united in one, and oppressive Customs come to an End.

Riches in the Hands of Individuals in Society, is attended with some degree of Power; and so far as Power is put forth separate from pure Love, so far the Government of the Prince of Peace is interrupted; and as we know not that our Children after us will dwell in that State in which Power is rightly applied, to lay up Riches for them appears to be against the Nature of his Government.

The Earth, through the Labour of Men under the Blessing of him who formed it, yieldeth a Supply for the Inhabitants from Generation to Generation, and they who walk in the pure Light, their Minds are prepared to taste and relish not only those Blessings which are spiritual, but also feel a Sweetness and Satisfaction in a right Use of the good Gifts of God in the visible Creation.

Here we see that Man's Happiness stands not in great Possessions, but in a Heart devoted to follow Christ, in that Use of Things, where Customs contrary to universal Love have no Power over us.

In this State our Hearts are prepared to trust in God, and our Desires for our Children and Posterity are, that they, with the rest of Mankind, in Ages to come, may be of that Number, of whom he hath said, I will be a Father to them, and they shall be my Sons and Daughters, 2 Cor. vi. 18.

When Wages in a fruitful Land bear so small a Proportion to the Necessaries of Life, that poor honest People who have Families cannot by a moderate Industry attain to a comfortable Living, and give their Children sufficient Learning, but must either labour to a degree of Oppression, or else omit that which appears to be a Duty.

While this is the Case with the Poor, there is an Inclination in the Minds of most People, to prepare at least so much Treasure for their Children, that they with Care and moderate Industry may live free from these Hardships which the Poor pass through.

Now this Subject requireth our serious Consideration: To labour that our Children may be put in a Way to live comfortably, appears in itself to be a Duty, so long as these our Labours are consistent with universal Righteousness; but if in striving to shun Poverty, we do not walk in that State where Christ is our Life, then we wander; He that hath the Son, hath Life, 1 John v. 12. This Life is the Light of Men, 1 John 1. 4. If we walk not in this Light, we walk in Darkness, and he that walketh in Darkness, knoweth not whither he goeth, John xii. 35.

To keep to right Means in labouring to attain a right End is necessary: If in striving to shun Poverty, we strive only in that State where Christ is the Light of our Life, our Labours will stand in the true Harmony of Society; but if People are confident that the End aimed at is good, and in this Confidence pursue it so eagerly, as not to wait for the Spirit of Truth to lead them, then they come to Loss. Christ is given to be a Leader and Commander of the People, Isaiah lv. 4. Again; The Lord shall guide thee continually, Isaiah lviii. 12. Again; Lord, thou wilt ordain Peace for us, for thou also hast wrought all our Works in us, Isaiah xxvi. 12.

In the Lord have we Righteousness and Strength, Isaiah xlv. 24.

In this State our Minds are preserved watchful in following the Leadings of his Spirit in all our Proceedings in this World, and a Care is felt for a Reformation in general. That our own Posterity, with the rest of Mankind in succeeding Ages, may not be entangled by oppressive Customs, transmitted to them through our Hands; but if People in the Narrowness of natural Love, are afraid that their Children will be oppressed by the Rich, and through an eager Desire to get Treasures, depart from the pure Leadings of Truth in one Case, though it may seem to be a small Matter, yet the Mind even in that small Matter may be embolden'd to continue in a Way of Proceeding, without waiting for the Divine Leader.

Thus People may grow expert in Business, wise in the Wisdom of this World, retain a fair Reputation amongst Men, and yet being Strangers to the Voice of Christ, the safe Leader of his Flock, the Treasures thus gotten, may be like Snares to the Feet of their Posterity.

Now to keep faithful to the pure Counsellor, and under trying Circumstances suffer Adversity for Righteousness Sake, in this there is a Reward.

If we, being poor, are hardly dealt with by those who are rich, and under this Difficulty are frugal and industrious, and in true Humility open our Case to them who oppress us, this may reach the pure Witness in their Minds; and though we should remain under Difficulties as to the outward, yet if we abide in the Love of Christ, all will work for our Good.

When we feel what it is to suffer in the true suffering State, then we experience the Truth of those Expressions, that, as the Sufferings of Christ abound in us, so our Consolation aboundeth by Christ, 2 Cor. i. 5.

But if poor People who are hardly dealt with, do not attain to the true suffering State, do not labour in true Love with those who deal hardly with them, but envy their outward Greatness, murmur in their Hearts because of their own Poverty, and strive in the Wisdom of this World to get Riches for themselves and their Children; this is like wandering in the Dark.

If we who are of a middle Station between Riches and Poverty, are affected at Times with the Oppressions of the Poor, and feel a tender Regard for our Posterity after us, O how necessary is it that we wait for the pure Counsel of Truth!

Many have seen the Hardships of the Poor, felt an eager Desire that their Children may be put in a Way to escape these Hardships; but how few have continued in that pure

Love which openeth our Understandings to proceed rightly under these Difficulties!

How few have faithfully followed that Holy Leader who prepares his People to labour for the Restoration of true Harmony amongst our Fellow Creatures!

In the pure Gospel Spirit we walk by Faith and not by Sight, 2 Cor. v. 7.

In the Obedience of Faith we die to the Narrowness of Self-love, and our Life being hid with Christ in God, our Hearts are enlarg'd toward Mankind universally; but in departing from the true Light of Life, many in striving to get Treasures have stumbled upon the dark Mountains.

Now that Purity of Life which proceeds from Faithfulness in following the Spirit of Truth, that State where our Minds are devoted to serve God, and all our Wants are bounded by his Wisdom, this Habitation has often been open'd before me as a Place of Retirement for the Children of the Light, where we may stand separated from that which disordereth and confuseth the Affairs of Society, and where we may have a Testimony of our Innocence in the Hearts of those who behold us.

Through departing from the Truth as it is in Jesus, through introducing Ways of Life attended with unnecessary Expences, many Wants have arisen, the Minds of People have been employ'd in studying to get Wealth, and in this Pursuit some departing from Equity, have retain'd a Profession of Religion; others have look'd at their Example, and thereby been strengthen'd to proceed further in the same Way: Thus many have encourag'd the Trade of taking Men from Africa, and selling them as Slaves.

It hath been computed that near One Hundred Thousand Negroes have of late Years been taken annually from that Coast, by Ships employed in the English Trade.

As I have travell'd on religious Visits in some Parts of America, I have seen many of these People under the Command of Overseers, in a painful Servitude.

I have beheld them as Gentiles under People professing Christianity, not only kept ignorant of the Holy Scriptures, but under great Provocations to Wrath; of whom it may truly be said, They that rule over them make them to howl, and the Holy Name is abundantly blasphemed, Isaiah lii. 5.

Where Children are taught to read the Sacred Writings, while young, and exampled in Meekness and Humility, it is often helpful to them; nor is this any more than a Debt due from us to a succeeding Age.

But where Youth are pinched for want of the Necessaries of Life, forced to labour hard under the harsh Rebukes of rigorous Overseers, and many Times endure unmerciful Whippings: In such an Education, how great are the Disadvantages they lie under! And how forcibly do these Things work against the Increase of the Government of the Prince of Peace!

Humphrey Smith, in his Works, p. 125, speaking of the tender Feelings of the Love of God in his Heart when he was a Child, said, "By the violent wrathful Nature that ruled in others, was my Quietness disturbed, and Anger begotten in me toward them, yet that of God in me was not wholly overcome, but his Love was felt in my Heart, and great was my Grief when the Earthly-mindedness and wrathful Nature so provoked me, that I was estranged from it.

"And this I write as a Warning to Parents and others, that in the Fear of the living God, you may train up the Youth, and may not be a Means of bringing them into such Alienation."

Many are the Vanities and Luxuries of the present Age, and in labouring to support a Way of living conformable to the present World, the Departure from that Wisdom that is pure and peaceable hath been great.

Under the Sense of a deep Revolt, and an overflowing Stream of Unrighteousness, my Life has been often a Life of Mourning, and tender Desires are raised in me, that the Nature of this Practice may be laid to Heart.

I have read some Books wrote by People who were acquainted with the Manner of getting Slaves in Africa.

I have had verbal Relations of this Nature from several Negroes brought from Africa, who have learn'd to talk English.

I have sundry Times heard Englishmen speak on this Subject, who have been at Africa on this Business; and from all these Accounts it appears evident that great Violence is committed, and much Blood shed in Africa in getting Slaves.

When three or four Hundred Slaves are put in the Hold of a Vessel in a hot Climate, their Breathing soon affects the Air. Were that Number of free People to go Passengers with all Things proper for their Voyage, there would

Inconvenience arise from their Number; but Slaves are taken by Violence, and frequently endeavour to kill the white People, that they may return to their Native Land. Hence they are frequently kept under some Sort of Confinement, by Means of which a Scent ariseth in the Hold of a Ship, and Distempers often break out amongst them, of which many die. Of this tainted Air in the Hold of Ships freighted with Slaves, I have had several Accounts, some in Print, and some verbal, and all agree that the Scent is grievous. When these People are sold in America, and in the Islands, they are made to labour in a Manner more servile and constant, than that which they were used to at Home, that with Grief, with different Diet from what has been common with them, and with hard Labour, some Thousands are computed to die every Year, in what is called the Seasoning.

Thus it appears evident, that great Numbers of these People are brought every Year to an untimely End; many of them being such who never injured us.

When the Innocent suffer under hard-hearted Men, even unto Death, and the Channels of Equity are so obstructed, that the Cause of the Sufferers is not judged in Righteousness, the Land is polluted with Blood, Numb. xxxv. 33.

When Blood hath been shed unrighteously, and remains unatoned for, the Cry thereof is very piercing.

Under the humbling Dispensations of Divine Providence, this Cry hath deeply affected my Heart, and I feel a Concern to open, as I may be enabled, that which lieth heavy on my Mind.

When the Iniquity of the House of Israel and of Judah was exceeding great, when the Land was defiled with Blood, and the City full of Perverseness, Ezek. ix. 9. some were found sighing and crying for the Abominations of the Times, Ezek. ix. 4. and such who live under a right Feeling of our Condition as a Nation, these I trust will be sensible that the Lord at this Day doth call to Mourning, though many are ignorant of it. So powerful are bad Customs when they become general, that People growing bold thro' the Examples one of another, have often been unmoved at the most serious Warnings.

Our blessed Saviour speaking of the People of the old World, said, They eat, they drank, they married, and were given in Marriage, until the Day that Noah went into the Ark, and the Flood came and destroy'd them all, Luke xvii. 27.

The like he spake concerning the People of Sodom, who are also represented by the Prophet as haughty, luxurious, and oppressive; This was the Sin of Sodom, Pride, Fulness of Bread, and Abundance of Idleness was found in her, and in her Daughters; neither did she strengthen the Hands of the Poor and Needy, Ezek. xvi. 49.

Now in a Revolt so deep as this, when much Blood has been shed unrighteously, in carrying on the Slave Trade, and in supporting the Practice of keeping Slaves, which at this Day is unatoned for, and crieth from the Earth, and from the Seas against the Oppressor!

While this Practice is continued, and under a great Load of Guilt there is more Unrighteousness committed, the State of Things is very moving!

There is a Love which stands in Nature, and a Parent beholding his Child in Misery, hath a Feeling of the Affliction; but in Divine Love the Heart is enlarged towards Mankind universally, and prepar'd to sympathize with Strangers, though in the lowest Station in Life.

Of this the Prophet appears to have had a Feeling, when he said, Have we not all one Father? Hath not one God created us? Why then do we deal treacherously every Man with his Brother, in prophaning the Covenant of our Fathers? Mal. ii. 10.

He who of old heard the Groans of the Children of Israel under the hard Task-masters in Egypt, I trust hath looked down from his Holy Habitation on the Miseries of these deeply oppress'd People. Many Lives have been shorten'd through extreme Oppression while they labour'd to support Luxury and Worldly Greatness; and tho' many People in outward Prosperity may think little of those Things, yet the gracious Creator hath Regard to the Cries of the Innocent, however unnoticed by Men.

The Lord in the Riches of his Goodness is leading some into the Feeling of the Condition of this People, who cannot rest without labouring as their Advocate; of which in some Measure I have had Experience, for, in the Movings of his Love in my Heart, these poor Sufferers have been brought near to me.

The unoffending Aged and Infirm made to labour too hard, kept on a Diet less comfortable than their weak State required, and exposed to great Difficulties under hard-hearted Men, to whose Sufferings I have often been a Witness, and under the Heart-melting Power of Divine

Love, their Misery hath felt to me like the Misery of my Parents.

Innocent Youth taken by Violence from their Native Land, from their Friends and Acquaintance; put on board Ships with Hearts laden with Sorrow; exposed to great Hardships at Sea; placed under People, where their Lives have been attended with great Provocation to Anger and Revenge.

With the Condition of these Youth, my Mind hath often been affected, as with the Afflictions of my Children, and in a Feeling of the Misery of these People, and of that great Offence which is minister'd to them, my Tears have been often poured out before the Lord.

That Holy Spirit which affected my Heart when I was a Youth, I trust is often felt by the Negroes in their Native Land, inclining their Minds to that which is righteous, and had the professed Followers of Christ in all their Conduct towards them, manifested a Disposition answerable to the pure Principle in their Hearts, how might the Holy Name have been honoured amongst the Gentiles, and how might we have rejoiced in the fulfilling of that Prophecy, I the Lord love Judgment, I hate Robbery for Burnt-offerings, and I will direct their Work in Truth, and make an everlasting Covenant with them. Their Seed shall be known amongst the Gentiles, and their Offspring amongst the People: All that see them shall acknowledge them, that they are the Seed which the Lord hath blessed, Isaiah lxi. 8, 9.

But in the present State of Things, how contrary is this Practice to that meek Spirit, in which our Saviour laid down his Life for us, that all the Ends of the Earth might know Salvation in his Name!

How are the Sufferings of our blessed Redeemer set at nought, and his Name blasphemed amongst the Gentiles, through the unrighteous Proceedings of his profess'd Followers!

My Mind hath often been affected, even from the Days of my Youth, under a Sense of that marvellous Work, for which God, in infinite Goodness, sent his Son into the World.

The opening of that Spring of living Waters, which the true Believers in Christ experience, by which they are redeemed from Pride and Covetousness, and brought into a State of Meekness, where their Hearts are enlarged in true Love toward their Fellow Creatures universally; this Work to me has been precious, and the Spreading the Knowledge of the Truth amongst the Gentiles been very desirable. And the professed Followers of Christ joining in Customs evidently unrighteous, which manifestly tend to stir up Wrath, and increase Wars and Desolations, hath often covered my Mind with Sorrow.

If we bring this Matter home, and as Job proposed to his Friends, Put our Soul in their Soul's stead, Job xvi. 4.

If we consider ourselves and our Children as exposed to the Hardships which these People lie under in supporting an imaginary Greatness.

Did we in such Case behold an Increase of Luxury and Superfluity amongst our Oppressors, and therewith felt an Increase of the Weight of our Burdens, and expected our Posterity to groan under Oppression after us.

Under all this Misery, had we none to plead our Cause, nor any Hope of Relief from Man, how would our Cries ascend to the God of the Spirits of all Flesh, who judgeth the World in Righteousness, and in his own Time is a Refuge for the Oppressed!

If they who thus afflicted us, continued to lay Claim to Religion, and were assisted in their Business by others, esteemed pious People, who through a Friendship with them strengthened their Hands in Tyranny.

In such a State, when we were Hunger-bitten, and could not have sufficient Nourishment but saw them in fulness pleasing their Taste with Things fetched from far:

When we were wearied with Labour, denied the Liberty to rest, and saw them spending their Time at Ease: When Garments answerable to our Necessities were denied us, while we saw them cloathed in that which was costly and delicate:

Under such Affliction, how would these painful Feelings rise up as Witnesses against their pretended Devotion! And if the Name of their Religion was mention'd in our Hearing, how would it sound in our Ears like a Word which signified Self-exaltation, and Hardness of Heart!

When a Trade is carried on, productive of much Misery, and they who suffer by it are some Thousands Miles off, the Danger is the greater, of not laying their Sufferings to Heart.

In procuring Slaves on the Coast of Africa, many Children are stolen privately; Wars also are encouraged amongst the Negroes, but all is at a great Distance.

Many Groans arise from dying Men, which we hear not.

Many Cries are uttered by Widows and Fatherless Children, which reach not our Ears.

Many Cheeks are wet with Tears, and Faces sad with unutterable Grief, which we see not.

Cruel Tyranny is encouraged. The Hands of Robbers are strengthened, and Thousands reduced to the most abject Slavery, who never injured us.

Were we for the Term of one Year only to be an Eye-witness to what passeth in getting these Slaves:

Was the Blood which is there shed to be sprinkled on our Garments:

Were the poor Captives bound with Thongs, heavy laden with Elephants Teeth, to pass before our Eyes on their Way to the Sea:

Were their bitter Lamentations Day after Day to ring in our Ears, and their mournful Cries in the Night to hinder us from Sleeping:

Were we to hear the Sound of the Tumult when the Slaves on board the Ships attempt to kill the English, and behold the Issue of those bloody Conflicts:

What pious Man could be a Witness to these Things, and see a Trade carried on in this Manner, without being deeply affected with Sorrow?

Through abiding in the Love of Christ we feel a Tenderness in our Hearts toward our Fellow Creatures, entangled in oppressive Customs; and a Concern so to walk, that our Conduct may not be a Means of strength'ning them in Error.

It was the Command of the Lord through Moses, Thou shalt not suffer Sin upon thy Brother: Thou shalt in anywise rebuke thy Brother, and shalt not suffer Sin upon him, Lev. xix. 17.

Again; Keep far from a false Matter; and the Innocent and Righteous slay thou not, Exod. xxiii. 7.

The Prophet Isaiah mentions Oppression as that which the true Church in Time of outward Quiet should not only be clear of, but should be far from it; Thou shalt be far from Oppression, Isaiah liv. 14. Now these Words, far from, appear to have an extensive Meaning, and to convey Instruction in regard to that of which Solomon speaks, Though Hand join in Hand, the Wicked shall not go unpunished, Prov. xvi. 5.

It was a Complaint against one of old, When thou sawest a Thief, thou consentedst with him, Psal. l. 18.

The Prophet Jeremiah represents the Degrees of Preparation toward Idolatrous Sacrifice, in the Similitude of a Work carried on by Children, Men, and Women: The Children gather Wood, the Fathers kindle the Fire, and the Women knead the Dough to bake Cakes for the Queen of Heaven, Jer. vii. 18.

It was a complaint of the Lord against Israel, through his Prophet Ezekiel, that they strengthen'd the Hands of the

Wicked, and made the Hearts of the Righteous sad, Ezek. xiii. 12.

Some Works of Iniquity carried on by the People were represented by the Prophet Hosea, in the Similitude of Ploughing, Reaping, and eating the Fruit; You have ploughed Wickedness, reaped Iniquity, eaten the Fruit of Lying, because thou didst trust in thy own Way, to the Multitude of thy mighty Men, Hosea x. 13.

I have felt great Distress of Mind since I came on this Island, on Account of the Members of our Society being mixed with the World in various Sorts of Business and Traffick, carried on in impure Channels. Great is the Trade to Africa for Slaves; and in loading these Ships abundance of People are employ'd in the Manufactories.

Friends in early Time refused, on a religious Principle, to make or trade in Superfluities, of which we have many large Testimonies on Record, but for want of Faithfulness some gave way, even some whose Examples were of Note in Society, and from thence others took more Liberty: Members of our Society worked in Superfluities, and bought and sold them, and thus Dimness of Sight came over many. At length, Friends got into the Use of some Superfluities in Dress, and in the Furniture of their Houses, and this hath spread from less to more, till Superfluity of some Kind is common amongst us.

In this declining State many look at the Example one of another, and too much neglect the pure Feeling of Truth. Of late Years a deep Exercise hath attended my Mind, that Friends may dig deep, may carefully cast forth the loose Matter, and get down to the Rock, the sure Foundation, and there hearken to that Divine Voice which gives a clear and certain Sound.

And I have felt in that which doth not deceive, that if Friends who have known the Truth, keep in that Tenderness of Heart, where all Views of outward Gain are given up, and their Trust is only on the Lord, he will graciously lead some to be Patterns of deep Self-denial, in Things relating to Trade, and handicraft Labour; and that some who have Plenty of the Treasures of this World, will example in a plain frugal Life, and pay Wages to such whom they may hire, more liberally than is now customary in some Places.

The Prophet, speaking of the true Church, said, Thy People also shall be all righteous.

Of the Depth of this Divine Work several have spoken.

John Gratton, in his Journal, p. 45, said, "The Lord is my Portion, I shall not want. He hath wrought all my Works in me. I am nothing but what I am in him."

Gilbert Latey, through the powerful Operations of the Spirit of Christ in his Soul, was brought to that Depth of Self-denial, that he could not join with that proud Spirit in other People, which inclined them to want Vanities and Superfluities. This Friend was often amongst the chief Rulers of the Nation in Times of Persecution, and it appears by the Testimony of Friends, that his Dwelling was so evidently in the pure Life of Truth, that in his Visits to those great Men, he found a Place in their Minds; and that King James the Second, in the Times of his Troubles, made particular Mention in a very respectful Manner of what Gilbert once said to him.

The said Gilbert found a Concern to write an Epistle, in which are these Expressions; "Fear the Lord, ye Men of all Sorts, Trades, and Callings, and leave off all the Evil that is in them, for the Lord is grieved with all the Evils used in your Employments which you are exercised in.

"It is even a Grief to see how you are Servants to Sin, and Instruments of Satan." See his Works, Page 42, etc. George Fox, in an Epistle, writes thus: "Friends, stand in the Eternal Power of God, Witness against the Pomps and Vanities of this World.

"Such Tradesmen who stand as Witnesses in the Power of God, cannot fulfil the People's Minds in these Vanities, and therefore they are offended at them.

"Let all trust in the Lord, and wait patiently on him; for when Trust first broke forth in London, many Tradesmen could not take so much Money in their Shops for some Time, as would buy them Bread and Water, because they withstood the World's Ways, Fashions, and Customs; yet by their patient waiting on the Lord in their good Life and Conversation, they answer'd the Truth in People's Hearts, and thus their Business increased." Book of Doctrinals, Page 824.

Now Christ our Holy Leader graciously continueth to open the Understandings of his People, and as Circumstances alter from Age to Age, some who are deeply baptized into a Feeling of the State of Things, are led by his Holy Spirit into Exercises in some respect different from those which attended the Faithful in foregoing Ages, and through the Constrainings of pure Love, are engaged to open the Feelings they have to others.

In faithfully following Christ, the Heart is weaned from the Desires of Riches, and we are led into a Life so plain and simple, that a little doth suffice, and thus the Way openeth to deny ourselves, under all the tempting Allurements of that Gain, which we know is the Gain of Unrighteousness.

The Apostle speaking on this Subject, asketh this Question; What Fellowship hath Righteousness with Unrighteousness? 2 Cor. vi. 14. And again saith, Have no Fellowship with the unfruitful Works of Darkness, but rather reprove them, Ephes. v. 11. Again, Be not Partaker of other Men's Sins, keep thyself pure, 1 Tim. v. 22.

Where People through the Power of Christ are thoroughly settled in a right Use of Things, freed from all unnecessary Care and Expence, the Mind in this true Resignation is at Liberty from the Bands of a narrow Self-Interest, to attend from Time to Time on the Movings of his Spirit upon us, though he leads into that through which our Faith is closely tried.

The Language of Christ is pure, and to the Pure in Heart this pure Language is intelligible; but in the Love of Money, the Mind being intent on Gain, is too full of human Contrivance to attend to it.

It appeareth evident, that some Channels of Trade are defiled with Unrighteousness, that the Minds of many are intent on getting Treasures to support a Life, in which there are many unnecessary Expences.

And I feel a living Concern attend my Mind, that under these Difficulties we may humbly follow our Heavenly Shepherd, who graciously regardeth his Flock, and is willing and able to supply us both inwardly and outwardly with clean Provender, that hath been winnowed with the Shovel and the Fan, where we may sow to ourselves in Righteousness, reap in Mercy, Hosea x. 12. and not be defiled with the Works of Iniquity.

Where Customs contrary to pure Wisdom are transmitted to Posterity, it appears to be an Injury committed against them; and I often feel tender Compassion toward a young Generation, and Desires that their Difficulties may not be increased through Unfaithfulness in us of the present Age.

CHAPTER II

On a Sailor's LIFE

In the Trade to Africa for Slaves, and in the Management of Ships going on these Voyages, many of our Lads and young Men have a considerable Part of their Education.

Now what pious Father beholding his Son placed in one of these Ships, to learn the Practice of a Mariner, could forbear mourning over him?

Where Youth are exampled in Means of getting Money so full of Violence, and used to exercise such Cruelties on their Fellow Creatures, the Disadvantage to them in their Education is very great.

But I feel it in my Mind to write concerning the Seafaring Life in general.

In the Trade carried on from the West-Indies, and from some Part of the Continent, the Produce of the Labour of Slaves is a considerable Part.

And Sailors who are frequently at Ports where Slaves abound, and converse often with People who oppress without the Appearance of Remorse, and often with Sailors employ'd in the Slave Trade, how powerfully do these evil Examples spread amongst the Seafaring Youth!

I have had many Opportunities to feel and understand the general State of the Seafaring Life amongst us, and my Mind hath often been sad on Account of so many Lads and young Men been trained up amidst so great Corruption.

Under the humbling Power of Christ I have seen, that if the Leadings of his Holy Spirit were faithfully attended to by his professed Followers in general, the Heathen Nations would be exampled in Righteousness. A less Number of People would be employed on the Seas. The Channels of Trade would be more free from Defilement. Fewer People would be employed in Vanities and Superfluities.

The Inhabitants of Cities would be less in Number.

Those who have much Lands would become Fathers to the Poor.

More People would be employed in the sweet Employment of Husbandry, and in the Path of pure Wisdom, Labour would be an agreeable, healthful Employment.

In the Opening of these Things in my Mind, I feel a living Concern that we who have felt Divine Love in our Hearts may faithfully abide in it, and like good Soldiers endure Hardness for Christ's Sake.

He, our blessed Saviour, exhorting his Followers to love one another, adds, As I have loved you. John xiii. 34.

He loved Lazarus, yet in his Sickness did not heal him, but left him to endure the Pains of Death, that in restoring him to Life, the People might be confirmed in the true Faith.

He loved his Disciples, but sent them forth on a Message attended with great Difficulty, amongst Hard-hearted People, some of whom would think that in killing them they did God Service.

So deep is Divine Love, that in stedfastly abiding in it, we are prepar'd to deny ourselves of all that Gain which is contrary to pure Wisdom, and to follow Christ, even under Contempt, and through Sufferings.

While Friends were kept truly humble, and walked according to the Purity of our Principles, the Divine Witness in many Hearts was reached; but when a Worldly Spirit got Entrance, therewith came in Luxuries and Superfluities, and spread by little and little, even among the foremost Rank in Society, and from thence others took Liberty in that Way more abundantly.

In the Continuation of these Things from Parents to Children, there were many Wants to supply, even Wants unknown to Friends while they faithfully followed Christ. And in striving to supply these Wants many have exacted on the Poor, many have enter'd on Employments, in which they often labour in upholding Pride and Vanity. Many have looked on one another, been strengthen'd in these Things, one by the Example of another, and as to the pure Divine Seeing, Dimness hath come over many, and the Channels of true Brotherly Love been obstructed.

People may have no intention to oppress, yet by entering on expensive Ways of Life, their Minds may be so entangled therein, and so engag'd to support expensive Customs, as to be estranged from the pure sympathizing Spirit.

As I have travell'd in England, I have had a tender Feeling of the Condition of poor People, some of whom though honest and industrious, have nothing to spare toward paying for the Schooling of their Children.

There is a Proportion between Labour and the Necessaries of Life, and in true Brotherly Love the Mind is open to feel after the Necessities of the Poor.

Amongst the Poor there are some that are weak through Age, and others of a weakly Nature, who pass through Straits in very private Life, without asking Relief from the Publick.

Such who are strong and healthy may do that Business, which to the Weakly may be oppressive; and in performing that in a Day which is esteem'd a Day's Labour, by weakly Persons in the Field and in the Shops, and by weakly Women who spin and knit in the Manufactories, they often pass through Weariness; and many Sighs I believe are uttered in secret, unheard by some who might ease their Burdens.

Labour in the right Medium is healthy, but in too much of it there is a painful Weariness; and the Hardships of the Poor are sometimes increased through Want of a more agreeable Nourishment, more plentiful Fewel for the Fire, and warmer Cloathing in the Winter than their Wages will answer.

When I have beheld Plenty in some Houses to a Degree of Luxury, the Condition of poor Children brought up without Learning, and the Condition of the Weakly and Aged, who strive to live by their Labour, have often revived in my Mind, as Cases of which some who live in Fulness need to be put in Remembrance.

There are few, if any, could behold their Fellow Creatures lie long in Distress and forbear to help them, when they could do it without any Inconvenience; but Customs requiring much Labour to support them, do often lie heavy on the Poor, while they who live in these Customs are so entangled in a Multitude of unnecessary Concerns that they think but little of the Hardships which the poor People go through.

CHAPTER III

On Silent Worship

Worship in Silence hath often been refreshing to my Mind, and a Care attends me that a young Generation may feel the Nature of this Worship.

Great Expence ariseth in Relation to that which is call'd Divine Worship.

A considerable Part of this Expence is applied toward outward Greatness, and many poor People in raising of Tithe, labour in supporting Customs contrary to the Simplicity that there is in Christ, toward whom my Mind hath often been moved with Pity.

In pure silent Worship, we dwell under the Holy Anointing, and feel Christ to be our Shepherd.

Here the best of Teachers ministers to the several Conditions of his Flock, and the Soul receives immediately from the Divine Fountain, that with which it is nourished.

As I have travelled at Times where those of other Societies have attended our Meetings, and have perceiv'd how little some of them knew of the Nature of silent Worship; I have felt tender Desires in my Heart that we who often sit silent in our Meetings, may live answerable to the Nature of an inward Fellowship with God, that no Stumbling-block through us, may be laid in their Way.

Such is the Load of unnecessary Expence which lieth on that which is called Divine Service in many Places, and so much are the Minds of many People employ'd in outward Forms and Ceremonies, that the opening of an inward silent Worship in this Nation to me hath appeared to be a precious Opening.

Within the last four Hundred Years, many pious People have been deeply exercised in Soul on Account of the Superstition which prevailed amongst the professed Followers of Christ, and in support of their Testimony against oppressive Idolatry, some in several Ages have finished their Course in the Flames.

It appears by the History of the Reformation, that through the Faithfulness of the Martyrs, the Understandings of many have been opened, and the Minds of People, from Age to Age, been more and more prepared for a real spiritual Worship.

My Mind is often affected with a Sense of the Condition of those People who in different Ages have been meek and patient, following Christ through great Afflictions: And while I behold the several Steps, of Reformation, and that Clearness, to which through Divine Goodness, it hath been brought by our Ancestors; I feel tender Desires that we who sometimes meet in Silence, may never by our Conduct lay Stumbling-blocks in the Way of others, and hinder the Progress of the Reformation in the World.

It was a Complaint against some who were called the Lord's People, that they brought polluted Bread to his Altar, and said the Table of the Lord was contemptible.

In real silent Worship the Soul feeds on that which is Divine; but we cannot partake of the Table of the Lord, and that Table which is prepared by the God of this World.

If Christ is our Shepherd, and feedeth us, and we are faithful in following him, our Lives will have an inviting Language, and the Table of the Lord will not be polluted.

SOME EXPRESSIONS OF JOHN WOOLMAN IN HIS LAST ILNESS.

LONDON:

Printed by Mary Hinde.

SOME EXPRESSIONS, &c.

Being in the Course of his religious Visit at York, and having attended most of the Sittings of the Quarterly-Meeting there, held in the Ninth Month, 1772, he was taken ill of the Small Pox, in which Disorder he continued about two Weeks, at Times under great Affliction of Body, and then departed in full Assurance of a happy Eternity, as the following Expressions, amongst others, taken from his own Mouth, do plainly evidence.

One Day being asked how he felt himself, he meekly answered, "I don't know that I have slept this Night: I feel the Disorder making its Progress, but my Mind is mercifully preserved in Stillness and Peace." Some Time after he said, "He was sensible the Pains of Death must be hard to bear, but if he escaped them now, he must some Time pass through them, and did not know he could be better prepared, but had no Will in it." Said, "He had settled his outward Affairs to his Mind; had taken Leave of his Wife and Family, as never to return, leaving them to the Divine Protection:" Adding, "And though I feel them near to me at this Time, yet I freely give them up, having an Hope they will be provided for." And a little after said, "This Trial is made easier than I could have thought, by my

Will being wholly taken away; for if I was anxious as to the Event, it would be harder, but I am not, and my Mind enjoys a perfect Calm."

In the Night a young Woman having given him something to drink, he said, "My Child, thou seemest very kind to me, a poor Creature, the Lord will reward thee for it." A while after he cried out with great Earnestness of Spirit, "Oh! my Father, my Father, how comfortable art thou to my Soul in this trying Season." Being asked if he could take a little Nourishment, after some Pause he replied, "My Child, I cannot tell what to say to it: I seem nearly arrived where my Soul shall have Rest from all its Troubles." After giving in something to be put into his Journal, he said, "I believe the Lord will now excuse me from Exercises of this Kind, and I see no Work but one, which is to be the last wrought by me in this World; the Messenger will come that will release me from all these Troubles, but it must be in the Lord's Time, which I am waiting for." He said, "He had laboured to do whatever was required, according to the Ability received, in the Remembrance of which he had Peace: And though the Disorder was strong at Times, and would come over his Mind like a Whirlwind, yet it had hitherto been kept steady, and center'd in everlasting Love." Adding, "And if that's mercifully continued, I ask nor desire no more."

At another Time he said, "He had long had a View of visiting this Nation; and some Time before he came, he had a Dream, in which he saw himself in the Northern Parts of it; and that the Spring of the Gospel was opened in him, much as in the Beginning of Friends, such as George Fox and William Dewsbury; and he saw the different States of People as clear as ever he had seen Flowers in a Garden; but in his going on he was suddenly stopt, though he could not see for what End, but looked towards Home, and in that fell into a Flood of Tears, which waked him." At another Time he said, "My Draught seem'd strongest to the North, and I mentioned in my own Monthly-Meeting, that attending the Quarterly-Meeting at York, and being there, looked like Home to me."

Having repeatedly consented to take a Medicine with a View to settle his Stomach, but without Effect, the Friend then waiting on him, said, through Distress, "What shall I do now?" He answered with great Composure, "Rejoice evermore, and in every Thing give Thanks." But added a little after, "This is sometimes hard to come at."

One Morning early he brake forth in Supplication on this wise; "Oh Lord! it was thy Power that enabled me to forsake Sin in my Youth, and I have felt thy Bruises since for Disobedience, but as I bowed under them thou healedst me; and though I have gone through many Trials and sore Afflictions, thou hast been with me, continuing a Father and a Friend. I feel thy Power now, and beg that in the approaching trying Moments, thou wilt keep my Heart steadfast unto thee." Upon his giving the same Friend Directions concerning some little Matters, she said, "I will take Care, but hope thou mayst live to order them thyself;" he replied, "My Hope is in Christ; and though I may now seem a little better, a Change in the Disorder may soon happen, and my little Strength be dissolved, and if it so happen, I shall be gather'd to my everlasting Rest." On her saying, "She did not doubt that, but could not help mourning to see so many faithful Servants removed at so low a Time," he said, "All Goodness cometh from the Lord, whose Power is the same, and he can work as he sees best." The same Day, after giving her Directions about wrapping his Corpse, and perceiving her to weep, he said, "I had rather thou wouldst guard against Weeping or Sorrowing for me, my Sister; I sorrow not, though I have had some painful Conflicts; but now they seem over, and Matters all settled, and I look at the Face of my dear Redeemer, for sweet is his Voice, and his Countenance comely."

Being very weak, and in general difficult to be understood, he uttered a few Words in Commemoration of the Lord's Goodness to him; and added, "How tenderly have I been waited upon in this Time of Affliction, in which I may say in Job's Words, Tedious Days and wearisome Nights are appointed unto me; and how many are spending their Time and Money in Vanity and Superfluities, while Thousands and Tens of Thousands want the Necessaries of Life, who might be relieved by them, and their Distresses at such a Time as this, in some degree softened by the administring of suitable Things."

An Apothecary who attended him of his own Accord (he being unwilling to have any sent for) appeared very anxious to assist him, with whom conversing, he queried about the Probability of such a Load of Matter being thrown off his weak Body, and the Apothecary making some Remarks, implying he thought it might, he spoke with an audible Voice on this wise: "My Dependance is in the Lord Jesus Christ, who I trust will forgive my Sins, which is all I hope for; and if it be his Will to raise up this Body again, I am content, and if to die I am resigned: And if thou canst not be easy without trying to assist Nature, in order to lengthen out my Life, I submit." After this, his Throat was so much affected, that it was very difficult for him to speak so as to be understood, and he frequently wrote when he wanted any Thing. About the second Hour on Fourth-day Morning, being the 7th of the Tenth Month, 1772, he asked for Pen and Ink, and at several Times, with much

Difficulty, wrote thus: "I believe my being here is in the Wisdom of Christ; I know not as to Life or Death." About a Quarter before Six the same Morning, he seemed to fall into an easy Sleep, which continued about half an Hour, when seeming to awake, he breathed a few Times with more Difficulty, and so expired without Sigh, Groan, or Struggle.

Note, He often said, "It was hid from him, whether he might recover, or not, and he was not desirous to know it; but from his own Feeling of the Disorder, and his feeble Constitution, thought he should not."

[1] When Crops fail. I often feel a tender Care that the Case of poor Tenants may be mercifully considered.

[2] See a Caution and Warning to Great Britain and her Colonies Page 31.

Printed in Great Britain
by Amazon